The Perennial Philosophy

Series

World Wisdom
The Library of Perennial Philosophy

The Library of Perennial Philosophy is dedicated to the exposition of the timeless Truth underlying the diverse religions. This Truth, often referred to as the *Sophia Perennis*—or Perennial Wisdom—finds its expression in the revealed Scriptures as well as the writings of the great sages and the artistic creations of the traditional worlds.

The Perennial Philosophy provides the intellectual principles capable of explaining both the formal contradictions and the transcendent unity of the great religions.

Ranging from the writings of the great sages of the past, to the perennialist authors of our time, each series of our Library has a different focus. As a whole, they express the inner unanimity, transforming radiance, and irreplaceable values of the great spiritual traditions.

Singing the Way: Insights in Poetry and Spiritual Transformation appears as one of our selections in the Perennial Philosophy series.

The Perennial Philosophy Series

In the beginning of the Twentieth Century, a school of thought arose which has focused on the enunciation and explanation of the Perennial Philosophy. Deeply rooted in the sense of the sacred, the writings of its leading exponents establish an indispensable foundation for understanding the timeless Truth and spiritual practices which live in the heart of all religions. Some of these titles are companion volumes to the Treasures of the World's Religions series, which allows a comparison of the writings of the great sages of the past with the perennialist authors of our time.

Singing the Way

Insights in Poetry
and Spiritual Transformation

by

PATRICK LAUDE

World Wisdom

Singing the Way: Insights in Poetry and Spiritual Transformation
© 2005 World Wisdom, Inc.

Parts of this book have been published
under the title The Way of Poetry,
Oneonta Philosophy Series, Oneonta, New York, 2002.

Library of Congress Cataloging-in-Publication Data

Laude, Patrick, 1958-
Singing the Way : Insights in Poetry and Spiritual Transformation / by Patrick Laude.
    p. cm. -- (The perennial philosophy series)
Includes bibliographical references and index.
ISBN 0-941532-74-7 (pbk. : alk. paper)
1. Religion and poetry. I. Title. II. Series.
PN1077.L38 2005
809'.93382--dc22

                                                          2004028850

Printed on acid-free paper in Canada

For information address World Wisdom, Inc.
P.O. Box 2682, Bloomington, Indiana 47402-2682
www.worldwisdom.com

CONTENTS

LIST OF ILLUSTRATIONS

INTRODUCTION

The connection between poetry and contemplation has been highlighted on many accounts and in many ways, so much so that it has become a sort of truism. In common parlance, the poet is often considered as an intuitive and meditative soul who enjoys a rare ability to contemplate reality in a more profound and subtle way than do most fellow human beings. Accordingly, one often deems poets to be endowed with a mediumistic ability that somehow allows them to gain access into the deepest layers of reality. By virtue of this ability, the poet was traditionally conceived as a mediator or a channel between the essence of things and the magic of words, crystallizing his perceptions into sounds and images that pierce through the veil of trivial usage and bring miracles out of language. However, the idea of poetic contemplation covers a wide spectrum of phenomena, and while all genuine poetry is in a sense "contemplative," it does not follow that the discipline of contemplative practice necessarily enters into the alchemy of poetic creation; hence the need to specify the scope of our understanding of contemplation.

*   *   *

In the Christian spiritual tradition, contemplation has often been defined in contradistinction to the reading of Scriptures (*lectio divina*), meditation, and the practice of vocal prayer. The latter is most often envisaged as a personal, volitional, and sentimental motion of the soul directed towards God. By contrast, meditation involves the discursive process of reason, even though this discourse may be accompanied by the evocation of images and ultimately results in emotional affects, as in the practice of Ignatian meditation. In contemplation, as suggested by the prefix "con-," motion and discourse are somehow superseded by a synthetic, immediate, and inarticulate mode of being— not mere thinking—that entails both totality and centering. Contemplation engages our entire being while rooting it in the unshakable ground of the Divine; it suggests union with God, and therefore Self-sufficiency and repose in Being.

*   *   *

By contrast with this self-contained and synthetic character of contemplation, poetry always implies, by definition, the idea of a production—poems or *poēmata*. Etymologically, the Greek word *poiēsis* literally means "creation," and specifically refers to creation in the realm of the *logos*. Although the scope of the term *logos* has tended to become more and more limited to the plane of rationality, its original meaning is far from exhausted by reference to the realm of the discursive mind. The etymology of the Greek word suggests the idea of a gathering or a collecting, thereby alluding to the distillation of a unity of understanding and discourse out of a multiplicity of perceptions.

In Christianity, the *Logos* was understood in the context of the Incarnation; it was therefore identified with Christ as both Divine and human manifestation of the redeeming Truth. In this context, the Word might best be defined as the perfection and prototype of Creation in God—the Model for all things, so to speak—while being also, from another standpoint, the perfection and culmination of Creation in man; hence the central position of mankind in the universe, a position that is symbolized in the Bible[1] by the human privilege of naming the creatures. The human ability to "name" beings clearly pertains to the Word as point of junction between the Divine and the human. The *Logos* is the nexus between these two realms, and thus the means of communication *par excellence* between the two; it is both divine Revelation and human Invocation. In the first case, God speaks in a human language as it were, while man's prayer is most fundamentally a divine idiom.

From the standpoint of the "descent" into being, the "poetic" Act of God through His Word is Creation, whereas in the perspective of the "ascent" toward God, this Act is to be understood as the theomorphic and deifying Norm[2] and the Way back to God. As is most directly expressed by the prologue of St. John's Gospel, God creates through His Word:

In principio erat Verbum,
Et Verbum erat apud Deum,
Et Deus erat Verbum.
Hoc erat in principio apud Deum.
Omnia per ipsum facta sunt:
Et sine ipso factum est nihil, quod factum est.[3]

---

[1] Genesis 2:19-20.

[2] Hence the Catholic idea of the "imitation of Christ" (*Imitatio Christi*).

[3] "In the beginning was the Word, and the Word was with God, and the Word was God. The same was in the beginning with God. All things were made by him; and without him was not any thing made that was made" (John, 1:1-3). As it is presented in St. John's prologue, the

Mankind, in his universal aspect, therefore constitutes the Divine "Poem" *par excellence*, and as such the prototype of the whole Creation.

* * *

In India, the sacred syllable *Omkara*, as a quintessence of Divine Revelation, constitutes the essence of all poetry. Similarly, in Islam, the Qur'ān is the Divine Revelation, and the Divine Name Allāh is—for Sufis—the synthesis of the Book. Each in its way can be viewed as the quintessence of poetry. The point of view of Far Eastern traditions is somewhat different in that they do not stem from Revelation as a Book or as an Original Utterance. In the Chinese and Japanese traditions—by virtue of the shamanistic roots of Taoism, Confucianism and Shintō—the word or the book is Nature, or it is synthesized by the fundamental "signatures" that are the combination of cosmic principles, *yin* and *yang*, as manifested first and foremost in the *I Ching*. It could be said that these traditions do not consider poetry as a prolongation of the verbal irruption of the Supreme in the world, but rather, that they envisage poetical creation as a mode of conformity to the immanent "traces" of the Divine in Nature.

* * *

Whether one considers the Divine Word as expressed through Revelation and Scripture or as manifested in the Book of Nature, the human poet is but an imitator of the Divine Poet since his "logical" (stemming from the *logos*) utterance is simultaneously a "poetical" work (referring here to *poiēsis* as creation or "making"). In their original root, "poetry" and "logic" are one and the same.[4] It is through a profound attention to this reality that Emerson asso-

relationship between *Deus* and *Verbum* is what Ananda Coomaraswamy proposed to define as a "distinction without difference." This expression is Coomaraswamy's translation for the Sanskrit *bhedabheda*. It is implied by the double function of *Verbum* as substantive "predicate" of *Deus* and as object of the preposition *apud* ("with" in the sense of abiding by). God is "no different" from His Word since the Word is, so to speak, the irradiation of God; but He is "distinct" from His Word in so far as the Word is the Prototype of Relativity.

[4] "According to traditional doctrines, logic and poetry have a common source, the Intellect, and far from being contradictory are essentially complementary. Logic becomes opposed to poetry only if respect for logic becomes transformed into rationalism, and poetry, rather than being a

ciated the Son of the Christian Trinity with the Sayer and with Beauty (the Father corresponding to the Knower and the True and the Spirit to the Good and the Doer). On the basis of this association, one may understand the deepest meaning of his elliptical formula: "Beauty is the creator of the universe." The Son is the Perfection of Creation and He is also its Door. Beauty is the Hidden Perfection of God from which all things are created. In its essence, or at its height, poetry is accordingly the echo of the Divine Logos.

Poetry may thus be understood as the essence of language, or it could also be said that the very root of language was—or is—poetry, before any distinction between poetry and prose be drawn. Every word, therefore, virtually partakes of poetry, even before being used in a line or a sentence, because every word is a symbolic treasury of virtually limitless implications. Whence flows Emerson's reminder concerning the synthetic character of poetry: "It does not need that a poem should be long. Every word was once a poem." And there is little doubt that when Mallarmé proposed to "give a purer meaning to the words of the tribe" (*donner un sens plus pur aux mots de la tribu*), he had some intuition of this original poetic vibration of the word, particularly of its root. The primordial power of this radical vibration—in which the auditory and semantic dimensions are as it were fused together—explains why poets are in fact the keepers of the symbolic richness of words. They both "attend to" the integrity of language and "open" it by unveiling the limitless potentialities of its foundations.

In all spiritual traditions, we find the idea that language was originally much richer and more synthetic than it is today. Language has tended to become reduced to its merely practical and communicative dimension—be it purely social or idiosyncratic—whereas its essence is actually symbolic. In other words, poetry is not only a means of communication with others and an expression of oneself; it is also—and above all—a way for transcendent Reality to manifest itself in and through words, images, and music. By virtue of this symbolic power not only to represent and communicate, but also to make present, it is fundamentally polysemic: it offers multiple strata of meaning and cannot be reduced to the single horizontal dimension of conceptual communication. This virtually unlimited multiplicity of meanings—unlimited

---

vehicle for the expression of a truly intellectual knowledge, becomes reduced to sentimentalism or a means of expressing individual idiosyncrasies and forms of subjectivism" (Seyyed Hossein Nasr, *Islamic Art and Spirituality*, p. 91).

in proportion to the depth of the poetry—must not however be confused with the relativistic claim that reduces poetry to a matter of subjective readings in the name of hermeneutic freedom. The very partial merit of this relativistic claim lies in the emphasis it places upon the individual as a locus of actualization of meaning. However, the "making" sense of the poem is not only a matter of subjective actuation; it is also—and primarily—one of objective and essential potency. Metaphysically speaking, one must maintain the radical objectivity and ontological power of the word both as *shaktic* or "magic" reality and as pure potentiality. In this sense, the Word is the very Act of Being.

*   *   *

As a way of access to the primordial richness of language, poetry is deeply connected to memory and *anamnesis*, memory being understood here in its profound and quasi-timeless connection with truth, and not simply as a psychic repository of ideas and images. Ananda Coomaraswamy has emphasized the fact that traditional literature—before the advent of modernity—was exclusively poetic:

> Ours is a prose style, while the traditional lore of all peoples—even the substance of their practical sciences—has been everywhere poetical.[5]

By contrast, the modern and contemporary disjunction between the intellective dimension of "logic" and the domain of poetry testifies to a desacralization of knowledge on the one hand, and to a debasement of poetry on the other hand. It is one of the major symptoms of what Gilbert Durand has proposed to call the "schizomorphic" sickness of modern man, i.e., the fragmentation of inner and outer reality that results in disintegration and irreconcilable oppositions.

In many cosmogonies, the process of creation is presented as an encounter between two complementary principles that are both necessary in order for the world to be. The Bible tells us that "the Spirit of God was hovering over the waters,"[6] whilst Hindu cosmology refers to *Purusha* and *Prakriti* as the two principles of manifestation. The first of these principles is active,

---

[5] Ananda Coomaraswamy, *Spiritual Authority and Temporal Power in the Indian Theory of Government*, p. 59, note 41.

[6] Genesis 1:2.

determinative, and "informing" while the second is plastic and receptive. Analogously, the poetical work tends to be conceived as the outcome of the encounter between "form" (*idea* or *eidos*, intelligible principle) and "matter" (*hylē*, substantial or hypostatic principle), or a "meaning" and a "form" (taken this time in the ordinary sense of the word). We find the same complementary pair of creative principles—with different emphases and nuances—in all major poetics, and the harmonic coincidence of the two elements involved is always understood as being brought out by the clear subordination of the substratum in relation to the intellective form.[7] This "crystallization" of the coincidence between intellective essence and linguistic substance is primarily effected through meter. As God "disposes everything according to measure, number, and weight" (*omnia in mensura, numero et pondere disposuisti*),[8] as He manifests the world through the qualitative measures of cosmic order, the poet analogously creates by manifesting the *eidos*, the spiritual meaning, within the domain of linguistic substance and through meter. In other words, the form is as if absorbed by the essence through the prosodic number. The latter is the very mode of poetic creation. It is not an arbitrary constraint but the expression of quality and intelligibility within the realm of quantity.[9] Number is the prototype of measure and it is therefore the manifesting and ordering principle of creation, the poem.[10]

In so far as number and measure are none other than expressions of unity, they also constitute the essence of rhythm as the "formal" pole of poetry. Rhythm, which plays such a central role in contemplative meditation and methods of invocation, must be understood as the expression of Unity within multiplicity; it is the very "vibration" of the One. In and through it the "other" participates in the "Same." In this connection, rhythm is closely asso-

---

[7] As Ray Livingston articulates the matter: "The universe itself, properly viewed by the Intellect, or the 'eye of the heart,' as it is often called, is the result of the marriage of Harmony (*sāman*) and the Word (*rc*) or, in another idiom, the union of essence and substance.... When there is a true union of those principles, the result is 'an effective harmony and the reproduction of the higher of the two principles involved'" (*The Traditional Theory of Literature*, p. 77).

[8] Wisdom of Solomon 11:20.

[9] In the words of René Guénon: "It can be said that the relation of measure to number corresponds, in an inversely analogical sense, to the relation of manifestation to its essential principle" (*The Reign of Quantity & the Signs of the Times*, pp. 36-7).

[10] "Number, gentlemen, number! Or else order and symmetry; for order is nothing else than ordered number, and symmetry is nothing but perceived and compared order" (Joseph de Maistre, *Les soirées de Saint-Petersbourg*, 2:125).

ciated with incantation as a spiritual method of return to the One. Through rhythm the One makes itself present in multiplicity, the Formless inhabits form: rhythm is the *barzakh* (the intermediary zone) between the instant of eternity and temporal sequence. From an animic standpoint, the mobility and perpetual "otherness" of the soul may be integrated by means of the "sameness" of the reoccurring patterns brought out by rhythmic practice. As Ananda Coomaraswamy has pointed out, the "singsong" reading of sacred texts is none other than the "performing" aspect of this rhythmic law. Monotony and absence of psychic expressiveness is a direct manifestation of the spiritual grounding of sacred chant in the One. This principle is central in sacred and liturgical psalmody, as is testified to by authentic Gregorian chant and traditional Qur'ānic recitation. In this connection, it is important to keep in mind that poetry should be read aloud, preferably sung. Poetry is not only a manifestation within the realm of multiplicity, it is also an exteriorization; and singing is the very symbol and means of this exteriorization. In this context, it should be recalled that the sacred text—essence or epitome of all poetical works, and always eminently poetic itself, as is the Qur'ān in the context of the Arabic language—proceeds by what Frithjof Schuon has characterized as a kind of "ruse."[11] It makes use of multiplicity and exteriorization in order to bring back the Ten Thousand Things to the One, and the Outward to the Inward. This is what could be called the alchemy of diversity. Accordingly, rhythm functions both as an expression of the One and as a necessity stemming from the spiritual and intellectual structure of our being. As a reflection of the *Logos*, it is the ebb and flow of Reality.

On the "substantial" plane of "words," rhythm, or meter, is like the imprint of the One; and in this connection it could be said that through rhythm, meter, or prosody, form participates in the essence. On the highest level, the essence is to be understood as the ineffable Principle—since God is the meaning of everything—the vibrant Silence that is the alpha and the

---

[11] "Like the world, the Qur'ān is at the same time one and multiple. The world is a multiplicity which disperses and divides; the Qur'ān is a multiplicity which draws together and leads to Unity. The multiplicity of the holy Book—the diversity of its words, aphorisms, images and stories—fills the soul, and then absorbs it and imperceptibly transposes it into a climate of serenity and immutability by a sort of 'divine ruse.' The soul, which is accustomed to the flux of phenomena, yields to this flux without resistance; it lives in phenomena and is by them divided and dispersed—even more than that, it actually becomes what it thinks and does. The revealed Discourse has the virtue of accepting this tendency while reversing its movement thanks to the celestial character of the content and the language, so that the fishes of the soul swim without distrust and with their habitual rhythm into the divine net" (Frithjof Schuon, *Understanding Islam*, pp. 47-8).

omega of all poetry and all music, of all worlds. However, we must also consider the relationship between essence and form from the standpoint of "meaning" or "content." The latter is always considered as more determinative or ultimately as more "real" than the formal structure.[12]

In Japanese poetry, for example, the *haiku* must fulfill some "formal" requirements that pertain to rhythm, as well as to the lexicon; but it cannot be a *haiku* without integrating an "essential" element without which it is not a *haiku*: the *hai-i*, the *haiku* spirit.[13] Similarly, Hindu poetics entirely revolves around the notion of *rasa* or "taste," a notion that evokes the divine and beatific infinitude as it is experienced by and through the Self.[14] It is a participation in the music of the Infinite.

Now such terms as *hai-i* or *rasa* refer to a somewhat "ineffable" and "indefinite" reality—although they may give rise to very specific descriptions and classifications in terms of their modalities—precisely because they pertain to Infinitude, as expressed in the Hindu concept of *Ānanda* or, in a different way and in Japanese parlance, in the term *fueki*, the "metaphysical ground," "non-articulated wholeness," (Izutsu's phrase), or Naught.[15] At whatever level and in whatever mode one may consider it, this infinite (opening onto the Boundless) and indefinite (that cannot be caught in the net of concepts and words) Reality is the end (in both senses of *telos* and limit) and the essence of poetry; but it is also transcendent in relation to the poem as a formal structure. Here, the analogy between the poem and the human

---

[12] As Livingston points out: "The letter or sound is the outward aspect which is of little importance compared to the spirit or meaning embodied in the words" (*The Traditional Theory of Literature*, p. 78).

[13] "… *Haiku* as a 17 syllabled verse is formally similar to the upper strophe of *waka*, except that every *haiku* must have *kigo* (season-word). However, the mere fulfillment of this formal requirement does not necessarily produce a *haiku*, if it is devoid of *hai-i* (*haiku* spirit), as is often the case. A verse of 17 syllabled words with the inner division of 5/7/5 without *hai-i*, even if it is provided with *kigo* (season-word), would not make a *haiku*; it could at the very most make an imperfect *waka*. That which makes a *haiku* genuinely *haiku* is not its formal structure but rather the *hai-i*, the *haiku* spirit" (Toshihiko and Toyo Izutsu, *The Theory of Beauty in the Classical Aesthetics of Japan*, pp. 64-5).

[14] "The savor is the essence, the 'self' (*ātman*) of the poem…. According to the *Agni Purana*, savor is derived from the third form of the tri-unity in its metaphysical aspect, *sat-chit-ānanda*, 'being-consciousness-bliss,' through the intermediary of the 'self' and pleasure in general" (René Daumal, *Rasa or Knowledge of the Self: Essays on Indian Aesthetics and Selected Sanskrit Studies*, p. 105).

[15] *Fueki* refers to the intrinsic nature of the infinite Void whereas *Ānanda* suggests the dynamic power of the infinite Self.

subject allows for a clearer understanding of the relation between "essence" and "form": in Hindu terms, just as *Ātman* is both transcendent and immanent in relation to the individual self, the "spirit of the poem" is both the very principle of the poem as well as being something situated beyond the poem as a formal entity. If poetry cannot be easily defined, it is not because it is vague or purely subjective, but because it is situated at the junction between form and essence, and opens onto the Infinite.

To express the matter in a paradoxical way: poetry "has something to say" which "cannot be said." It "has something to say": it may not be didactic in the negative sense of the word, but it is still, if genuine, the result of a kind of necessity, the outcome of a pressure or a need to crystallize a "meaning" into a "form." A contemporary poet such as Rainer Maria Rilke was still very keenly aware of this urgent and necessary character of poetry—the best name for which is inspiration—when he wrote to a would-be poet:

> This most of all: ask yourself in the most silent hour of the night: *must* I write? Dig into yourself for a deep answer. And if the answer rings out in assent, if you meet this solemn question with a strong, simple "I must," then build your life in accordance with this necessity.[16]

Poetry is "given to" or rather "imparted upon" the poet, whether it has the crystalline brevity of *haiku* or the powerful grandeur and length of the epic.[17] This is the inspiration from the "gods" or from the "muses" that the twentieth-century surrealists caricatured with their "automatic writing," confusing the light of the super-conscious with the darkness and chaos of the sub-conscious. Being literally "in-spired," true poetry is therefore a rare occurrence, especially in times of spiritual scarcity such as ours.

"Which cannot be said": poetry is akin to experience, or let us say to presence. Poetry is the articulation of a contemplative perception; it is the result of an encounter between a subject and an object, and ultimately the

---

[16] Rainer Maria Rilke, *Letters to a Young Poet*, p. 6.

[17] As Seyyed Hossein Nasr comments on one of the masterpieces of Sufi poetry: "Shaykh Mahmud Shabistarī, the author of the *Gulshan-i rāz* (*The Secret Rose Garden*), which is one of the greatest masterpieces of Persian Sufi poetry, writes: 'Everyone knows that during all my life, I have never intended to compose poetry. Although my temperament was capable of it, rarely did I choose to write poems.' Yet in spite of himself, Shabistarī, in a period of a few days, and through direct inspiration (*ilhām*) composed one of the most enduring and widely read poetical masterpieces of Oriental literature. Moreover, he composed in perfect rhyming couplets and the *mathnawī* meter while remaining oblivious to the canons of prosody as contained in the classical works on the subject" (*Islamic Art and Spirituality*, pp. 93-4).

verbal crystallization of an identification between them. In the modern world, poetry is often conceived as "subjective" and purely "emotional" because of a misunderstanding or an abuse of this principle. Normatively, poetry is the crystallization of what Daumal quite suggestively calls "an objective emotion." Objective in the sense that it is grounded in an archetype—the essence of a phenomenon or a perception—and emotional in the sense that the soul reacts to this archetype in which she recognizes, more or less clearly, her very substance. In this way, sentiment can be quite objective, and certainly more so than an ineffective reasoning severed from its intellective and intuitive root.

Let us consider Japanese *haiku* as an example: in it, the subject participates in the very mode of nature's operations. The poem is like a glimpse into the emergence of the Whole, of the Infinite, into a given form, a given ambience. In a sense, *haiku* constitutes a limit of poetry: language is reduced to its minimal manifestation in order to suggest the full Reality of That from which the phenomenon emerges. In this regard, poetry must suggest the very ineffability of the object that it attempts to convey. It is a form of the Formless. Baudelaire had an intuition of this function of poetry when he defined it as a capacity to recover childhood and perceive a given phenomenon "in all its freshness, as the very symbol of reality." One could say of the true *haiku* what Titus Burckhardt so suggestively wrote of Far-Eastern landscape painting:

> … in landscape paintings of a Buddhist (*ch'an*) inspiration … all the elements, mountains, trees and clouds, are there only in order to emphasize by contrast the void out of which they seem to have arisen at that very instant, and from which they are detached like ephemeral islets.[18]

Of course, not all poetry must conform to this "minimalist" pattern. However, even the most expansive plenitude of expression, if truly poetic, tends to resonate with contemplative Silence—that vibrant essence which is none other than the Heart as source of all songs.

*   *   *

In the six studies that follow, our purpose has been to highlight the relationship between poetry and contemplation by uncovering the nexus that binds traditional poetics, metaphysical principles, and spiritual practice. In other words, what we propose is to examine traditional patterns of association between

---

[18] Titus Burckhardt, *Sacred Art in East and West*, pp. 183-84.

contemplative practice and contemplative poetry while situating these practices within the metaphysical framework of each spiritual tradition.

Our manner of proceeding varies: we have sometimes chosen to enter a traditional world through the gate of one of its most authoritative representatives and most celebrated poetics. In this respect, the examination of Lu Chi's *Wen Fu* constitutes an appropriate introduction to both Chinese poetry and the specifically Confucian-Taoist understanding of the relationship between poetry and contemplative practice. By contrast, our approach to Hindu poetics emphasizes the study of metaphysical principles as they derive from scriptural sources. In an analogous way, we examine the Islamic and Sufi understanding of poetry primarily through the prism of Qur'ānic religious concepts and Sufi speculative metaphysics. As for Japanese poetry, we envisage it from the standpoint of Japanese civilization as it results from the conjunction of the Buddhist *weltanschauung* and the Shintō perspective on nature. In this chapter, we also emphasize the spiritual and technical contrast between the *waka* and *haiku* forms of poetry in order to highlight the complexity of the relationship between perception and language in the context of Zen Buddhism.

As for our analyses of Western poetics, a word needs to be said about the relatively limited scope of our study. The reader will notice that we have deliberately excluded the canon of Christian mystical poetry—from Meister Eckhart to Saint John of the Cross—from our inquiry. Such exclusion may seem inappropriate on account of the qualitative and quantitative weight of contemplative Christian poetry. However, it has seemed a daunting task to try to reconstruct a Christian poetics. It may be that the theology of the Word Incarnate is in fact the only fundamental and ultimate "poetics" of Christianity. Let us remark, moreover, that the diversity of liturgical languages and the lack of a sacred language in the Christian tradition may account for the lack of a unified or homogeneous "poetics" by contrast with the linguistic situation that prevails in India, Islam, or China. We may therefore wonder whether the Christian tradition, in spite of its poetical summits in the works of Dante and the Counter-Reformation mystics, has given rise to a cohesive poetics that may account for the diversity of mystical and contemplation production in the Christian context. In this regard, a discussion of Jacques Maritain's evaluation of poetry in light of Thomistic principles will allow us to examine the parallels and divergences between the poetic and mystical experiences.

From a literary standpoint, the relative heterogeneity of the mystical tradition, and its correlative post-Renaissance association with philosophical and literary movements, which arguably lie outside the traditional Christian understanding of the world, make it difficult to unveil a fundamental unity in Western poetics, apart from the creative and mystical life that has flowed from union with the Word Incarnate. Moreover, given the extraordinary diversity of Western discourses on poetry—a diversity that may be interpreted in itself as a manifestation of the fragmentation of knowledge which characterizes the modern era—we have chosen to restrict our purpose to a small number of themes that fundamentally bear on the poetic practice of contemplation: inspiration, self-knowledge, and spiritual presence. Our hope is that they will help illuminate some of the main tenets of the relationship between poetry and contemplative vocation in the European literary tradition.

A final chapter is devoted to the archaic and shamanistic roots of poetry. It focuses on the fundamental function of song as a spiritual point of convergence between man and nature. Its terminal placement may help to recapitulate the deepest dimensions of poetic inspiration through an inquiry into its most primordial layers.

Our main objective, in the pages that follow, will be to highlight the manner in which poetry lies at the intersection of doctrine and method, which are respectively the conceptual network of metaphysics as a pointer to Reality and the spiritual means of assimilating It. The conjunction of doctrine and method in poetry is already very apparent in primordial and mythological traditions in which foundational myths describe the manifestation and structure of the universe in relation to the Divine—metaphysics and cosmology—while providing ritual, incantatory, or "sacramental" means of junction with the Higher World. Foundational poetry—the "musical" narratives that account for the nature of reality—is therefore contemplative *par excellence* in both the sense of a theoretical "vision" of Reality, and a methodical or "magical" assimilation of It. If wisdom can be considered, as for example in Buddhism, as the union of doctrine (*prajñā*) and method (*upāya*), poetry may well be defined as the very language of contemplative wisdom. In poetry, Truth and Presence meet.[19] As we will see in the six essays following, a given type of poetry will emphasize—depending on its religious, traditional, and cultural context—one element at the expense of the other, but the two will always remain relevant. This double aspect of poetry makes it akin to Revelation, and to prophecy, so that it could indeed be said, as is taught in the Islamic and North American shamanistic traditions, that Revelation is in a sense the epitome of poetry, while all genuine poetry is in a way Revelation.

---

[19] "The saving manifestation of the Absolute is either Truth or Presence, but it is not one or the other in an exclusive fashion, for as Truth It comprises Presence, and as Presence It comprises Truth. Such is the twofold nature of all theophanies" (Frithjof Schuon, *Form and Substance in the Religions*, p. 1).

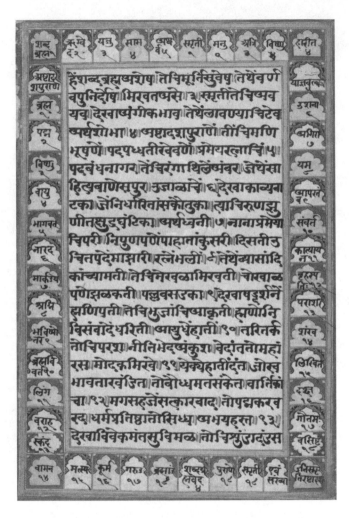

I. Page from an illustrated manuscript of the *Jñāneshvari*,
a commentary on the *Bhagavad Gītā*
Nagpur (18th century)

1. HINDU POETICS
The Liberating Word

When discussing the philosophy and the methods of Hindu poetics, it is important at the outset to situate poetry within its anthropological and spiritual context. In this respect, one of the first principles that must be highlighted is the fact that Hindu poetics stands in sharp contrast with the ordinary contemporary European concept of poetry in that it cannot be dissociated from the goal of life, in view of which it is only a means. As René Daumal has rightly pointed out in his *Rasa or Knowledge of the Self*, "art ... is not an end in itself. It is a medium in service of sacred understanding."[1] As modern men we tend to place an emphasis on the individual as the locus of creativity and potential or actual happiness; our perception of poetry is that of a free, spontaneous, and self-enhancing activity that draws its worth from allowing us to express ourselves independently of the constraints of a perceived usefulness or specific finality. In fact, poetry has tended to become a kind of antonym for the useful and the purposeful, while being on the other hand all the more closely associated with self-expression.

Hindu poetics is predicated upon principles that are directly contrary to these assumptions. First, it lends reality and "seriousness" to poetry inasmuch as it may lead to what it perceives as the ultimate goal of life; and secondly, this goal is fundamentally identified with the transcending of the particular limitations of the egoic individuality, whether it be that of the poet, the auditor, or the reader. The Hindu *weltanschauung* and anthropology is articulated in a cohesive understanding of what makes human life worth living and gives to it its purpose. Traditionally, the Hindu world enumerates and acknowledges four of these "purposes": *kāma* (pleasure), *artha* (wealth), *dharma* (duty or function), and *moksha* (spiritual liberation from existential bondage).[2]

As with most Indian quaternaries, however, these four goals should not be understood primarily as a hierarchical set of four elements (which they undoubtedly are on a certain level), but rather as a relative hierarchy of three

---

[1] René Daumal, *Rasa or Knowledge of the Self*, p. 9.

[2] These four existential goals also correspond to the four "castes" or *varnas*: "The four castes correspond to four fundamental and naturally-occurring human types, characters or temperaments. This differentiation or hierarchization is a fact of nature, not nurture; of heredity, not environment" (William Stoddart, *Outline of Hinduism*, p. 45).

terms that are both transcended and synthesized by a fourth. Accordingly, moksha clearly stands above any other purpose in Hindu life, and it also eminently includes in its realization the fulfillment of all other existential goals. In essence, *moksha* transcends and recapitulates all the other goals because the strength of the instinct of self-preservation "… is there to be overcome by the higher faculties of reason and self-control" and "reason itself must be disintegrated and transcended in the pure vision of the One which is the real 'self' and true Being."[3] All positive aspects of reality are "legitimate" in the overarching scheme of manifestation; but man, in so far as he is a locus of consciousness of *Ātman*, the immanent and absolute Subject, needs to outgrow his lower aspirations. According to this view of reality, the "I" that ordinary consciousness posits as the *de facto alpha* and *omega* of its identity, is nothing but a mistaken distortion of the real "I," the only Subject that is. From this principle, it results that the ego-consciousness cannot be the fundamental end of artistic and poetic creation. René Daumal, who is quite aware of the fundamental gap separating the two visions we have sketched above, draws a suggestive contrast that highlights their diverging orientations:

> Modern man believes himself adult, complete, having no more to do until death, than to gain and spend goods (money, vital forces, learning), without these transactions affecting that which calls itself "I." The Hindu regards himself as an entity to complete, a false vision to rectify, a composite of substances to transform, a multiplicity to unify.[4]

If such is the finality of human destiny, how should poetry be situated within the process of development affecting human consciousness? To begin with, let us remark that the exercise of poetry appears able to be an instrument of fulfillment with respect to the first three goals that we have mentioned. Poetry is undoubtedly a source of delight (*kāma*) both operatively and aesthetically; it may also be (albeit in a less direct manner) the means of acquisition of wealth or goods (*artha*); and it undoubtedly corresponds to a vocational function (*dharma*) for the poet who exercises his gift. More importantly however, poetry corresponds to a way of access to *moksha* in its own right. In other words, the purely contemplative understanding and practice of poetry constitutes the entelechy of that art. Poetry, an activity that modern thinking associates with individual and self-justifying enjoyment, is in fact a path of liberation from the bondage of the individual ego in so far as the latter is experienced as a veil upon the nature of the true Subject.

[3] R.C. Zaehner, *Hinduism*, p. 63.

[4] René Daumal, *Rasa, or Knowledge of the Self*, p. 7.

As an intermediary realm between formal relativity and the formless absoluteness of *Ātman* (a provisional way of speaking, since the non-dualistic perspective of *Advaita Vedānta* considers such a distinction to be ultimately "unreal"), art may be considered as either a formal projection that is as if modeled after its Source, or as a participation in or fusion with that Source. The first approach, which could be referred to as mathematical or geometric, is expressed *par excellence* in the art of architecture, since traditional architecture is understood as a reproduction of a divine model. We see that the square in Hindu architecture, which is at the foundation of the temple, is conceived as the symbol of *Purusha*, the Divine Essence.[5] The etymological association between "temple" and "contemplation" points to the symbolic function of art, the temple being the place where the divine Invisible may be "contemplated" in its formal reflection. The second approach, which could be called as musical or unitive, proceeds through a kind of identification with its goal. This is particularly relevant to the realm of poetry. René Daumal has encapsulated the manner in which this second approach differs from, but also complements, the first:

> Two directly related principles are at the foundation of the aesthetic. The one—analogous recreation of the universe—is particularly apparent in the plastic arts. The other—the establishment of an emotional concord between the individual and the universal laws—manifests itself in music, dance, and poetry. The first is expressed through the concept of *pramāna* (right proportion, analogic precision, conformity to the ideal model) in architecture, sculpture, and painting. The second is expressed through the concept of *rasa*, "savor," direct apprehension of a state of being.[6]

We must note, firstly, that the two terms *pramāna* and *rasa* belong to tellingly different registers. The first has a predominantly epistemological import and has been translated by Eliot Deutsch as "means of valid knowledge." A good definition of *pramāna* is provided in the following lines:

> According to Indian philosophy, and especially as developed in the Nyāya system, a *pramāna* is a "means of valid knowledge." A *pramāna* is that

---

[5] "According to the Hindu tradition the square obtained by the rite of orientation, which summarizes and circumscribes the plan of the temple, is the *Vāstu-Purusha-mandala*, that is to say the symbol of *Purusha*, in so far as he is immanent in existence (*vastu*), or the spatial symbol of *Purusha*" (Titus Burckhardt, *Sacred Art in East and West*, p. 35).

[6] René Daumal, *Rasa, or Knowledge of the Self*, p. 9.

which produces knowledge that is in accord with reality; it is that by which the subject knows the object.[7]

The *Vedānta* acknowledges six such *pramānas*: sensory perception, comparison, judgment of non-existence, inference, logical assumption, and testimony (mainly revelation). What seems to us important is the fact that the *pramānas* can be characterized in terms of "accord," harmony, proportion, or conformity, thereby entailing a relationship between a subject and an object. According to this approach to Reality, one has always to rely upon analogies to "represent" the object, whilst the object remains forever at a distance. In considering *pramāna*, account has to be taken of a discontinuity between what is, and that by which one may come to know it. Even in the case of shruti, or direct audition of the revealed *Veda*, the relationship with truth appears in the form of an external apprehension.

By contrast with the epistemological implications of *pramāna*, *rasa* refers *a priori* to the vocabulary of emotions and sensations. *Rasa* is characterized by its directness, its immediacy, as also by its totality. This totality proceeds from the fact that it operates through a kind of identification between subject and object. The term *rasa* has many connotations, but it indicates primarily a "mood" or a "savor." Let us take note of the fact that a "mood" is like a subjective "savor" in the sense that it is a subtle psychic quality emanating from a subject, while the "savor" is a kind of objective "mood" that "qualifies" an object. *Rasa* is in a sense more appropriately rendered by "emotion" than by "sentiment": the latter would correspond rather to *sthayi bhava* or "the abiding sentiment which can develop into emotion (*rasa*) when confronted by appropriate stimuli."[8] Or again, in Krishna Chaitanya's terms: "The *sthayin* is not *rasa*; sentiment is not emotion, but the possibility and promise of it."[9] *Sthayin* is akin to the sense of taste while *rasa* is more like the actual savoring.

"Savor" and "mood" do not lend themselves to an analytical and rationally based discourse, which does not mean that they do not have an intellective dimension. They actually correspond to qualitative modifications that have an epistemological bearing upon *buddhi* or the immanent intellect, but not upon *manas*, which is the discursive and analytical mind. Both "mood" and "savor" are understood to proceed from within the nature of a being, whence the meaning of "quintessence" that is sometimes attributed to *rasa*. *Rasa* also refers to

---

[7] Eliot Deutsch, *Advaita Vedānta*, p. 69.

[8] Krishna Chaitanya, *Sanskrit Poetics*, p. 8.

[9] *Ibid.*, p. 8.

the sap of a plant, i.e., the immanent principle of its nutrition and growth. The implications of "taste" also point to the idea of absorbing and assimilating, whence a spiritual interiorization that is at the same time a means of transformation. Along the same lines, Ananda Coomaraswamy remarks that one must be mindful of the two main uses of *rasa*: in the plural it refers to the various emotional moods that characterize a given work; and in the singular it pertains to the act of gustation.[10] In other words, the "objective" dimension of *rasa* is manifold since it entails a spectrum of emotional modalities that recapitulates on its level the totality of the unfolding *Māyā*, whereas its "subjective" aspect remains singular in the sense that it requires that a single self may "taste" the savor of the work. This is not to say that the singularity of *rasa* has nothing to do with the work itself since it obviously "emanates" from that work; it simply means that *rasa* cannot by any means be equated with one objective quality, aspect, or part of the work. *Rasa* as a synonym for the multiplicity of the emotional moods of a work may in this sense be related to the famous Scholastic adage, *"de gustibus and coloribus non disputatur"*;[11] in other words, the very ordinary notion of personal "taste" refers to the same principle that enjoins us not to confuse "modal" *rasa* with "quintessential" *rasa*. As far as the latter is concerned, the singularity of *rasa* as savoring of the quintessence of the work is a direct reflection of the unity of the Supreme Self. When René Daumal writes that "the savor is the essence, the 'self' (*Ātman*) of the poem" he clearly points to the fact that the savoring of *rasa* in the poem is no different from Self-consciousness. The *Sāhitya Darpana* refers to this highest dimension of the poetic experience when describing the very act of aesthetic contemplation. In Coomaraswamy's translation:

> Pure aesthetic experience is theirs in whom the knowledge of ideal beauty is innate; it is known intuitively, in intellectual ecstasy without accompaniment of ideation, at the highest level of conscious being; born of one mother with the vision of God, its life is as it were a flash of blinding light of transmundane origin, impossible to analyze, and yet in the image of our very being.[12]

"Ideal beauty" is here a translation of *rasa*, which is a fairly Platonic rendering of the idea of essential savor that has the inconvenience of emphasizing

---

[10] See Ananda Coomaraswamy, *The Transformation of Nature in Art*, pp. 47-8.

[11] Tastes and colors cannot be topics of rational debate.

[12] Cited in Ray Livingston, *The Traditional Theory of Literature*, p. 94.

the aspect of transcendence of what is primarily an immanent reality. To speak of knowledge in the context of aesthetics is implicitly to refer to a science of forms that entails a perfect adequacy and leaves no room for subjectivist arbitrariness. As for the assertion that this knowledge is innate, this must be understood against the background of the metaphysical and epistemological doctrine of the all-encompassing and exclusive reality of *Ātman*. Every individual subject is endowed with a potential knowledge of aesthetics given the fact that it "is" only by virtue of the Essential Subject of that knowledge, the transpersonal Substance that is the real "I" beyond the illusory veils of egoic consciousness.

The knowledge here at issue can by no means be referred to as "intellectual" in the ordinary sense of the word since it is not effected through mental representation: it may however be understood in its full import as pertaining to the realm of intelligence (*buddhi*) if one remains keenly aware of the distinction between intuitive intellection—that is, a direct apprehension of the "known" through identification between the "knower" and it—and the discursive or rational process, the latter being always indirect and reflective. The consubstantiality of this type of intellectual knowledge with the very nature of God is another aspect of the directness we have mentioned since intellection may amount to situating oneself within a "ray" of divine knowledge. The "ray" we have in mind should not however be conceptualized as a kind of illumination coming from without, but rather as an uncovering of the Light that is permanently shining within the human subject. In this instance, the permanence of the Light of the Self must be sharply contrasted with what is described as an instantaneous "flash of blinding light of transmundane origin." The instantaneousness of the aesthetic perception is not without relationship to the blinding character of light as well as to the very nature of the poetic experience. On the one hand, the disproportion between the Self and the soul cannot but result in the incapacity of the latter to be a constant and perfect mirror of the former, whence the instantaneous and relatively unstable character of the experience. On the other hand, the contemplative mode of such an aesthetic perception is more akin to an abrupt but circumstantial removal of the egocentric veil than to a methodical and intellective path as such.

Be that as it may, we could also say that in the experience of poetic savoring, what is effected (virtually or actually) is the transcending of the polarity between subject and object or, what amounts to the same, the unveiling of the true Self. Quoting Visvanātha, Daumal states, "poetry is a word whose essence is savor."[13] Specifying that savor is not to be reduced to the status of a mere

---

[13] René Daumal, *Rasa, or Knowledge of the Self*, p. 11.

individual emotion, Daumal pursues his analysis by proposing the suggestive concept of an "objective emotion." *Rasa* is therefore not purely and simply an emotional response for it implies an objective grounding that transcends mere psychic affects. In other words, *rasa* is a mode of being through which an objective reality that pertains to the archetypical realm of bliss (*Ānanda*) comes to be realized "subjectively" by a given individual. If one has recourse to the tri-unity of aspects that characterizes the Supreme *Brahman*, *Sat* (Being), *Cit* (Consciousness) and *Ānanda* (Beatitude), one can then understand that poetic savor is related to the third of these aspects since it produces pleasure and rides the dynamics of emotions.

The close association of *rasa* with love and devotion pertains to the same dimension of beatitude: "*rasa* is the river that flows from the eternal Vrindaban—the secret place where Krishna plays—to earth, where it 'manifests as the stream of *rasa* flowing between men and women.'"[14] *Rasa* is therefore like the manifestation of the Infinite, which draws beings together and unites them in blessed happiness. This "flow" of erotic interaction between men and women is the very substance of the love that unites everything in the dynamics of manifestation. The universal congruence of poetry and love finds its highest significance in this mystery. If love is most often expressed through and in poetry, it is precisely because poetry is a mode of participation in the elating and transforming flux of *rasa*. Thus, in the contemplative way of love, *bhakti-marga*, *rasa* is an emotional state of devotional love that suffuses the longing of man for Krishna. It expresses the highest function of contemplative poetry as means of union with the One. In the case of human love, as in that of devotion, *rasa* must not be reduced to the status of a kind of self-suggestion or self-inflation: its foundations are always objective even though its modes of manifestation entail subjective practices and strategies.

The *modus operandi* of *rasa*, in poetry as in music and dance, consists in triggering this type of objective and spiritual perception. Essentially, such a perception can, and in fact should, lead to the center of consciousness that is *Ātman*, the indestructible Substance of the subject; it is such a vibration that must be followed all the way to the Self. The contemplative experience of *samādhi*, or spiritual "enstasis" that was said to result from Ramakrishna's encounters with beautiful works of art and natural beings refers to this very possibility. As Grazia Marchiano points out, Indian art and poetry can be conceived as "a process leading from selfish attachment to the source of pleasure

---

[14] Charles Cameron, "In the Words of a Tibetan Geshe," http://home.earthlink.net/~hipbone/IDTWeb/Geshe.html.

to an unafflicted mental state."[15] Although the terms "selfish" and "mental states" may unfortunately limit the scope of the Indian aesthetic experience because of their moral and discursive connotations, the main point made here is that poetry proceeds, so to speak, in the way of a ruse or a trick: raising intense emotional responses in our individual being, it takes us beyond that egoic "self" through a sort of enstatic experience that allows us to establish a connection with the deepest core of our being.

Poetry makes use of the means and ways of *Māyā* to liberate us from *Māyā*: alluring the psychic entity, it brings us to a state of "fusion" that makes us participate in the pure substance of Being. The fact that the Upanishads refer to *rasa* in the same way as to the essence of the subject—while the meaning of aesthetic emotion seems posterior—clearly indicates that *rasa* is of the most profound mystical and metaphysical import. In a kind of unitive and immediate knowledge, the poetical experience that it entails takes us away from mere emotional engrossment with aesthetic objects and enables us to gain access to the Source from which both the aesthetic quality and the sense of self stem.

The Javanese concept of *rasa*—inspired by Indian philosophy and culture—that has been studied by Clifford Geertz[16] can help us gain further in-

---

[15] "By aesthetic experience Indian rhetoricians, who have been systematically exploring it since the 7th century, mean a dynamics of subjective consciousness which does not identify itself with the source of pleasure by which it is triggered, but becomes a totally absorbing experience. Whoever experiences this process is absorbed in it to the point of transcending his own limited subjectivity. The climax reached through the transcendence of pleasure is described as 'selfless sympathy' (Sanskrit. *sahrdayatā*). The concept of selfless sympathy is based on two poles which the classical Indian mind considers wholly compatible: the first is 'heart' (*hrid*), conceived as the root-source of emotion; the other is selflessness, the dimension where subjectivity and pleasure are transcended. Aesthetic experience is therefore a process leading from selfish attachment to the source of pleasure to an unafflicted mental state" (Grazia Marchiano, "What to Learn from Eastern Aesthetics," *Canadian Aesthetics Journal / Revue canadienne d'esthétique* 2 (Winter 1998) http://www.uqtr.uquebec.ca/AE/vol_2/marchiano.html).

[16] "As 'feeling' it is one of the traditional Javanese five senses—seeing, hearing, talking, smelling, and feeling, and it includes within itself three aspects of 'feeling' that our view of the five senses separates: taste on the tongue, touch on the body, and emotional 'feeling' within the 'heart' like sadness and happiness. The taste of a banana is its *rasa*; a hunch is a *rasa*; a pain is a *rasa*; and so is a passion. As 'meaning,' *rasa* is applied to the words in a letter, in a poem, or even in common speech to indicate the between-the-lines type of indirection and allusive suggestion that is so important in Javanese communication and social intercourse. And it is given the same application to behavioral acts generally: to indicate the implicit import, the connotative 'feeling' of dance movements, polite gestures, and so forth. But in this second, semantic sense, it also means 'ultimate significance'—the deepest meaning at which one arrives by dint of mystical effort and whose clarification resolves all the ambiguities of mundane existence. *Rasa*, said one of my most articulate informants, is the same as life; whatever lives has *rasa* and whatever has *rasa* lives. To translate such a sentence one could only render it twice: whatever lives feels

sight into this notion, so essential for the understanding of Indian poetry and its philosophical background. In this anthropological context, the term *rasa* follows two semantic directions: that of feeling and that of meaning, echoing the Indian implications of "mood" and "essence." The sense of feeling encompasses both sensory perception and emotional responses, therefore implying a character of immediacy; the lexical lack of differentiation between physical and psychic experiences may also refer to a sense of the concrete unity of human experience that is often overlooked by the schizomorphic tendencies of Western discursive practice. In this sense, *rasa* is also given the meaning of an implicit, underlying quality or "presence" that is the fundamental key for the understanding of a speech, a text, or a poem. It is at this juncture that the senses of "feeling" and "meaning" meet: the subtle and unexpressed connotative dimension of a poem is both "felt," in the sense of not being susceptible of an analytic deciphering, and "understood," by virtue of its power of cultural and spiritual resonance. If *rasa* is the hidden and resounding dimension of the poem that allows one to make sense of it, it is because it is both immanent and transcendent to the text. It needs the text as a linguistic substance in order to be manifested, but its essential reality escapes any technical structure or formal characteristic. This essential reality is the ultimate meaning of the poem and it is also what gives unity to the whole poem.

When considered from the point of view of transmission and experience, *rasa* is attained through the vehicle of what Indian rhetoricians refer to as *dhvani*. Paraphrasing the *Vyaktivāda*, Ananda Coomaraswamy translates this complex concept as "the reverberation of meaning that arises through suggestion."[17] *Dhvani* is the primary concept of what constitutes the inner essence of good poetry, poetry capable of emanating or awakening *rasa*. The auditory connotation of "reverberation" also suggests the inward import of *dhvani*. From this inward standpoint, the concept of *dhvani* is akin to the Javanese idea that we have mentioned above, and that alludes to a mysterious resonance which is the overall character of *rasa*. According to Coomaraswamy, *dhvani* is neither denotation nor connotation (although it is certainly closer to the latter given its indirectness), but rather it refers to a suggestion. In other words it is neither literal nor allegoric, but anagogic, the latter pertaining to the higher spiritual meaning toward which one must "ascend" (*ana*: upward). *Dhvani* can be understood as the harmonic note that suggests the way of a given *rasa*;

and whatever feels lives; or: whatever lives has meaning and whatever has meaning lives" (Clifford Geertz, *The Religion of Java*, quoted in Cameron, "In the Words of a Tibetan Geshe").

[17] Ananda Coomaraswamy, *The Transformation of Nature in Art*, p. 53.

it could also be said that *dhvani* is simply the auditory or semantically suggestive manifestation and means of experience of that *rasa*. Rakesh Gupta complements this definition by stating that "the suggested sense blossoms, as it were, out of the primary denotation or secondary indication."[18] This image of blossoming implies that the denotative sense functions as the starting point of the suggestion but that the latter comes to obliterate the former, which becomes purely accessory. Anandavardhana considers this obliteration of the explicit by the implicit—or the subordination of the former to the latter—as a central characteristic of effective poetry, a feature that actually serves as a specific difference for the definition of a poetic genre:

> That kind of poetry, wherein the [conventional] meaning renders itself secondary or the [conventional] word renders its meaning secondary and suggests the [intended or] implied meaning, is designated by the learned as *dhvani* or "suggestive poetry."[19]

In fact however, the definition of *dhvani* has been an extremely complex question in Indian poetics, one of the main points at issue being that of the relationship between the explicit and the implicit in poetry. The comparison of *dhvani* with "charm in ladies"—in the *Dhvanyāloka* of Anandavardhana—brings to the fore the complexity of the relationship between explicit forms and suggestion: "In the words of first-rate poets (the implicit aspect) shines supreme and towers above the beauty of the striking external constituents even as charm in ladies."[20] The relationship between "charm" and physical beauty points to a subtle connection between inner suggestion and outer depiction. "Charm" cannot be reduced to physical beauty, but it is undoubtedly related to the resonance or echo of elements that pertain to the latter.[21] *Dhvani* is most commonly conceived, as in Gupta's definition, as being the implicit element that proceeds from the explicit; but it may actually refer to a variety of such implicit elements such as meaning, figures of speech, or sentiments. In any case, there is little doubt that *dhvani* is most profoundly suggestive, being therefore the determining factor of beautiful poetry, to the extent of its being most mysteriously connected to explicit denotation. In other words, the

[18] Rakesh Gupta, *A Dictionary of Sanskrit Poetics*, p. 51.

[19] Anandavardhana, *Dhvanyāloka*, I. 13, p. 19.

[20] *Ibid.*, I. 3, p. 7.

[21] Physical beauty may enhance or prolong charm, but it does not create it. Charm can even compensate for a lack of physical beauty.

quality of *dhvani* is mostly determined by its capacity to foster interiorizing associations of meaning and feeling.

In a sense that is often parallel to the mysterious suggestiveness and the instantaneous effect of *dhvani*, Hindu poetics also refer to the original sounds that are the seeds of all utterances, *sphota*. The image conveyed by the term *sphota* is that of a bud which contains *in potentia* the whole development of the flower. This potentiality can also be understood in terms of power, as suggested by the French word *puissance*. Power is finally manifested in a kind of "explosion" or "budding" that unveils the "potential" meaning. Krishna Chaitanya equates this event to that of a phenomenon in quantum physics:

> ... according to the *Sphota* doctrine, the meaning holds itself back from self-revelation till the last phoneme of the word is uttered, or the last word in the sentence, thus completing the etymological and syntactical shapes. Then the revelation takes place in a *Sphota* [literally, explosion]. *Sphota* is the integral significance, which makes its discontinuous, quantal appearance when the phonetic shape is complete. The phonetic shape is the suggestor (*Abhivyanjaka*); the *Sphota* is the suggested (*Abhivyangya*).[22]

The distinction that is drawn by Chaitanya runs parallel to the distinction between an explicit utterance (from *explicare*, to unfold) and its suggestive effects, the latter being discontinuous with respect to the former: *dhvani* appears on the basis of explicit denotation but it also represents a qualitative leap. The element of discontinuity entailed is a hallmark of the transcendence of the poetic meaning and points in the direction of the contemplative unveiling of the essence. Moreover, the instantaneousness of the sphotic explosion is not without analogy with the ultimate liberation that occurs when the karmic sequence has been unfolded and therefore exhausted.

Considering *sphota* from the standpoint of its productive dynamics, one may also emphasize the fact that language is a shaktic reality, in the sense that there is in words, and in each of the letters that form these words, a power that is a principle of dynamic manifestation issuing from a particular divine agency. The extrinsic distinction between the Divine as being and as manifesting, as *Brahman* and as *Shakti*, has been encapsulated by Ramakrishna in the following way:

> When I think of the Supreme Being as inactive, neither creating, nor preserving, nor destroying, I call him *Brahman* or *Purusha*, the impersonal

---

[22] Krishna Chaitanya, *Sanskrit Poetics*, p. 68.

God. When I think of him as active, creating, preserving, destroying, I call him *Shakti* or *Maya* ... the personal god. But the distinction between them does not mean a difference. The personal and the impersonal are the same Being, in the same way as are milk and its whiteness, or the diamond and its luster, or the serpent and its undulations. It is impossible to conceive of the one without the other. The Divine Mother (Kali) and *Brahman* are one.[23]

The letter and the word, in so far as they manifest themselves as sounds, constitute through analogy secondary expressions of this dual dimension of the Divine. Sanskrit letters are thus considered as "seeds" that are associated with the specific energy of a given divine aspect.[24] As for names of worshiped deities (*ishta devata*), they properly constitute "sacramental" means of union with the Divine or one of Its aspects, the latter being ontologically identified with It. "God and His Name are one," as Ramakrishna also said. This is the principle upon which the yoga of invocation (*japa-yoga*) is founded: by virtue of steadfast and sincere repetition of the Name, the soul is permeated by the Divine Presence and, on the basis of the essential unity between the Supreme Self and the Name, the latter becomes the gradual means of the unveiling of the former. Inasmuch as poetry can be identified with sacred utterance, it therefore becomes the vehicle of a spiritual disclosure.

From the complementary standpoint of manifestation, the operative and shaktic dimension of sound is based on the very concept of universal unfolding and cosmogony. We find a particularly direct expression of this process and its spiritual corollaries in the verses of the 14th century Kashmiri *yogini* and popular saint Lalla Yogeshwari:

> Shiva is the horse and Vishnu the saddle
> Brahma adorns the stirrups,
> The yogi, by the art of yoga, recognizes Him.
> Who is the god that rides the horse?
> It is the perpetual, unobstructed sound [OM],
>   beyond time and space,

[23] Ramakrishna, cited in Romain Rolland, *Prophets of the New India*, pp. 42-3.

[24] "Every letter of the Sanskrit alphabet is also a *bija* mantra—a seed syllable—whose energy is that of a particular *deva* or *devi* (god or goddess). These syllables manifest pure energy—sound in its direct derivation. For the practitioner they dissolve into light—his true nature—thus allowing him to transcend the mundane world as perceived by his ego-mind and to experience his absolute non-dual nature, the self or *atma* in Sanskrit terminology" (René Daumal, *Rasa or Knowledge of the Self*).

Permeating everything, the principle of absolute vacuity,
Whose abode is the Void [of the Sahasrāha],
Who has no name, no complexion, no pedigree
   and no form;
Who by Its own reflection on Itself emerges as "I-ness,"
First as the Sound and the Dot, and is called as such,
He is the God who will mount the horse.[25]

The Shivaite perspective presented here clearly "subordinates" the personal manifestations of the Divine to the Supreme *Ātman*, the unqualified and universal Substance and Consciousness of all beings and all subjects. There is little doubt that such subordination is intended to draw a sharp contrast with passages from the Upanishads that describe Vishnu as the charioteer or the rider and the syllable OM as the chariot. Lalla Yogeshwari's understanding of the Sound appears to refer primarily to metaphysical principles, by contrast with yogic determinations of the sacred syllable. To say that Vishnu "rides" and "drives" the chariot of OM[26] implicitly amounts to considering the latter as a methodical means, and not as the supra-formal principle of all manifestation. For Lalla Yogeshwari, the primordial Sound is considered as the Rider because it is identified with the Supreme, which is beyond all determination: it is only through a self-reflective act that the Supreme determines Itself as Being and Power. The first of these determinations is symbolically and operatively referred to as the Dot, i.e., is the static principle of being (*sat*) which may be identified with the god Shiva. It is also considered as the Sound or the Primordial OM. By virtue of a complementary aspect—but without in the least introducing any duality within the non-dual Reality—the auditory manifestation of the Divine, the primordial OM (or AUM), is identified with the *Shakti* or Divine feminine. It remains true that these two aspects are essentially one, i.e., that they form the *Nāda-Bindu* or primordial Sound. Moreover, we should pay attention to the fact that both Shiva and *Shakti* must be considered on two different levels, the Supreme and the Non-Supreme: Shiva is the horse as personal divine manifestation, but He is also and above all the rider of the horse insofar as He is understood as the transcendent and non-qualified dimension of the Divine, that which Lalla designates as Paramashiva.

---

[25] B.N. Parimoo, *The Ascent of Self: A Reinterpretation of the Mystical Poetry of Lalla Deb*, pp. 144-45.

[26] "Riding this chariot that is the syllable OM, having Vishnu as charioteer, the adept who is devoted to the service of Rudra, moves forward on the path that leads to the Brahman's heaven" (*Amrtanāda Upanishad*, 2 [my translation, here and in following citations, is based on Jean Varenne's French translation in *Upanishads du Yoga*, p. 148]).

Analogously, we can distinguish between *Mahāshakti*—the Divine Essence in Its aspect of Infinite Power—and the productive *Shakti* that presides over universal manifestation.[27] *Shakti* is the principle of becoming and change; as such, it is the immanent aspect of the Divinity, in contradistinction to the transcendent dimension, which is the realm of Shiva. As we have suggested, and as illustrated by Lalla's verses, the Divine Sound is particularly associated with the dynamic aspects of manifestation and transforming energy. On the other hand, the Dot is associated with Light, and it is ultimately with this Light that the *yogi* must identify. Sound leads to Light, or to use Daumal's expression, It so to speak "dissolves" into Light. Sound can therefore be understood in this connection as the all-pervasive reality that both reveals and reintegrates. In the *Bhagavad Gītā*, the sacred syllable OM is explicitly referred to as a central means for the realization of *moksha*, the supreme deliverance that is the highest goal of human life as a way of return to the non-dual Supreme Self:

> Uttering the single-syllable "OM" Brahman (*om ity ekāksaram brahma*)
> Meditating on Me,
> He who goes forth, renouncing the body,
> Goes to the supreme goal (*paramām gatim*).[28]

Quite suggestively, Brahman, the Supreme Reality, is here qualified by the word "*ekāksaram*," which means "having one syllable." OM is properly speaking the Absolute in the form of one syllable. As such, it is traditionally referred to as the sheath of *Brahman*, since it constitutes the outer "shell" of the imperceptible "Void" of *Ātman*. It is also referred to as *pranava*, the vital breath that penetrates and permeates all things, thereby suggesting that OM is the most direct symbol of the omnipresence of the Divine. In it, the limitless expanse of universal manifestation coincides with the most concentrated and synthetic expression of reality. This coincidence of opposites amounts to the minimal degree of intelligibility allowable by the *pranava*, which is not properly speaking "understandable" in terms of purely intellective discrimination.

In the *pranava*, intelligence is as if reduced to its pure aspect of being or presence; but it follows from this reduction that the whole universe of letters

---

[27] "In the Absolute, the *Shakti* is the aspect of Infinitude that coincides with All-Possibility and gives rise to *Māyā*, the universal and efficient *Shakti*" (Frithjof Schuon, *Roots of the Human Condition*, p. 29).

[28] *Bhagavad Gītā* VIII.13, trans. Winthrop Sargeant, p. 361.

and sounds, indeed the whole universe as such in so far as it comes into existence through the "vibration" of the primordial Sound, is but the unfolding of this seed. It is interesting to note in this respect that Sri Shankaracharya, the supreme authority of *Advaita Vedānta*, after having quoted several passages from the Upanishads (in his commentaries on the *Bhagavad Gītā*)[29] that highlight the saving power of the sacred *pranava* OM, specifies that such passages are intended for "persons of dull and middling intellects," the inference being that most practitioners are unable to concentrate their intelligence and being on the supra-formal Supreme by means of intellective discrimination (*viveka*). This somewhat belittling statement is to be understood within the context of Shankara's spiritual perspective, a perspective that is based upon the transcending of *avidyā*, ignorance, the source of which is none other than the superimposition (*adhyāsa*) of the qualities of one being upon another. In other words, the liberation from ignorance is the recognition of the non-reality of *Māyā*, and the exclusive attribution of Reality to *Ātman*. According to this view, the way of the *pranava* is somewhat indirect in that it does not immediately reach the core of the problem: the superimposition of appearance upon Reality and the ensuing error of attributing reality to appearance. From Shankara's point of view, instead of sharply cutting through the illusion of a self-existence of *Māyā*, the concentration on OM bypasses discrimination and "dully" follows the detour of mystic identification with the Self as sheathed in an auditory symbol. The Word is already a projection of *Ātman*; focusing on It is therefore only appropriate for those who lack the discriminative ability to see through the veil of *Māyā*.

By contrast with Shankara's purely intellective emphasis, the perspective of yoga is very much connected with the spiritual integration and methodical use of sacred sound. In the *Yogatattva Upanishad*, we find an extensive discussion of the reality of the *pranava* OM. The Upanishad states the radical dimension of the tri-vocal OM as a matrix of all triads:

---

[29] "He who will meditate on the Supreme Purusha by the three-lettered syllable 'OM'—he is borne up by the Sama-hymns to the Brahma-loka, to the region of Brahman" (*Prasna Upanishad*, 5.5). Let us take note of the fact that the previous passage does not refer to *moksha* (deliverance) as such, but only to a rebirth in the proximity of *Brahman*. However, the *Katha Upanishad* (2.14) refers to the sacred syllable as the supreme goal of existence, i.e., unconditioned deliverance: "that goal which all the Vedas speak of (i.e., are intended for), which all the austerities speak of, desiring which they lead the life of Brahmacharya (celibacy), that goal I tell thee in brevity: It is this, the syllable 'OM'" (quoted in *The Bhagavad Gītā with the Commentary of Sri Sankaracharya*, p. 228).

Three are the worlds, three the Vedas,
Three the ritual junctions, three the tones;
Three are the sacrificial fires,[30]
    three the natural qualities (*guna*);
And all these triads have the three phonemes
    of the syllable OM as foundation.[31] (verse 134)

It is essential to recall that the Sanskrit syllable OM is actually formed of three phonemes: these are the vowels A and U which are diphthongized as O and the nasalized M, which is also prolonged as a final resonance. In Yoga, this concluding prolongation is identified with the supreme state of *turīya*, which transcends the three states of deep sleep (*prājña*), dream (*taijasa*), and wakefulness (*vaishvānara*). In other words, the final resonance that evokes the return of all relative forms to the one and only Reality of *Ātman* transcends all differentiation and multiplicity. It is Silence as the essence of all sounds. It is also the formless and impersonal Divine that transcends the *Trimurti* of Brahmā, Vishnu, and Shiva. The *Dhyānabindu Upanishad* states that the final resonance of OM gives access to spiritual liberation while the vocalic syllable in itself has only more extrinsic effects: when envisaged as a brief syllable it effaces sins, whereas it provides wealth when it is lengthened.[32] It is difficult to say whether the distinction between a short and a long form of the sacred syllable should be understood as referring to the single vowels versus the diphthong that they form together (Jean Varenne's view), or as hinting at two different modes of elocution. In both cases, however, one may infer that the brief syllable is related to a relatively quick rhythm and a repetitive mode, whereas the long syllable is akin to "acquiring" and "possessing" a share of good or energy. In other words, the deliberate repetition of the formula is a steadfast washing away of impurities while the lengthened version is characterized by a replenishing of virtue. Be that as it may, both processes can only be understood as preparations for a radically higher goal, *moksha*, which is actualized exclusively through the infinitely deepening effect of the final resonance.

[30] Indo-Aryan sacrificial fires were traditionally numbered as three: a western fire area was round and represented the earth; an eastern area was square and represented the heavens; and a southern area in the shape of a half-moon, representing the "dome of circle between earth and heaven" (Cf. David and John Noss, *A History of the World's Religions*, p. 89).

[31] Jean Varenne, *Upanishads du Yoga*, p. 91.

[32] "As a brief syllable, OM consumes sins; as a long syllable, OM, without effort, gives wealth; with the nasal resonance, it provides liberation" (verse 17) (Jean Varenne, *Upanishads du Yoga*, p. 97).

This distinction is highly relevant to a contemplative practice of poetry—if one is to understand the latter as a prolongation of the sacred word—since it allows us to distinguish between three different spiritual functions of words-sounds: on the one hand, the word-sound of a spiritually oriented poetry, as epitomized by sacred incantations, is akin to a lustral exercise that can be conceived as a doing away with psychic knots and obstacles that obstruct the way to the Heart. The Word is an ablution in two senses: in that it proceeds from the Substance with which it is essentially identified, and also because its presence in the mind and heart of the reader-auditor-practitioner excludes extraneous mental and animic crystallizations that would be contrary to the contemplative climate which the pronunciation of the syllable fosters. As for the effortlessly acquired "wealth" that the Upanishad associates with *Omkāra*, it is also not without importance with regard to poetry as a spiritual practice. In this connection, the Word should be interpreted as a formidable repository of power. On whatever level one may wish to understand the meaning of that "wealth," it is always a question of increasing one's capital of reality in order to better realize one's goal. The effortless aspect of this work stems from the spiritual principle that the Japanese tradition of Pure Land Buddhism refers to as *tariki*, the "power of the other" as opposed to the *jiriki*, the "power of one-self." The "power of the other" amounts in fact to the inner transformative efficacy that dwells at the core of the sacred syllables. Accordingly, true poetry "enriches" one in that it stores up treasuries of spiritual power within us. The Word penetrates us and "capitalizes" its spiritual energy in ourselves.

These two complementary modes of the influence of the Word allow of further clarification if we consider the fact that the brief and analytic mode of the sacred syllable proceeds on the basis of differentiation, multiplicity, and repetition whereas the long and diphthongized version operates by means of conjunction, accumulation, and synthesis. However, it must be emphasized that the third mode, that of resonance, is the only one that touches upon the essential meaning and final end of poetry. As we have already seen, Hindu poetics highlights "resonance" both as a practical and semantic principle. The *Dhyānabindu Upanishad* stresses the first of these principles by comparing the "ineffable resonance" of *Omkāra* with the profound and far-reaching resonance of a large bell.[33] It is important to emphasize that this "resonance" is ever continuous in the heart of man, whether he is aware of it or not. In this view, *Omkāra* is not involved in the process of spiritual realization as an external tool—as it is in other passages—but, more fundamentally, is the very

---

[33] *Dhyānabindu Upanishad*, 18.

Center of consciousness that is to be disclosed. In Hindu metaphysics, spiritual realization is not so much something to be *acquired* or sought after as it is an eternally present reality that has only to be *unveiled*. The major implication of this contemplative principle is that Hindu poetics tend to view poetry less as a creation, in the sense of the western European model of *poiēsis*, than as an utterance of That (*Tat*) which is.

In addition to these equivalences that relate to the modes and phases of spiritual realization, traditional sources associate the various letters, as we have stated above, with the power of a particular deity. Each of the three letters is also, as such, a principle of manifestation and reabsorption. The ternary AUM is thus correlated to each of the major gods: A corresponds to Brahmā, the god who creates; it is therefore related to the beginning phase of manifestation and the almost imperceptible initial vocalic aspiration (as well as with the final vowel-sound of the God's name); U refers to Vishnu (note the final sound of His Name) and the conservative function of the Divine, which is the intermediary pause between manifestation and reabsorption; finally, the M sound refers to Shiva, the transformer and destroyer who brings back the whole spectrum of *Māyā* to the non-dual *Ātman*. Each phoneme is also associated with a given color: A is yellow and is identified as such with manifesting energy. It implicitly refers to the cosmic quality of *guna rajas*, which is ordinarily associated with another warm color, red. U is akin to white and to light, while M is connected to black and to darkness.[34] These last two colors are ordinarily and respectively related to *sattva* and *tamas*, the ascending and luminous quality, and the descending and dark quality. One may at first be puzzled by the associations U-*sattva* and M-*tamas*; it must, however, be borne in mind that light is related to manifestation or the "coming into the open" of Reality, whereas darkness is a symbolic dimension of the mystery of the non-dual Essence. Moreover, *tamas* as demiurgic principle of manifestation is a reverse analogue of the Infinitude of Shiva, since it is essentially by virtue of this infinitude that manifestation takes place.

What has been illustrated by considering the auditory symbols inherent to each part of the *pranava* is also traceable in the graphic representation of OM. René Guénon has judiciously pointed to the fact that the three graphic forms which constitute the *pranava* also recapitulate the "breathing" process of manifestation: there is first the straight line as affirming manifestation, then the semi-circle, which corresponds to a "state of envelopment relative to that unfolding [of manifestation], but nevertheless still developed or mani-

---

[34] *Dhyānabindu Upanishad*, 9-13.

fested,"[35] and finally the non-manifested state. The *pranava* is therefore the essential synthesis of the whole process of manifestation, and it is as such that it can perform its role as a fundamental means of spiritual contemplation. It is actually the sacramental symbol of the Hindu contemplative path since it recapitulates the whole becoming of man; to know it is to know That (*Tat*), since manifestation is nothing but the manifold "ontological magic" of *Tat*.

Akin to the number three, the *pranava* OM corresponds to the Earth and to the domain of manifestation, as is implied by the Veda that places "four above and three below." From this point of view, four represents the stability of the Divine domain (*Ātman* has four "feet" or *pādas*, i.e., states) and three points to the instability and lack of self-sufficiency of the manifestation that precisely calls for the need of a fourth component. Now this fourth element is not situated on the same level as the first three, in the same way as the "nasal resounding" that prolongs the three vocalic phonemes also transcends them. This "resounding," as described in the *Yogatattva Upanishad*, is identified with *turīya*, the unconditioned state of *Ātman*, i.e., *Ātman* in itself and independently of any conditioning whatsoever. An OM without final resonance would be like the three conditioned states of *Ātman* without an unconditioned state; in other words it would not be what it is as spiritually operative *pranava*.

This last remark is of the utmost importance in understanding the ultimate principle of Hindu poetic utterance: the Word (the creative *Vāc* from which everything proceeds) is not only the unfolding of the seed of *Brahman*, it is also the means of a way of return to the latter by virtue of the immanence of that resonance, which is like the presence of silence in sound. Poetry, as sacred chant, is therefore never to be understood as a way of no return; or, to put it differently, as "art for art's sake": it is on the contrary always subordinated to a spiritual goal that orients its unfolding and coincides with its ultimate end. As the *pranava* OM, contemplative poetry is a means of bringing back manifestation to its source, of bringing duality and multiplicity back to the non-dual silence. That is the reason why the Upanishads of Yoga associate the pronunciation of the sacred syllable with the inversion of the lotus of the heart; thus we read in the *Yogatattva Upanishad*:

> As fragrance is in the flower, butter in milk,
> As oil is in sesame, and gold in nuggets,
> A lotus is in the heart:
> Pointing downward, it sets up its stem

---

[35] René Guénon, *Man and his Becoming according to the Vedānta*, p. 96.

and bears a mark at its basis:
In the middle of it the spirit dwells;
When saying "OM!," the adept utters the vowel A,
The lotus raises itself upward,
    it is pierced when U is pronounced;
With the nasal sound M, OM is complete,
Prolonged by the resonance in the shape of a crescent.[36]

The process of inversion that is described in this passage allows us better to understand the contemplative function of the Word. The initial downward direction of the lotus has to do with manifestation as a centrifugal emanation coming out of the seed of *Ātman*, the downward motion being here a symbolic synonym of the outward one. It is only by contact with the *pranava* that the direction of the lotus is reversed; upon being pierced, the lotus opens up to the liberating and limitless inner space of the spirit that had until then remained enclosed in the lotus. The yogic use of OM may therefore be equated with the reversal of an inversion, or in other words a spiritual magic of exteriorization in view of interiorization: the *pranava* is the envelope of *Brahman* as the lotus is the sheath of the spirit—both *Brahman* and the spirit are identical with *Ātman*. Now it is through the "formal" mediation of the sacred syllable—as manifestation of the "supra-formal"—that the "formal" envelope of the heart may be pierced and opened to give access to the limitless immanence of the Self. The sacred syllable is the intermediate reality that connects, as through an inversion, manifestation and non-manifestation. Considering this from the standpoint of methodical Yoga, the *Dhyānabindu Upanishad* also designates OM as a "bow," the spirit being the arrow and *Brahman* the target. This image is important in that it clearly defines the syllable as a principle of energy and motion. It is through a repeated contact with OM's power that the soul is able to transcend itself. On more speculative grounds, the same text expresses this intermediary status of OM in a suggestive metaphysical paradox:

The seed syllable is crowned with a dot and a crescent;
It is sonorous, but if one destroys the syllable,
There only remains the absolute, silent.
The Sound that does not resound
    because it is beyond sound,
The adept that finds it is delivered of any doubt.[37]

[36] *Yogatattva Upanishad*, 136-39, cited in Jean Varenne, *Upanishads du Yoga*, p. 92.

[37] *Dhyānabindu Upanishad*, 2-3, cited in Jean Varenne, *Upanishads du Yoga*, p. 94.

The real Sound is the essence of Sound that lies beyond auditory manifestation. Through the extreme brevity of its phonetic substance and through its resounding prolongation—an entrance into silence—the *pranava* OM becomes the bridge that allows one to pass beyond the screen of phenomena to reach the "magnetic field" of Atmic presence. This bridge is instrumental, but it is not an end in itself. The *Amrtanāda Upanishad* also identifies it with the chariot that leads to the end of the way, and it underscores that this chariot is of no use beyond that point:

> When the adept reaches the end of the path
> He abandons the chariot and goes his way.[38]

Some Upanishads even explicitly subordinate OM to silence, indicating that the latter is actually more effective to reach the goal than the former. The *Amrtabindu Upanishad* states, for example, that "silence produces in fact a greater benefit" than OM.[39] At the other extreme, the formal repetition of a mantra is like an indefinite extension of the *pranava*; it allows one to reach its essence by encompassing duration and sequence within it. The *Hamsa Upanishad* teaches us that "one can also realize the Sound by repeating the *mantra* ten millions times."[40] The hyperbolic and maximal quantitative extension of the repeated *mantra* is like the complementary reverse of the synthetic power of the *Omkāra*. However, the repetition of a *mantra* is often considered as a method that is better fitted for the "adept who is little gifted intellectually."[41]

Throughout the preceding pages, we have highlighted, on different levels and in various modes, a fundamentally complementary relationship between a transcendent and non-manifested principle that is the essence of being, and a manifested, auditory, or semantic reality that functions as a support for the former. Our examination of the relationship between *rasa* and *dhvani* as well as our references to the rapport between the ineffable Sound and the OM utterance have allowed us to unveil what may be the most important principle of Hindu poetics and poetry. Ananda Coomaraswamy comments upon the marriage *mantra* of the High-Priest and the King as a most direct expression of the type of dual relationship that we have presently in mind:

---

[38] *Amrtanāda Upanishad*, 3, cited in Jean Varenne, *Upanishads du Yoga*, p. 148.
[39] *Ibid.*, p. 157.
[40] *Hamsa Upanishad*, 16, cited in Jean Varenne, *Upanishads du Yoga*, p. 146.
[41] *Yogatattva Upanishad*, 20-22, cited in Jean Varenne, *Upanishads du Yoga*, p. 72.

(The High-Priest addresses the King saying) I am That (*ama*, "He"), thou art This (*sa*); thou art This, I am That. I am Sky, thou art Earth. I am the Harmony (*sāman*), thou the Words (*rc*). Let us twain here unite our houses (*samvahavahai purāni*). Thou art the body, thou my body from this Great Dread.[42]

The duality described in this passage refers, in the poetic domain, to the necessary "marriage" of intellective form and linguistic and auditory matter. The second is akin to *Vāc*, i.e., productive speech, *Vāc* being also the name that is sometimes given to the *Shakti* of *Brahmā*, the Creator. *Vāc* is the substantial and dynamic principle of manifestation, in the same way as *rc* fulfills this function with regard to poetry. As for *sāman*, the first "spouse" of the poetic marriage, it is identified with music, chant, or harmony—these notions being understood here in their intellective implications as informing *rc*.

In a sense, the Western reader may be *prima facie* puzzled by the fact that music is identified with the "form" while words are considered as mere "matter."[43] We ordinarily tend to associate "content" with words and music with a sort of aesthetic "vehicle" for that "content." It may be that a Western overemphasis on discursive thought, and on language as an exclusive means toward the discovery of truth, has resulted in a quasi-identification between intellective life and argumentative and verbal expression, whereas music and harmony have been, so to speak, confined to the realm of artistic enjoyment, having little if anything to do with the intellect. It goes without saying that this point of view was not at all that of the great philosophers of ancient Europe as testified by Pythagoras' "music of the spheres." In the full sense of these words, music and harmony are profoundly intellectual realities since they refer, on the highest level, to the transcendent "structure" of reality, its archetyp-

---

[42] Ananda Coomaraswamy, *Spiritual Authority and Temporal Power in the Indian Theory of Government*, pp. 51-2.

[43] "The spirits who bestowed on us songs with words have given a great gift. These songs express our knowledge of and joy in the Creator, using an earthly language with rational terms. They have particular meaning and purposes and are sung accordingly. But the mind cannot think 'Great Spirit' (*Wakan Tanka*), or conceive reality as it truly is. Thus, additional songs have been given to us—songs with music only—praise expressed through a few sacred syllables which go beyond the mind, beyond language and say the inexpressible, sing what is intellectually unutterable. These are perhaps the very chants which the spirits themselves sing—similar to the hosannas and hallelujahs of another tradition. Therefore, although the philosopher, the musicologist and the anthropologist may have little or nothing to say of these wordless melodies, it should be recognized that these are our highest and most treasured hymns because they go above the intellect and kindle the heart directly" (Ben Black Bear Sr. and R.D. Theisz, *Lakota Ceremonial Songs*).

ical essences; the word *harmonia* is akin to the Greek verb *harmottein*, which means to arrange or to dispose in order. Now the supreme "ordering" reality is the Divine Intellect and music is therefore nothing but the reflection of this Intellect on a variety of planes. The "music of the spheres" is the language of the Intellect; as Martin Lings puts it:

> The "music of the spheres" is the transcendent rhythm and melody to which the soul of unfallen man had access, and which may therefore once again become accessible.... The art of music presupposes some such access, for its primal purpose is to give us a foretaste of that which now "we cannot hear"; and its power to stir us to the depths of our being depends on the fidelity with which it echoes the transcendent harmony that underlies our nature.[44]

The Hindu *sāman* is closely related to this "transcendent harmony" and it also implies that, at its highest level, music is independent of any verbal vehicle (i.e., the "wordless Chant" of Prajāpati), its association with the latter taking place only on the level of manifestation. As the non-manifested *Brahman* manifests itself in and by *Vāc*, so in the same way, *sāman* is manifested by and through *rc*. As a "material" substance for poetry, the latter cannot be separated from the former. In this respect, Ananda Coomaraswamy quotes the *Jaiminīya Upanishad Brāhmana* to illustrate how *rc* without *sāman* amounts to the "evil (*pāpman*) of the Chant, and whoever seeks to take refuge in such a toneless *Rc* (*rcy asvarāyām*) is found out by Death."[45] That is to say, words do not convey "eternal life" independently from the intellective intuition of harmony that makes them the receptacle of That which is. To speak of evil in this connection is not the expression of an hyperbolic moralism: in fact, since the source of all "evils"—from a Hindu standpoint—flows from the neglect of *dharma*, it could be argued that the disconnection of words from intellective harmony is actually a betrayal of the very goal of poetry. The adjective "toneless," used in reference to *Rc*, refers to the absence of tonal quality in the sense of a lack of the qualitative differences that are expressive of intellective music. The connotations of the concept of tone must also lead us in the direction of "height" and "pitch," symbol references to the qualitative order that is expressed by the Intellect, and also to the "vertical inflection" of words along

---

[44] Martin Lings, *Symbol and Archetype: A Study of the Meaning of Existence*, p. 65.

[45] *Jaiminīya Upanishad Brāhmana*, I.16.10, cited in Ananda Coomaraswamy, *Spiritual Authority and Temporal Power in the Indian Theory of Government*, p. 53.

the axis of reality. Words in and of themselves are only a quantitative substratum that may fulfill some formal conditions in order to be able to function as a vehicle for harmony. Words do not approach the Supreme because they cannot say what It is, as opposed to music and harmony which can be Its direct reflections and methods of access.

If we refer to the aforementioned notion of *rasa*, we can easily understand why words in themselves are unable to give access to Reality: they cannot reach the inner essence, and that is precisely why the highest form of theology and autology is apophatic; the *via negativa* does not refer to Reality by verbal affirmations; it seeks only to "uncover" Its nature by asserting what It is not. As for the affirmative or cataphatic dimension of theology, it is only useful to point to a Reality that is infinitely beyond all pointers. In poetry, words are cataphatic tools that are needed to approach Reality; but as one moves closer to the goal, the tools become more and more accessory. The best poetry is that in which *sāman* has subordinated *rc* to itself, to the point of making it its own: form is so to speak absorbed by the essence. By contrast, the "death" that threatens him who would rely on words alone while neglecting harmony refers to the clinging to "forms" as a substitute for the "essence," which is consequently ignored or rejected.

In this very connection, we should also take note of the fact that the Hindu "poetic marriage" we have just been examining constitutes in itself an indictment of much of what has passed for poetry in the contemporary development of Western literature. In other words, and to follow the profound meaning of Hindu poetics, there is no genuine poetry that does not primarily stem from a contemplative attention to music. Poetry cannot simply be reduced to the flow and arrangement of words; it cannot result from a mere syntactic relationship between words, nor is it merely dependent upon a linguistic structure immanent to the text. At the most extreme end of the spectrum, the surrealists' automatic writing is pure poetic "death" since it does not involve even the least "information" of words by "harmony." The "chaotic" dimension of much of surrealist poetry has undoubtedly to do with the substitution of the unconscious for the Intellect. The former does not deal with objective qualitative proportions; rather, it capitalizes on an indeterminate confusion of potentialities that comes into being through a process of "symbolization" that makes them objects of consciousness.

There is no doubt an analogy between the process that takes place in modern poetry, which is founded upon the unconscious, and the emergence of *Ātman* as triggered by a profound poetic experience. In both cases, what cannot be perceived "reveals" itself through a kind of symbolic objectification.

However, in the case of Hindu poetics, the "marriage" of harmony and words is comparable to the unification of multiplicity: the *sāman* is the qualitative principle that holds together the words, just as a string is the common thread that passes through the beads of a necklace and insures the unity of the whole. By contrast, in the type of contemporary poetry that is influenced by the understanding of creation as a free flow of images and words gushing forth from the unconscious, one must take note of the absence of any real relationship between unity and simplicity; by failing to be animated by the Intellect that interconnects them and relates them to a principle of unity, words become "dead" segments of linguistic "matter." "Death" is the lack of this common thread which ends in the disintegration of the poem. This death can also be understood as a "divorce," in the sense that it results from cutting off the formal manifestation from its divine essence.

In order to fully understand the import of this divorce, one has to take into account the fact that the Hindu understanding of poetry as creation involves the reduplication of a cosmogonic act. The sacrifice of the One, *Purusha* or *Prajāpati*, is presented as a dismemberment that results from an initial sacrifice; the central cosmogonic figure being a supreme God "whose sacrificial death gives rise to the manifold cosmos."[46] The One that is to be dismembered may take very different forms (Serpent, Ancestor, Mountain) and the dismemberment may be effected in different modes (according to the will of the One, or against his will), but it always comes back to the issue of the "sacrifice" of the One in order to produce the worlds: a "death" of God so that manifestation having man at its center—may be. The manifestation of the potentialities of the One initiated by the sacrifice does not ensue in an arbitrary and disorderly manner: each possibility is actually assigned a "measure" (*mātra*). This Sanskrit term is etymologically akin to the English meter and provides us with an important key for an understanding of poetry as modeled after cosmogony. The term is also used to refer to the three components of the *Omkāra*, i.e., precisely, the manifested dimension of the sacred syllable. On the contrary, the fourth component, the resonance identified with the essence of OM, *Ātman*, is considered as *amātra*, i.e., without measure, character, or assignation. This is another way of saying that the realm of the "cosmic poem"[47] does not belong to the domain of manifestation. In a sense, the three characters of the *prānava* are the first seminal *mātra* from which proceed all other manifested realities.

[46] R.C. Zaehner, *Hinduism*, p. 40.

[47] On this point, one may refer to René Guénon's *Man and his Becoming according to the Vedānta*, p. 69.

As we have suggested above, the concept of *mātra* denotes an assignation or an allotment, therefore an idea of limitation or measure: *mātra* is the principle of quantitative determination. It may be understood as the most direct reflection of quality in the realm of quantity; it could also be referred to as "qualitative quantity" if such an expression be allowed. Ananda Coomaraswamy has suggested that the presence of *mātra* is the element which distinguishes poetry from prose. He quotes the assertion of the *Aitareya Āranyaka* that "vain talk is unmeasured."[48] This is not only a way of saying that language should obey certain constraints of order and measure; it is also a means of placing the emphasis on the fact that poetry is the only language—in this respect akin to sacred scripture—that conforms to the productive ways of being. Hindu poetry, like art in general, is not only concerned with *mimesis* in the Aristotelian sense but also, and above all, with the process of creation. Poetry is good poetry insofar as it espouses the modes of this process. On the contrary, any literary production that confines itself to the reproduction of nature as it appears to the eyes condemns itself to the dispersing platitudes of naturalism. True poetry is a re-membering of the original unity that so to speak "reconciles" *vāc* and *çabda*, speech and meaning. The restored co-unity of words and meaning is the major element in early definitions of poetry in India. In one of the first attempts at defining poetry, Bhāmaha describes poetry as "a form of composition in which word and meaning co-exist."[49] While other later definitions—like that of Visvanātha—tend to emphasize an understanding of poetry wherein the infusion of the utterance with *rasa* constitutes the key factor, it should be noted that these two definitions converge on a situation in which the accidental nature of language is subsumed under the ultimate meaning that is the Self; in Visvanātha's words:

> *Rasa* is a state of intelligence and is free from any other form of perception or knowledge. It is akin to the blissful realization of the Supreme Self and is animated by a kind of transcendental or super-mundane imaginative pleasure.[50]

This blissful realization amounts to the union of meaning and words since, in the Supreme Brahman, speech (*vāc*) and meaning (*çabda*) are one and in-

[48] Ananda Coomaraswamy, *Spiritual Authority and Temporal Power in the Indian Theory of Government*, p. 57.

[49] Nirmala Jain, *A Dictionary of Sanskrit Poetics*, p. 78.

[50] *Ibid.*, p. 132.

distinguishable. It is only at the level of the causative Word (*sūkshma kārana*) that one can speak of a "distinction without difference" (*bheda-bheda*), to use Coomaraswamy's terminology. However, duality occurs only on the level of the manifested utterance (*vaikharī-çabda*). This is the most extreme phase of the process of dismemberment we have mentioned above. Poetry is a means of restoring the situation that prevails on the level of the causative and subtle *çabda*: in it, the distinction between words and meaning may be perceived, but it does not amount to a real "difference" since the two components are brought together in the unity of the poetic utterance. However, the level of "material" language may also be that where *vāc* becomes "emancipated" from *çabda* and loses a genuine sense of qualitative orientation. In a sense, daily and prosaic language, to the extent that it is not informed by the models of sacred scripture and the reflective parsimony stemming from a consciousness of the One, is a dilapidation of language. The "talkativeness" of modern discourse is a symptom of a loss of sight of the poetic essence of language. From the technical standpoint of poetic "diction," Ananda Coomaraswamy sees in the substitution of "expressiveness" for "intoned incantation" another symptom of the isolating and individualistic character of most of our modern use of language:

> … our substitution of stress for tone, our "expressive" and informal manner of reading and singing—so different from the measured "singsong" of traditionally spoken verse—are essentially profane developments characteristic of an age that can no longer think of song as an evocative or creative (*poetikos*) art in any literal sense of the words, or of Sacrifice as necessary for our daily bread.[51]

The inexpressive self-effacement of traditional recitation or incantation constitutes a key to the contemplative practice of poetry reading. Individually "expressive" composition and reading amount to a substitution of one's idiosyncrasy for the ontological power of words themselves. According to this vision of things, and as Julius Evola has suggested with regard to the function of *mantra*, it could be said that poetry—both as production and as reading—constitutes a kind of "purification" of words through which the unity of speech and meaning is restored. Effective poetry is a way (*marga*) of analogic reversion of the process of divine creation. Meter is one of the primary in-

---

[51] Ananda Coomaraswamy, *Spiritual Authority and Temporal Power in the Indian Theory of Government*, p. 59.

struments of this restoration in that it informs a linguistic multiplicity with a sense of integrating and liberating unity. The units of poetic measure reproduce on the level of quantity the qualitative unity of the principle. It is for this very reason that poetic language may be deemed as "primordial": most Indian theoreticians of poetry agree that the language of poetry is of a different quality than that of common discourse.[52] This qualitative difference stems from a closer relationship of poetry to the essence of language. Poetry exemplifies the language of truth as it brings back the analytical diversity of words to their essential unity, thereby functioning as a way of spiritual liberation.

Having highlighted this highest contemplative function as it is vested in poetry, the question arises as to the compatibility of the apophatic and ascetic dimensions of Hindu metaphysics—especially in the *Vedānta* and Yoga *darshanas*—and the worldly roots of poetic creation as a means of pleasure and enjoyment. Chaitanya puts it in a nutshell: the "basic issue here is … whether or not existence in the world is an authentic mode of being."[53] In other words, there exists *a priori* a certain tension between a doctrine that denies the full reality of the phenomenal world and an activity that is fundamentally based upon an integration of this world. However tempting it may be to simplify matters by opposing "world-affirming" types of spirituality to "world-negating" forms of contemplation, the fact of the matter remains that this distinction can be deemed valid only as a matter of emphasis, and certainly not in exclusive terms. A pure Advaitin like Sri Rāmana Maharshi was, after all, able to write poetic hymns in honor of the sacred mountain Arunachala, and the great Shankaracharya left us devotional poetry dedicated to Krishna (*Bhajagovindam*). It must be stressed that *Advaita Vedānta*—the most consistently non-dualistic metaphysical perspective of India—does not consider worldly phenomena "unreal." Eliot Deutsch has clearly delineated the problem in referring to two levels of being that are often confused: that of "appearance" and that of "unreality." Although only the Self can be considered as fully real in the sense of not being susceptible of underrating, negation, or contradiction by anything else, the world of phenomena cannot be purely reduced to the status of unreality. Deutsch's interpretation of the Advaitin concept of appearance is in this respect particularly helpful:

---

[52] "One aspect of poetry has been emphasized by nearly all the scholars in their definitions: they all agree that though poetry employs the standard language as its medium, it differs from the everyday spoken language qualitatively" (Nirmala Jain, *A Dictionary of Sanskrit Poetics*, p. 78).

[53] Krishna Chaitanya, *Sanskrit Poetics*, p. 308.

Appearance, then, comprises that about which doubts can arise. It is that which is, or in principle can be, a datum of experience within the subject/object situation. *The Apparent* is that which is the content of sense-mental experience. It is the differentiated multiplicity of being.[54]

Although the preceding considerations and quotations should keep us from the pitfalls of oversimplification, one must acknowledge that the world of poetic creation may reveal more affinities with the spiritual perspective of Tantric or Shaktic Hinduism than discriminative *Advaita Vedānta*. To speak in very general terms, we may draw a contrast between the two approaches in the following way: whereas Advaitin discrimination consists in a methodical intellective reduction of phenomenal existents—envisaged as multiple aspects of *Māyā*—to the universal Substance that underlies them, the Tantric approach is intent on using the productive energy of *Māyā* (*Shakti*) as a means for the realization of *Ātman*. In other words, the Advaitin perspective emphasizes the discontinuity between *Ātman* and *Māyā* by "subrating" (Deutsch's term) the reality of the latter, while the Tantric point of view considers the continuity between the two by highlighting the function of *Māyā* or *Shakti* as productive power of *Ātman*. It is clear that the importance ascribed to phenomenal reality and terrestrial existence cannot but be very different on the basis of such diverging premises. A Tantric approach is more likely to make use of emotional reactions to the ambience as a source of interiorizing energy than would the more static and intellective school of *Advaita Vedānta*.

In Indian poetics, one of the major questions related to this particular problem has been that of knowing whether the supreme state of peace and bliss that is concomitant with the realization of *Ātman* can be the object—or subject—of a specific kind of *rasa*. Such a *rasa* would be expressive of *Shanti*, the great peace. As Krishna Chaitanya puts it, "those who rejected the *Santa Rasa*, the tranquility of liberation, as impermissible for literary delineation, used the argument that it implied the total absence of all feelings and action—'desiccation of sense and inoperacy of spirit.'"[55] Such a view considers *moksha* as a state of utter indifference toward phenomena as well as an inner disposition that transcends all emotional modifications.

However, the most common view of the supreme state, and one that seems to be more in agreement with the anthropological and spiritual viewpoint of Hinduism, consists in distinguishing between *Ātman* and the *jīvātman*, or the

[54] Eliot Deutsch, *Advaita Vedānta*, p. 24.
[55] Krishna Chaitanya, *Sanskrit Poetics*, p. 333.

Universal Spirit and the individual soul. The essential identification of the liberated subject with the transpersonal essence does not entail a total disappearance of the individual soul. There is a kind of subtle interplay between the inner Center that is at peace and the variable motions of the soul that is involved in the diversity of the world. This vision of the relationship between the universal and the individual is, for example, proposed by Visvanātha in his concept of "bonded-liberated state" (*yukta-viyukta-dasa*), "similar to that of Vyāsa who had given the brilliant clarification that the Yogi and the poet are poised in that interface between pure being and becoming, absolute existence and historical existence, which enables the relishing of both."[56]

The very concept of a "bonded-liberated state" indicates, through its highly paradoxical character, how *moksha* is difficult to express through words, and the extent to which its manifestation has to reconcile extremes that the mental and discursive faculty cannot fathom. Since the realization of *moksha* cannot be interpreted as a mere destruction of the psycho-mental entity of the individual, as is sometimes done in the West, one must infer—and such inference is in fact confirmed by the testimony of great contemporary sages like Rāmana Maharshi or Mā Ananda Moyi—that it is a state where a profound identification with the Self allows the person to receive impressions and emotions, reacting to the world of phenomena without being affected in depth by the moving or troubling diversity of that world. However, the emotions that are conveyed by poetry can also be experienced by the delivered sage—in fact more acutely than by ordinary men—while they may be, for others, the channels leading to a state of spiritual realization. From the standpoint of the *jīvan-mukta*, the various *rasas* that can be experienced in works of poetry reflect so many aspects of the soul's quest for the Self, or so many manifestations of delusion and error. Each emotion becomes a way to relate to the Supreme, either as a reflection of one of its aspects, or as a negation of Reality that calls for an emotional response: love *rasas* will thus evoke the dimension of beatitude that pertains to the Supreme, whereas mindless human activities and passions will evoke laughter or anger, comical moods, or combative dispositions. It can therefore be said that while it is true that there cannot be properly speaking a *rasa* that expresses *moksha*, given that *moksha* transcends all forms and bonds, it is nevertheless plain that the various *rasas* evoke a diversity of dispositions of the soul with respect to *Ātman* by virtue of the metaphysical principle of the unity of being.

[56] *Ibid.*, p. 311.

The metaphysical and spiritual status of emotions resulting from this principle is also the key to an understanding of the way in which poetry may fulfill the function of a central spiritual means in Hindu contemplative practice. By virtue of *rasa*, poetry produces an emotional reaction that must be converted into a spiritual energy. In other words, a contemplative practice of poetry requires that its practitioners make use of the reactions that poetry triggers in them by disconnecting these responses from the limiting objects that are their immediate source in order to be able to establish a contact with the inner core of Reality. Poetic suggestions and vibrations should lead to the inward way that opens into the heart, the hidden lotus wherein *Ātman* awaits to pour Itself forth.

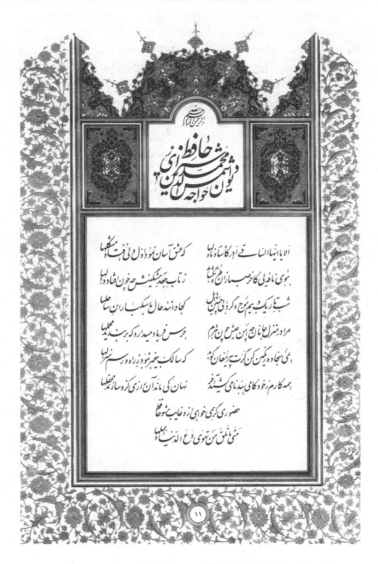

II. *Sāqī Nāmeh*, from the Dīwān of Hāfez Shirazi (1300-1389)

2. ISLAM
Sufism and Poetry

At a first reading, the Qur'ān does not seem to favor poets. Sūrah 26, entitled "The Poets" (*al-Shu'arā'*), concludes with four verses that appear to contain strong words against poetry:

> And the poets—the deviators follow them.
> Seest thou not that they wander in every valley,
> And that they say that which they do not?
> Except those who believe and do good and remember Allāh much, and defend themselves after they are oppressed. And they who do wrong, will know what final place of turning they will turn back.[1]

Circumstantially, these reproaches are addressed to those among the poets who opposed the Prophet of Islam by casting doubts on his message. These verses should therefore not be read as an indictment of poetry as such, as is moreover clearly indicated by the "exception" (*illā alladhīna āmanū wa 'amilū as-sālihāti*, "except those who believe and perform good deeds"). Actually, there were among the Prophet's contemporaries, poets such as Hassan ibn Thabit who put their talents in the service of Islam.[2] Moreover, as Toshihiko Izutsu has demonstrated in his works on the Qur'ān, the Islamic revelation was, in a certain sense, circumstantially situated within a poetic context that was conducive to it. Some major Qur'ānic themes and expressions can be interpreted as a spiritual counterpoint and a response to pre-Islamic poetry.[3] In addition, the linguistic usage of Arabic words in pre-Islamic poetry has become in Islam a basic principle of Qur'ānic commentary (*tafsīr*).[4]

---

[1] *The Holy Qur'ān*, trans. Maulana Muhammad Ali, pp. 224-27.

[2] See Anne-Marie Schimmel, *As Through a Veil, Mystical Poetry in Islam*, p. 14.

[3] Commenting on the pessimistic conception of earthly life that prevails in pre-Islamic poetry, Izutsu states as follows: "It is important to remark also that this bitter consciousness of the absolute impossibility of finding 'eternity' in this world was at once the dead end into which heathenism drove itself and the very starting point from which Islam took its ascending course" (*Ethico-Religious Concepts in the Qur'ān*, p. 48).

[4] "Ibn 'Abbās ... is given the credit for having emphasized one of the basic principles of *'ilm al-tafsīr* which has remained important to this day, namely, that the meaning of words, especially

47

Notwithstanding these qualifications, it should be added, on a more profoundly spiritual plane, that the reproach of "wandering" that is addressed to poets in the aforementioned verses points to the lack of direction that characterizes poetry in the absence of faith or contemplative intellection. Moreover, a poetry that is disconnected from a sense of the Ultimate Reality reveals its futility in that it entails spiritual "hypocrisy" by positing two separate and irreconcilable realities, that of "saying" (*yaqulūna*) and that of "doing" (*yaf'alūna*). Divorced from "doing," "saying" amounts to little more than nothing; it is deprived of ontological and spiritual reality and therefore pertains to the domain of "vain talk" (*bātil*). This "vain talk" is the fundamental opposite of the Qur'ān, since it is basically deprived of any ontological reality. As with the Greek poets at the time of Plato, the deluded poets whom the Qur'ān chastises are producers of a phantasmatic reality which they substitute for God's works. Given the tension between the poetic power of the Qur'ān—as well as the poetic vigor of the Bedouin culture that envelops its outer manifestation—and the fundamental "associationism" (*shirk*) and negation of transcendence that is the fatal bent of the worldly poetry of the time, there is no category of human activity—painting excepted—that is considered with more ambivalence than poetry, while yet having been exalted and practiced in a most varied and original way by Muslims as early as the first centuries of Islam.

Arab poetry, as manifested prior to the development of Islamic poetry, appeared to most Muslims as a kind of semi-magical and semi-prophetic manifestation of idolatry, chiefly characterized by its individualistic and passionate tendencies; but also—whence its ambiguity—as a repository of tribal virtues that Islam alone was able to bring to spiritual fruition. On the one hand, poetry was associated with an exaltation of the individual ego and worldly life—as epitomized by wealth and wine—that is the very antithesis of contemplative extinction. Moreover, passions and occult powers seemed to rule poetical practice, and the latter was therefore perceived as a potential—if not actual—locus of rebellion against God's law. On the other hand, Islam found consonant elements in the moral undertones and modes of expression of pre-Islamic *Jāhilīyah* poetry. Accordingly, and with a keen sense of awareness of the extraordinary creativeness of Muslim civilization in the domain of poetic expression, a foremost expert on Islam such as Anne-Marie Schimmel has justifiably asserted that "despite the attempts by later poets to

of unusual words in the Qur'ān ought to be traced back to their usage in the language of pre-Islamic poetry" (Ahmad Von Denffer, *'Ulūm al-Qur'ān*, p. 126).

rehabilitate poetry and despite the fact that 'no people in the world … are so moved by the word … as the Arabs' (Philip Hitti), it cannot be denied that the words of Sūrah 26 point to an important truth, namely, the strong tension between the words of revelation and the words of poetry."[5]

In such a problematic and ambivalent context, genuine prophecy is at the same time culturally embedded in a certain poetic and moral climate that "predisposes" its themes and modes of expression, while it is still constantly summoned to distinguish itself from profane poetry. The Islamic Revelation appears in the form of a book, i.e., in a verbal form of the Word, in contrast to Christianity, where the Word is made flesh in Christ. In a cultural climate in which poetry is central, this is both an asset and a danger. On the one hand, the level of inspiration of the Qur'ān is taken by Muslims to be directly reflected in the poetic incomparability (*i'jāz*) of the Qur'ānic text. In this connection, the Qur'ān may be considered as the major "miracle" of Islam, a testification to its supernatural origin. On the other hand, however, the all-pervasiveness of poetic inspiration in the pre-Islamic era allows for the possibility of dismissing the Revelation as one more occurrence of the verbal magic of poetry. Poetry is therefore both exalted and rejected, and in this respect the Qur'ān is both a reference and a counter-model for poetry.

The positive and "prophetic" status of poetry is primarily actualized in Islamic spirituality: the intimate relationship between poetry and the Qur'ān is clearly highlighted—although not exclusively so—by the fact that poetic texts are often intertwined with Qur'ānic quotations. It would actually be more accurate to consider these quotations as being integrated into these contemplative poems in a way that reflects a profound interiorization of the Qur'ānic revelation.[6] Qur'ānic "poetry" has become the very substance of the contemplative soul to such an extent that it becomes, so to speak, the very texture of its utterances. In Islam, the contemplative poetry of the mystics is both a commentary upon the Qur'ān and a kind of prolongation of the sacred text; the integration of Sufi poetry—along with Qur'ānic passages—within the mystics' ceremonial gatherings bears witness to this fact. The case of Rūmī is particularly instructive in this regard since much of his poetry is interspersed with Qur'ānic passages, such that Anne-Marie Schimmel has argued that "it

---

[5] Anne-Marie Schimmel, *As Through a Veil*, p. 13.

[6] "Being the inner dimension of the Islamic revelation, Sufism is related in both form and content to the Noble Quran, and the language of the Sacred Text, its rhythms and rhymes, its metaphors and symbols, has continued to echo in Sufi literature throughout the centuries" (Seyyed Hossein Nasr, *Sufi Essays*, p. 171).

would be useful to read Mawlana's [i.e., Rūmī's] poetry as a kind of *tafsir*, a commentary on the Koran, and to reconstruct his interpretations from the numerous quotations."[7] In parallel, some experts have been able to show that thousands of verses from both the *Diwān* and the *Mathnawī* can be considered as translations of Qur'ānic verses into Persian poetry.[8]

*   *   *

Seyyed Hossein Nasr has emphasized the relationship between logic and poetry in Islam by highlighting the fact that the two domains have become separated in the West in the wake of the Renaissance and post-Renaissance split between the thinking "I" and the world of nature. The Cartesian separation between *res cogitans* and *res extensa* is one of the major philosophical episodes of that scission, as are also—in an even more radical way—the epistemological conclusions of Kant's critical idealism. In the pre-modern world, by contrast, the anthropocosmic unity of man and nature was characterized by a situation in which the domain of discourse on the one hand, and that of the archetypes as manifested in the cosmos on the other hand, was still profoundly connected. In Islam, and particularly in the world of Sufism or *tasawwuf*, the term *āyāt* refers both to the cosmic "signs" that are like the "signature" of God upon Creation, and to the verses of the Qur'ān. Intelligence (*'aql*) is conceived as a fundamentally contemplative faculty since it is manifested primarily in the ability to read these *āyāt*. The unbeliever is repeatedly characterized in the Qur'ān as one who is unable to read the signs of God on the horizon; this incapacity being both the cause and the consequence of his lack of *islām*, or "submission" to God.

The Qur'ān and the book of Creation are the two fundamental aspects of the Word of God. They are "poetry" in the highest sense. Logic and poetry are therefore intimately connected as complementary modes of knowing in Islam: they both manifest the Divine Intelligence in the realms of nature and language. Michel Foucault's concept of a "prose of the world" that would have the semantic "transparence" of a book to be read should actually be prolonged here by that of a "poetry of the world," since the latter refers more

---

[7] Anne-Marie Schimmel, *I am Wind, You are Fire, The Life and Work of Rumi*, p. 116.

[8] "One of the greatest living authorities on Rumi in Persia today, Hadi Ha'iri, has shown in an unpublished work that some 6,000 verses of the *Dīwān* and the *Mathnawī* are practically direct translations of Qur'ānic verses into Persian poetry" (Seyyed Hossein Nasr, *Islamic Art and Spirituality*, p. 145).

explicitly to the idea of a qualitative and orderly correspondence between nature and language. Seyyed Hossein Nasr expresses the meaning of this correspondence in the following terms:

> According to the traditional doctrine, the inner reality of the cosmos, which unveils itself to the inner eye or to intellectual vision—for which the inner eye is the instrument of perception—is based upon a harmony which imposes itself even upon the corporeal domain. This harmony is, moreover, reflected in the world of language, which is itself a reflection of both the soul of man and of the cosmos.[9]

On its highest level, poetry therefore reproduces the qualitative order of the cosmos. God can be contemplated both in the order of nature and in the harmonic structures of poetic language.

As with the signs of God on the horizon, the phenomena that constitute poetic language may be considered from two standpoints: they can be envisaged on the one hand as a set of formal appearances and structures, as they may also be interpreted in light of their inner significance. Islamic poetics therefore distinguishes between two components of poetic expression: that of form (*sūrah*) and that of meaning (*ma'nā*). As George Cave puts it:

> *Sūrah* means the appearance of the poem, and comprises all that is not inherent in the meaning of the poem. By this is meant structure, metrical arrangement, rhyme scheme, rhetorical devices, etc., in other words all that can be concretely viewed and objectively treated. *Ma'nā* simply means "meaning" or that which must be subjectively treated or intuited.[10]

Notwithstanding its clarity and relevance, this definition may present the inconvenience of lending itself to a misinterpretation of the two adverbs "objectively" and "subjectively." It would in fact be erroneous to reduce *ma'nā* to a kind of equivalent of "feeling" or "emotion": if *ma'nā* is to be "subjectively treated or intuited" it is not by reason of its purely emotional character, but simply because the "meaning" has to be apprehended by the intelligence and the sensibility of the auditor—therefore "subjectively"—in order to be actualized. *Ma'nā* is an inner reality whereas *sūrah* is like the outer shell through which the latter may manifest itself. *Ma'nā* is akin to

[9] Seyyed Hossein Nasr, *Islamic Art and Spirituality*, pp. 88-9.
[10] George Cave, *Sufi Poetry*, p. 3.

the intelligible seal (*eidos*) that informs the material substratum (*hylē*). The combinatory fusion of these two principles is effected in a variety of proportions: the more clearly determinative *ma'nā* is, the more integrally the intelligible radiance of the poem may be unveiled:

> As this impression of *ma'nā* upon *sūrah* increases, the external form becomes transparent and reveals more readily its inner meaning.[11]

As with the most expressive forms of human and natural beauty, the poetic ideal is therefore one in which *sūrah* has been completely crystallized by *ma'nā*. Sufi poetry is in no way intent on allowing language freedom from the intellective form of *dhawq*, or intuitive taste of reality. A true poem is one in which a profound spiritual intuition manifests itself in the perfect clothing of a prosodic gem. Mystical poets like Rūmī have utter disdain for poetry conceived as an art for art's sake, as a formal perfection in kind: "in face of meaning, what is form? Very contemptible."[12] If it is so, it is most fundamentally because meaning is akin to God's informing and intellective power, or because, as William Chittick quite plainly puts it: "in the last analysis the meaning of all things is God."[13] The complementary relationship between *sūrah* and *ma'nā* does not, however, amount to a situation where *sūrah* has no intellectual dimension in itself. In fact, the form of the poem tends to reproduce a structure that is entailed by the spiritual vision of the world. In other words, the material substratum cannot but "reproduce" in its own way the qualitative essence of the archetype. This reproduction is primarily effected through quantitative structures that pertain to the form of the poem. Form and essence cannot be completely severed from one another since reality is one. Poetry is a "logical" language, but one in which the symbolic potentialities of the latter are brought to exceptional heights. Symbolic meaning is a capacity to reveal the formless in and by a form. In this connection, Seyyed Hossein Nasr quotes Jāmī as a poet who is most explicit about this union of form and essence in poetry:

> What is poetry? The song of the bird of the Intellect.
> What is poetry? The similitude of the world of eternity.

---

[11] Seyyed Hossein Nasr, *Islamic Art and Spirituality*, p. 89.

[12] Rūmī, *Mathnawī* I. 3330, cited in William Chittick, *The Sufi Path of Love, The Spiritual Teachings of Rūmī*, p. 19.

[13] William Chittick, *The Sufi Path of Love*, p. 19.

The value of the bird becomes evident through it,
And one discovers whether it comes from the oven of a bath house or a
    rose garden.
It composes poetry from the Divine rose garden;
It draws its power and sustenance from that sacred precinct.[14]

The Intellect (*'aql*) is the reality through which man connects with higher realities, and particularly with the Divine realm. As the song of a bird, poetry is therefore a spontaneous expression of that connection. In a sense—and with the exception of jaculatory prayer and other possible modes of spontaneous utterances of the Self—poetry is for mankind the closest utterance there is to what singing is for birds. Rūmī emphasizes this parallel when longing for an expression that would match bird songs in their "meaning" and not simply in their "form":

Birdsong brings relief
To my longing.
I am just as ecstatic as they are,
But with nothing to say!
Please, universal soul, practice
Some song, or something, through me![15]

The ideal of poetic creation to which Rūmī aspires is therefore one in which the *modus operandi* of nature occurs in the animal realm: it consists in a perfect receptivity toward the spiritual and animic resonances of nature as God's message. However, in contrast to birds, it may be that the difficulty experienced by the mystic in finding "something to say" is in fact paradoxically a consequence of the metaphysical and epistemological privileges of mankind. Birds always have "something to say" because the very form of their "saying" is "meaningful": it is only in man, by virtue of his "poetic" freedom and as a consequence of his ability to "disassociate" levels of reality by cutting himself off from the One, that formal expression may not necessarily fit consciousness. Man has potentially more to say than animals since he is able to pronounce the Name of God and to gain access to a wide array of images and words to crystallize the central metaphysical consciousness that a full awareness of this pronunciation entails. In him, intellective intuitions "want"

---

[14] Jāmī, cited in Seyyed Hossein Nasr, *Islamic Art and Spirituality*, p. 91.

[15] Rūmī, *Birdsong*, trans. Coleman Barks, p. 13.

to be "fixed" in poetic forms whose function in relation to truth is analogous to that of a crystal with respect to light. The poetic crystal transmits the light of truth while focusing and refracting it by virtue of its particular mode of perfection.

The spiritual implications of the contemplative function of poetry that have just been sketched have been most suggestively encapsulated by Hafiz:

> Good poetry
> Makes a beautiful naked woman
> Materialize from words
> Who then says,
> With a sword precariously waving
> In her hands,
> "If you look at my loins
> I will cut off your head,
> And reach down and grab your spirit
> By its private parts,
> And carry you off to heaven,
> Squealing in joy."
> Hafiz says,
> "That sounds wonderful, just wonderful."[16]

First of all, the experience of poetry implies the ability of words to make spiritual reality "materialize." In other words, it is through words that contact is effected with the "imaginal world" (*'ālam al-khayāl*) where spiritual realities take on form. The imaginal world—the locus of the images that are expressed by poetry—is the intermediary realm that mediates between the supra-individual kingdom of the Spirit and the zone of multiplicity and matter. On this imaginal level, the "beautiful naked woman" is the most direct image of the hidden beauty of God, which intoxicates those who contemplate it. Her nakedness is all the more significant in that poetry seems to imply, by definition, a formal "clothing" of truth: good poetry proceeds in such a way as to reveal naked reality through the "clothing" of words. Poetry makes words transparent: it unveils the body of the goddess through a dance of a thousand words. When actualized by words, this most direct image of ecstasy and union with God is depicted as a terrible reality, through an evocation that almost conjures up visions of the Goddess Kali, the destroyer. Beauty holds a sword

---

[16] Hafiz, "That Sounds Wonderful," cited in *The Subject Tonight is Love, 60 Wild and Sweet Poems from Hafiz*, trans. Daniel Ladinsky, p. 32.

as an attribute of rigor and justice that will not tolerate any complacency or weakness. Interestingly however, the punishment that awaits the one who looks at the woman's loins is also, quite paradoxically, a reward. In fact, the matter is not so much one of indiscretion and passion which would result in a symbolic castration of man; it is rather as if the "head," organ of the discursive faculty, were to be neutralized by the more direct experience of rapture that results from the contemplation of the naked woman, the inner ecstatic power of poetry. Accordingly, the ambiguity of the vision is akin to the ambivalence of eroticism in general; the "beheading" is also a liberation; what is dangerous and painful is also a key to delivering the most precious reality of the self. The translation "squealing in joy" is also highly significant in this respect since it evokes both feelings of pain and pleasure, therefore suggesting that on the highest level, poetry is jointly an experience of beatitude and an inner torment that is related to the limitations of the human self. In a sense, poetry functions as a kind of ruse: it exerts a fascination upon its reader or auditor; but this fascination must find its outcome in a "sacrifice" of the rational faculty, which entails a total abandonment of oneself to the pull of grace.

Sufism, in its methodical or operative dimension, makes use of artistic means to awaken and strengthen a psychophysical consciousness of the Divine that may open body and soul to the irradiation of celestial archetypes. In this respect, the contemplative role of poetry can be defined as a prolongation of the act of remembrance through the invocation (*dhikr*) of the Name of God. No practice is more central to Sufi spirituality than the remembrance of God through the methodical and, in principle, constant invocation of His Name. Essentially, the practice of the invocation is the very act of the Spirit (*Ruh*); but, from the standpoint of the soul, it may also be supported and heightened by artistic means. Poetry, music, and dance are particularly apt to foster this type of existential remembrance and they may even be combined in the *samā'*, or session of the Mevlevi and Jarrahiyyah orders, the former tracing its ceremonial practices to Jalāl ad-Din Rūmī. Mystical verses from Mawlānā may thus be accompanied by melodies while dervishes perform their traditional whirling dance. In such a context, poetry may be deemed a prolongation of the Divine Name itself; the synthetic mode of presence actualized by a Divine Name, whether it be the Supreme Name Allāh or one of the ninety-nine traditional names that express some of the countless qualities of the Divine, is so to speak analytically unfolded in the poetical text. The latter proceeds in a certain sense from the former: the contemplative concentration on the most synthetic expression of the Divine brings about a kind of spiritual unification and "simplification" of the soul that "cleanses" the human consciousness from the complex network of dispersing and peripheral thoughts and feelings, thereby making way for the "simple complexity" of inspired poetry. By using the paradoxical expression "simple complexity," we refer not only to the multiplicity of the imaginative, linguistic, and auditory components of the poem, but also to the flowing unity of the whole work as it freely and spontaneously springs forth from the consciousness suffused with grace.

Such considerations help us understand why poetic creation constitutes in a sense a criterion of the spiritual maturity of the contemplative. This is so because the free and inspired flow of words can result only from a perfect conformity to the Divine Presence; such conformity is referred to by Sufis as *faqr* (spiritual poverty), whence the name of *faqīr* and *fuqarā'* that is often used in the Arab world to refer to practitioners of *tasawwuf*. The "centrifugal" creative motion that characterizes Sufi poetry can therefore be characterized as an overflowing or outpouring of grace through the channel of words. There is no trace of virtuosity in such a practice of poetry: the poet is too overwhelmed by the flow of images and words to be able to manipulate them in a technical way. The formal cohesiveness and regularity of the poetry is less the result of a conscious and painstakingly skillful composition on the part of the contemplative poet, than the "quantitative" reflection and manifestation of a qualitative perfection. As Frithjof Schuon has pointed out, the art of poetry is characterized—by contrast with music—as one in which the "essence" moves toward the form in order to meet with it. The form is therefore like a kind of outer crystallization of the very unfolding or "exteriorization" of the essence. In music on the other hand, it is rather the form that moves toward the essence, the former echoing the "vertical music" of the latter.

The exteriorization of the poem, which is the literary fruit of contemplation and union with the Divine, is quite evidently not an end in itself. It is, to use Schuon's phrase, an "exteriorization with a view to interiorization." It could also be added that, strictly from the standpoint of contemplation, poetry is in no way "needed"; in fact silence could be deemed—and is actually deemed—by many mystics as the only language fit for the contemplative experience.[17] The exteriorization that poetry implies must therefore be understood as a sort

---

[17] Writing about the first manifestations of Sufi poetry, Anne-Marie Schimmel gives voice to some of the mystics' concerns: "Who could and who would tell what was going on in the blissful solitude of love, in prayer and ecstasy, when the lover does not want anything *from* God but only God Himself? Was not poetry therefore a treason to mystical experience, and complete silence the only legitimate way a Sufi could choose?" (*As Through a Veil*, p. 16).

of complementary realization that "projects" the inward into the outward. It is in this sense that Seyyed Hossein Nasr has perceived Shams ad-Dīn al-Tabrīzī as a kind of catalyst who prompted Rūmī to "exteriorize" his purely inner state of being into contemplative poetry.[18] In this connection, mystics tend to emphasize the "necessity" of "words," even though that necessity might be elsewhere denied by the same mystics in view of the distance separating union from its utterance. Rūmī may thus refer to poetic language in an almost derogatory way, while writing elsewhere that "faith may be in the heart, but if you do not express it in words, it has no profit."[19] In this sense poetry becomes an occurrence of testimony, which is the very principle of belonging to Islam. A faith not expressed in a testimony is not a fully "profitable" faith in the sense that it lacks the actualizing "magic" of the vow, while being incommunicable to others. In Islam, speech is the very principle of being, even though a "witnessing" of the tongue is not in itself sufficient in the absence of a correct intention.

This "exteriorization in view of interiorization" that is at the core of contemplative poetic utterances may however be considered from a slightly different standpoint, depending on whether one envisages the point of view of the contemplative poet or that of the contemplative reader or auditor. Let us remark in this connection that the contemplative, in normal circumstances, will most likely be an auditor rather than a reader. As Dana Wilde has rightly indicated,[20] the actual reading aloud of poetry entails a mode of spiritual assimilation that is much stronger and much more direct than that which would be offered simply by the more discursive and indirect mode of silent reading. Oral communication entails a more direct spiritual, and also animic and physical, imparting of reality than does the written word. In this sense, poetry may be considered as the "wine" of Islam. There is a profound

---

[18] "It seems that Shams ad-Dīn was a divinely sent spiritual influence which in a sense 'exteriorized' Rūmī's inner contemplative states in the form of poetry and set the ocean of his being into a motion which resulted in vast waves that transformed the history of Persian literature" (Seyyed Hossein Nasr, *Jalāl ad-Dīn Rūmī: Supreme Persian Poet and Sage*, p. 23).

[19] Rūmī, *Fīhi mā fīhi*, cited in William Chittick, *The Sufi Path of Love*, p. 269.

[20] "Poetry can literally be intoxicating. A brief anecdote, one among many that might be told: Years ago a couple of friends and I were reading poems of Robert Frost aloud in the living room, and although we were temperately drinking black tea (not beer or wine as we well might have been), I began to feel quite tipsy, the early sweet fuzzy stages of drunkenness that incite one to intensify the pleasure by drinking more" (Dana Wilde, "Poetry and Sufism: A Few Generalities," www.unc.edu/depts/sufilit/Wilde.htm).

analogical correspondence between the "wine" of Christ's blood and the "poetry" of the Qur'ānic substance.

The connection between the methodical use of the Divine Name and that of poetry in Islam allows us to place this fact in a clearer light. The Name not only corresponds to a graphic sign and to the mental associations that it entails, it also and above all is an auditory form that recapitulates the Presence of the Divine. The graphic representation of the Name is in this respect more akin to the dimension of truth as consciousness, whereas its auditory vibrations point to the ontological presence of God in His Name. In the case of the contemplative poet, the poetic vibrations that result in the creation of a poem "trace" a cyclical whole that involves both a manifestation and a reintegration through the word.

The poet is also an auditor, in the sense that he may listen to the voice of inspiration as he would listen to the voice of God speaking through him. In the *Wasiyah 'arūsiyah*, we read that the Sufi Sheikh, when God speaks through his mouth, must listen as if he were himself one of his own auditors. In fact, the all-pervasiveness of God is the very key to the de-centering of the subject; for, as Rūmī expresses it, "when I write letters to my friends, He (the Beloved) is paper, pen and ink-well."[21] The poetic experience is therefore a wonderment and an awe: it points to a transcendent voice that is the real "I" or the supreme Self or Witness (*shuhūd*); or, as Rūmī puts it, "That voice which is the origin of every cry and sound: that indeed is the only voice, and the rest are only echoes."[22] Sometimes, this metaphysical priority of the Divine voice is a source of confusion for the Sufi poet who does not seem to retain a clear perception of the respective identities of the speaker and the hearer. A poem of al-Hallāj's *qasida* highlights this kind of indecision and the disorienting inversion it entails:

Here I am, I am, my secret, my bliss
Here I am, here I am, my goal, my thought
I call you, no you call me, how can
I call you if you do not whisper to me?
O eye of my being's eye, O end of my wish
O my speech and my terms and my stammering.[23]

---

[21] Rūmī, *Dīwān-i Shams-i Tabrīzī* 2251, cited in William Chittick, *The Sufi Path of Love*, p. 234.

[22] Rūmī, *Mathnawī* I.2107, cited in *Rumi Daylight*, trans. Camille and Kabir Helminski, p. 55.

[23] Al-Hallāj, *Selections from the Poems of Zuhair ibn Abi Sulma and Husain ibn Mansur al Hallaj*, trans. Arthur Wormhoudt, p. 79.

The ambiguity of the status of the poetic utterances implicitly refers to levels of subjectivity. The Qur'ān states: "We are nearer to him (man) than his jugular vein" (Sūrah Qaf, 50:16), whence a recognition that speech ultimately stems from that profoundly hidden source of being which is the core of the self. It is when considered from the standpoint of this immanent ocean of being that the work of poetry and all its components may be referred to as being aspects of the Divine itself. Conversely, it could also be said that in this respect poetry may constitute for the writer an experience of objectification and extinction. The contemplative is "extinguished" in the flow of words and images emanating from the Word. This utterance becomes the center of his consciousness to the point of making his ordinary self (*nafs*) peripheral. Rūmī has emphasized this pervasive immanence of God in the very act of poetic creation, highlighting both the material immanence and the productive efficiency of the Divine:

> And when I write a letter
> To my beloved friends,
> The paper and the inkwell,
> The ink, the pen is He.
> And when I write a poem
> And seek a rhyming word—
> The one who spreads the rhymes out
> Within my thoughts, is He![24]

"He" is the very substance and fundamental reality of all poetic manifestation, just as He is also the creative Act that is immanent to all creation. To be a poet, as to be an artist in general, ultimately consists in "participating" in the Divine Act on a given level of being. The Divine Word as Act is the essence of poetic creation in Sufism; William Chittick has also underlined the importance of this reality for Islam at large:

> Moslem thinkers have always stressed the importance of God's creative Word in the natural order of the universe and man, just as they have emphasized the central role of His written Word in guiding man to salvation.[25]

---

[24] Rūmī, cited in Anne-Marie Schimmel, *I am Wind You are Fire*, p. 45.
[25] William Chittick, *The Sufi Path of Love*, p. 268.

The poet is not so much a creator as he is a transmitter of That which is expressed through Him. In his *Dīwān*, a contemporary Sufi Master such as Sheikh Ahmad al-'Alawī, expresses this de-centering in the following distich:

> Allāh! Allāh! I speak only of Him
> My whole and only word is His Splendor.
> (*Nahnī bihi, kulli nutqī bisanāhu*)[26]

All contemplative utterances may ultimately be reduced to the Divine Name, which is the essence of all words; and the Divine Name is nothing other than the very voice of God, the utterance of Reality.

From another standpoint, poetry may be considered as a means of bridging the gap of absence. In his article entitled "Mystical Poetry," Martin Lings has emphasized this important aspect of poetry in the world of Sufism, highlighting its role as a means of actualizing presence in absence. The Sufi way is often described as an alternation of contraction (*qabd*) and expansion (*bast*), these two states of the soul corresponding respectively to separation and union, or absence and presence. As distinct from the Divine Substance, the soul of the contemplative experiences separation and distance from God; fear and longing are two most common expressions of this sense of absence. The soul is in a state of contraction because it is "sent back" so to speak to its limited identity, severed from the Source that gives being and life to it. However, this separation is never absolute in itself; it is not due to the radical absence of God—since God is ever present—but to a state of "absence," distraction (*ghaflah*), or lack of consciousness in the soul itself.

On the other hand, the soul may also experience a profound sense of union and participation in the Divine life, which is the expansion of love that dispels limitations and lifts the veil of separation. In such a state, the soul is so penetrated by the Divine presence that it cannot even reflect upon itself as a separate being. However, given the rhythm of alternation that presides over all manifestation—since the latter cannot have the same degree of being and permanence as God himself—the soul is necessarily subjected to variations that alternate between *qabd* and *bast*. Even in the case of the highest contemplative mode of being and consciousness, the very participation of the soul in the sequential nature of time and the fragmented reality of manifestation entails some measure of animic "unevenness" due to

[26] Ahmed Ben Mustapha al-'Alawī, *Extraits du Dīwān*, pp. 54-5.

the unavoidable consequences of the transcendence of the Divine. As Martin Lings puts it:

> Mystical systems are in agreement that for one who reaches the end of the path itself in this life, the divine presence, which constitutes that end, is a framework that admits of temporary "absences" of the Beloved, although these are relative and illusory.[27]

As an expression of separation from the One, poetry is at the same time a way of experiencing His presence in a so to speak symbolic and indirect manner. A poignant cry may sometimes fulfill this function, as in the *Dīwān* of al-Hallāj:

> O surfeit of sadness, that I should forever
> Be calling upon Thee as if I were far
> Or as if Thou wert absent![28]

The distance between the Divine and the human is only an appearance, as indicated by the conditional mood, but it remains nevertheless true that the soul must experience it in a very concrete way. The sighs of love that are immanent in the wording of the poem are not only a discourse addressed to God, they are also an attempt at making Him present. We could also synthesize this function of poetry by relating it to that of the Divine Name which is invoked by the Muslim mystic. According to this contemplative approach, God makes Himself present in His Name, and the contemplative may participate in this presence through his invocation of the Name.[29] God "bridges" the gap between Himself and His creature by uttering His Name. This utterance is immanent in the sacred scripture of Islam in so far as the name Allāh is part of the Qur'ān, and is actually considered by Sufis as constituting its very essence. The whole tradition can be understood, in a certain sense, as the outward manifestation of the Divine Name: from Allāh to the testimony of faith, the *shahādah*, from the latter to the whole Qur'ān, and

---

[27] Martin Lings, "Mystical Poetry," in *The Cambridge History of Arabic Literature: 'Abbasid Belles-Lettres*, Julia Ashtiany et al. (ed.), p. 236.

[28] *Le Dīwān d'al-Hallāj*, 44, cited in Martin Lings, "Mystical Poetry," p. 237.

[29] Louis Massignon, and after him Louis Gardet, have rejected the idea that this concept of the Name is the result of a Hindu influence. In fact, as Anawati and Gardet point out, this idea refers to a "specifically Semitic meaning attached to the value of the Name" (Cf. G.C. Anawati and Louis Gardet, *Mystique Musulmane*, p. 199).

from the sacred scripture to the entire traditional world that derives from it, both directly and indirectly, Islam may be interpreted as an outer and complex manifestation of the Word.

As we have just seen, poetry may be conceived as a way of filling the gap that separates the human soul from the Divine Presence: we could say that this function of poetry is akin to *tashbīh* or analogy, i.e., to the mode of thinking and speaking based upon an affirmative and symbolic definition of the One. However, in keeping with the overall spiritual economy of Islam, Sufism remains keenly aware of both dimensions of *tanzīh* and *tashbīh*, of "other-ness" and analogy. The latter refers to the continuity between God and the world, referring to its symbolic and theophanic dimension—and being therefore related to an understanding of poetry as "making God present," whereas *tanzīh* establishes a clear distinction between the One and His creatures, thus stressing the discontinuity between the Divine Essence and manifested forms. The second perspective is decidedly emphasized in some of the most elliptic expressions of Sufi gnosis, particularly in the *Book of Spiritual Stations* and in the *Book of Spiritual Addresses* by Muhammad Ibn 'Abd al-Jabbār al-Niffarī. The *Mawqif* (Station) of the Ineffable in the *Kitāb al-Mawāqif* is particularly interesting in this respect:

> Expression is a swerving: when thou witnessest that which never changes,
> thou wilt not swerve.
> The divine word turns unto ecstasy: and using the divine word to induce
> ecstasy turns unto the raptures induced by words.
> Raptures induced by words are an infidelity according to definition.
> Listen to no letter concerning Me, and receive no information of Me from
> any letter.
> Letter cannot inform of itself: how then should it tell of Me?[30]

Even though this text is not technically poetic, its aphoristic form is quite akin to the symbolic and gem-like modality of contemplative poetry. The concise and elliptic form of expression that is used by Niffarī appears to be in full consonance with the fundamental tenet of his concept of language and expression. Whereas the word may be conceived *a priori* as a way in which God reveals Himself to men through the Scriptures and through His Name, thereby allowing for a sacramental participation of mankind in His nature, it

---

[30] Al-Niffarī, *Kitāb al-Mawāqif*, 4-8, in *The Mawāqif and Mukhātabāt of Muhammad Ibn 'Abdi'l-Jabbār al-Niffarī*, ed. and trans. A.J. Arberry, pp. 69-70.

may also be envisaged, as it is here by Niffarī, as a separative reality that leads one astray from the One, causing the contemplative to "swerve" instead of realizing the unity of being. As Rūmī puts it, "although in one respect speech removes veils, in ten respects it covers and conceals."[31] Words have more chance of covering than unveiling precisely because they most often proceed from a human subject and not from the Divine Word. When stemming from the individual, words encounter the ocean of dissimilitude, the gap between the many and the One. It is only when they proceed from the Divine Source, or let us say from a zone of profundity that borders on the Divine, that words may become a means of unveiling the Mystery. That is why in Niffarī's text, the divine word that "turns unto" ecstasy refers to the Qur'ānic scripture: its mystical use is "infidelity" when considered from the standpoint of mere definition, or according to the exoteric outlook that sees the letter and not the spirit.

In another passage, Niffarī alludes to these two opposite outcomes of the use of words when he states "by it (the Ineffable) thou art concentrated in the effable" and "if thou witnessest not the ineffable, thou art confused by the effable." In other words, there is no real "concentration" on the Word, or words in general, except through That which lies beyond It, or beyond them, and that is their essence and their principle of unity. The actual understanding of the linguistic, aesthetic, and poetic forms presupposes a centering upon That which transcends all forms and all language. To be "concentrated" upon the effable amounts to being conscious of its essence, i.e., its formless root. By contrast, a relationship with language—and particularly with poetic language—that is not rooted in a clear perception of the One can only be a source of ignorance and straying.

In Islam, as indicated by Niffarī, spiritual centering takes the form of a "witnessing" (*shahādah*) that relates everything to its Source. The supreme *shahādah* is a witnessing of the Ineffable (*mā lā yanqāl*) that is the precondition for the validity of all other utterances. In parallel, God as *Logos*, God as effable, is the very principle of creation. To understand the Word is therefore, by way of consequence, to understand things in their determinative and limiting reality, as well as in the concatenation and relationships that bind one to the other. The Word "utters" and "spells out" the various created realities, and these realities result from a compound of archetypical reality and substantial form. However, a true understanding of the limitless and

---

[31] Rūmī, *Mathnawī* I. 2973, cited in William Chittick, *The Sufi Path of Love*, p. 269.

inner meaning of beings can only be reached through a consciousness of the ineffable:

> The ineffable causes thee to witness in everything my Self-revelation towards it, and causes thee to witness of everything the places of its gnosis.[32]

On the level of the ineffable, which is supreme and unmediated contemplation, both dimensions of knowledge are revealed: the Divine Self knows Itself in every being, and every being is known through the Divine Knower and as a particular mode of knowledge of the latter. "I" is the Divine Self who is ultimately the only Knower; "thou" is the human self as central and conscious refraction of the One; while "everything" refers to all other creatures whose modes of knowledge of the One are both more peripheral and more limited than that of man as primary interlocutor of God. In the contemplative silence of pure consciousness, man witnesses God as the Only Knower and everything as a mode of knowledge of Reality. Such a "witnessing" can take place only through and in the ineffable, for any discourse would necessarily introduce a duality that would sever the human self from the Divine Self-revelation. In pure contemplation, man knows things as they are known by God and, in a concomitant way, he then knows God as He is "known" by things in the form of their archetypical necessity.

Niffarī pursues this exposition of contemplative gnosis by referring to the delicate relationship between writing and contemplation:

> Thou wilt write so long as thou reckonest: when thou reckonest no more, then wilt thou write no more.
> When thou no more reckonest nor writest, I shall assign to thee a portion of illiteracy: for the illiterate Prophet neither writes nor reckons.
> Neither write nor study nor reckon nor examine.
> Study writes true and false alike, and examination reckons taking and leaving alike.
> He belongs not to Me nor to my lineage who writes truth and falsehood, and reckons taking and leaving.
> Every scribe recites his scripture, and every reciter reckons his recitation.[33]

[32] Al-Niffarī, *The Mawāqif and Mukhātabāt*, ed. and trans. A.J. Arberry, p. 69.

[33] Al-Niffarī, *Kitāb al-Mawāqif*, 12-17, in *The Mawāqif and Mukhātabāt*, ed. and trans. A.J. Arberry, p. 70.

Writing and reckoning are intellectual activities that presuppose multiplicity: the former takes place by virtue of the sense of multiplicity that is entailed by the latter. The very act of reckoning presupposes a kind of quantitative and analytical consideration of Being that is infinitely transcended by its object. As Rūmī also expresses it:

> Speech is an astrolabe in its reckoning.
> How much does it really know of the sky and the sun?
> Or of that sky which holds this heaven as a speck;
> And the Sun which shows this sun to be a grain of sand?[34]

In addition to this "faltering" in the face of the Absolute, reckoning also implies an individual subject who wants to account for realities for the sake of his own sense of being and centrality; "every scribe" and "every reciter" limits reality by his own "reciting" and his own "reckoning." Writing implies truth and falsehood insofar as it adulterates reality with representation; it cannot encompass the sphere of reality with the planimetric surface of its graphic wording. Similarly, reckoning presupposes more and less, addition and subtraction, whereas everything is infinitely present in the actuality of the Divine Ineffability. Such perspectives are therefore incompatible with the simplicity and totality of the Supreme Subject, the essential "I." Considered primarily as a consequence of reckoning, writing is envisaged in its aspect of self-fulfillment, as a way of substituting individual consciousness for Self-consciousness of the One. In a sense, writing has no intrinsic meaning when considered from the exclusive standpoint of gnosis: its function can only be extrinsic, either as an "accounting for" spiritual consciousness to itself or as an imparting of that consciousness to others.

The mention of illiteracy, as opposed to reckoning and writing, is most telling in that it points both to the inner "virginity" of the Prophet, and to the primacy of oral expression over the written word. The "illiteracy" of the Prophet is in fact the passive or receptive dimension of his spiritual perfection. The "illiteracy" of the Prophet (*an-nabī al-ummī*) refers to the utter "poverty" of his soul before the divine inspiration and command. If the Prophet were not illiterate, he would not be the perfect recipient of the divine Word; human interferences would affect the integrity of the Message. For that reason, writing may appear as a potential act of spiritual betrayal. As a

---

[34] Rūmī, *Mathnawī* II. 3013-15, cited in *Rumi Daylight*, trans. Camille and Kabir Helminski, p. 172.

guarantee of fidelity and legitimacy, what matters most of all, from a human standpoint, is the integrity of the oral transmission (*isnād*). Even from a ritual standpoint, "the whole experience of the Qur'ān for Muslims remains to this day first of all an auditory experience and is only later associated with reading in the ordinary sense of the word."[35] The superiority of the spoken word over the written word is most profoundly connected to the intimacy of the Divine Word with the heart of man when the latter is in a state of primordial purity. In his *Mathnawī*, Rūmī can thus write:

> The book of the Sufi is not black lines and words,
> It is none other than the whitened heart which is like snow.[36]

Beyond its aspect of graphic exteriority, writing becomes identified—in its essence—with the very heart of the contemplative, but that heart is white as snow: it is both blankness and silence, a silence that is however vibrant with the Divine Word. Arberry reminds us, in this connection, that at times "Rūmī signed his verses with the soubriquet Khāmūsh, the Silent, a reference to the ineffable nature of the mysteries."[37] Symbolically and operatively speaking, the absence of writing is not so much a lack of graphic representation as it is a lack of appropriation of the Divine that would result from a sort of fixation of consciousness. In Islam, writing is God's privilege, so to speak: He is the One who, with the Calamus, writes destinies on the supreme Tablet. When studying and writing are associated with the pair of opposites truth and falsehood, the implication is that writing takes us away from the pure Presence in which, through the contemplative life, there is neither truth nor falsehood but only pure Being. Writing introduces the writer into the realm of distinction and opposition while making it possible to lose spiritual contact with the Divine. As Arberry very profoundly points out when referring to Niffarī's doctrine of the letter (*harf*):

> Letter does not reach Presence (*hadrah*), and the people of presence transcend letter and banish it: those that depart from letter are the people of presence, and those that have departed from themselves have departed from letter. God is nearer than the letter, though it should speak, and He

---

[35] Seyyed Hossein Nasr, "Oral Transmission and the Book in Islamic Education: the Spoken and the Written Word," *Journal of Islamic Studies* 3:1 (1992):1.

[36] Rūmī, *The Mathnawī of Jalālu'ddīn Rūmī*, ed. and trans. R.A. Nicholson, pp. 40, 59.

[37] A.J. Arberry, *Mystical Poems of Rūmī*, p. 2.

is farther than the letter, though it should be silent: for he is the Lord of *harf* and *mahrūf*.[38]

It should be noted that letters occupy a very important place in Islam, and especially in Sufism, in that the Arabic alphabet, as graphic means of the transmission and calligraphy of the Qur'ān, is imbued with profound symbolic and mystical significance. The science of letters (*'ilm al-hurūf*) is actually one of the most central hermeneutic disciplines of Sufism: it is fundamentally based on the correlation between Divine Names and letters and, operatively, upon the correlation between letters and numeric values. It is noteworthy that, in the perspective of radical gnosis which is Niffarī's, the theophanic letter becomes a veil, as also is the name—and even the meaning and the thing named—since "when thou departest from meanings, thou art fit for My gnosis."[39] On a methodical level, it is important to notice that, in the passage of Niffarī which we have quoted above, the mystic appears to suggest that there exists a profound solidarity between the letter and the self. The letter is not the "name" that was taught by God to Adam (Qur'ān, 2:31).[40] By contrast with the "names" that were taught to Adam in his state of primordial perfection, "letters" are utterly dependent upon the individualized self; as a "separated" and rational being, the individualized self is situated within the realm of limitations, determinations, and articulations that are part and parcel of the world of relativity:

> I have joined every pair of letters with one of my qualities, and the existences have been brought into existence through the qualities joining them together.[41]

To transcend letters therefore consists in transcending the domain of exclusivity, a domain of differentiation whose unity is guaranteed only by the "ineffable" and by divine qualities. It is also in a certain sense to return to a primordial state of perfection that precedes the descent (*ahbitū*) into "water and clay" and the expulsion from the Garden. In this sense, it is the realm of multiplicity as negation of Unity, not as theophany. We must however note that the verb which is used to refer to this "descent" has also the meaning

---

[38] A.J. Arberry (ed.), *The Mawāqif and Mukhātabāt*, p. 22.

[39] Al-Niffarī, *The Mawāqif and Mukhātabāt*, ed. and trans. A.J. Arberry, p. 47.

[40] *Ibid.*, p. 269.

[41] Al-Niffarī, *The Mawāqif and Mukhātabāt*, ed. and trans. A.J. Arberry, p. 105.

of "living" and "settling" so that it would be more accurate to speak here of a separation rather than a fall. The Qur'ān also strongly emphasizes that this "settlement" in the terrestrial world can only constitute an abode for an ephemeral time (2:36), therefore giving a legitimacy to human terrestrial endeavors while being no less adamant—to say the least—of the very constraining limits imposed upon these endeavors in light of the primacy of transcendence and the hereafter. In Islam, there cannot be a Fall in the sense of a fundamental loss that would leave mankind as if crippled and unable to enjoy its theomorphic norm. Man remains God's *khalīfah* or vice-regent of Creation. He is therefore allowed to "live" and "settle" in the world inasmuch as he remembers who he is and also that he must needs return to God. He is "real" because he still participates in the Reality of God, and the reality of what he creates is dependent upon a fuller consciousness of that participation. On all levels of creation, "reality" is therefore contingent upon God's "holding together," as silent and ineffable Principle, the multiplicity of letters, names, and meanings. Now God's ineffability is primarily experienced in the mode of presence; it is God's presence that "guarantees" the mysterious unity of everything.

By contrast, letter, as name, implies a qualitative determination that has to do with intelligence as consciousness. God's intelligence spells out the multiplicity of beings in their respective uniqueness. The spiritual orientation to which Niffarī alludes in the passages we have quoted seems to be akin to the unity of presence rather than to the unity of consciousness: it is related to intelligence as presence, i.e., to a mode of apprehension of reality which is more centered upon the pole of "being" than upon the pole of "consciousness," these two poles being fundamentally one on the highest level while still quite distinct at all lower planes. This emphasis on presence is to some extent akin to the spiritual bent of poetry—at least by comparison with other domains of literary expression: poetic language is less discursive than it is synthetic and in this capacity it may better recapitulate the contemplative mode of presence. This is the reason why poetry is, in Sufism, more often associated with love as a mystical reality of a higher order than with intelligence as a mental phenomenon. Rūmī founds this superiority of poetry over other modes of expression by suggesting its affinity with the essentiality of a central desire:

> Love lit a fire in my chest, and anything
> That wasn't love left: intellectual
> Subtlety, philosophy
> Books, school.

All I want now
To do or hear
Is poetry.[42]

Poetry appears in this connection as an essential language, the language that is left when all other types of language are powerless on account of the limits of language. It is the language of Love, the "language that cannot be said, or heard." Poetry is the tentative and liminal language of the supra-formal realm where the individual "expires" in Pure Being. As such poetry is always on the verge of being extinguished or silenced by the contemplative experience: "Love has come and covered my mouth: 'Throw away your poetry and come to the stars.'"[43]

Notwithstanding the fact that poetry is an attempt at the expression of presence, it also presupposes a mode of keen consciousness of this presence, a consciousness that necessarily involves the mental mirror of the contemplative poet. As such, poetic expression may be defined as a kind of intermittent projection of spiritual presence onto the mirror of mental and imaginal consciousness. Rūmī is once again our guide in approaching this subtle interplay between presence and consciousness, between existential love and intellectual vision:

In your light I learn how to love.
In your beauty, how to make poems.
You dance inside my chest,
Where no one sees you,
But sometimes I do, and that
Sight becomes this art.[44]

The "dance" that takes place within the chest of the contemplative is akin to the penetrating infusion of presence that is like a breathing in of the divine ether: this presence no one can see or define, for grace eludes any attempt at appropriating it. It can only be glimpsed in the instant of consciousness that is fixed into poetry, when "sight becomes this art."

*   *   *

[42] Rūmī, cited in *Birdsong*, trans. Coleman Barks, p. 20.

[43] Rūmī, *Dīwān-i Shams-i Tabrīzī* 182, cited in William Chittick, *The Sufi Path of Love*, p. 226.

[44] Rūmī, cited in *Birdsong*, trans. Coleman Barks, p. 41.

Between absence and presence, the theme of love and its spiritualization, occupies a central position in Sufi poetry and literature. The famous story of Laylā and Majnūn typifies the complexity and depth of the dialectics of absence and presence in love, and the subtlety of its relationship with poetic expression. Majnūn represents the figure of a lover who is "possessed" by the *jinn* of love to the point of becoming insane. Intoxicated with his inner image of the beloved, Majnūn flees into solitude and wilderness. There, his interiorization of Laylā's image is so profound that he is led to exclude the physical presence of his beloved. When Laylā comes to visit him in the desert, Majnūn refuses to see her under the pretext that she would distract him from the essential reality, the imaginal form of Laylā that he contemplates.

The Sufi tradition has generally interpreted Majnūn's loving madness as a metaphor for the individual's extinction in God's presence. The "alienation" of Majnūn therefore refers to the contemplative station of *fanā'* or disappearance. The figure of the beloved, whose name refers to the Night of the Divine Essence, embodies or symbolizes the Divine Presence and Divine Wisdom. The seat of individual consciousness becomes so powerfully and profoundly "occupied" by the Divine that it amounts to a radical "alienation" in which "I" becomes "Thou."

Jad Hatem has opposed this traditional understanding of Majnūn's intoxication with the love of Laylā by suggesting that far from reducing Majnūn's ego to utter nothingness, his erotic experience leads to the dissolution of the very being of Laylā. In other words, the extinction is not Majnūn's but rather Laylā's.[45] There is but little distance from such an understanding to the interpretation of Majnūn's love as an exaltation of his own ego. In fact, such an opposition is fundamentally illusory, in that it participates in a discursively dualistic reduction of a profoundly non-dualistic experience. It is certainly possible to interpret Majnūn's loving madness in terms of an "exaltation," but reducing the latter to an expression of the egoic identity would be missing the point. The fact is that, through his loving experience, Majnūn is not the "same" as he was: he has been made "other," "alien" and he has abandoned

---

[45] "Le désir ne manque plus de rien, s'engendre pour accroître le sentiment de soi. C'est plutôt la personne de Laylā qui subit l'extinction, car en dépit de son irréductibilité, elle est entièrement transie par le Moi puisque, par l'intériorisation, elle se mêle à l'affectivité de l'amant [Desire does not lack anything, it engenders itself to increase the feeling of oneself. It is rather the person of Laylā who undergoes a process of extinction, for notwithstanding her irreducible reality, she is entirely deserted by the Ego since, through interiorization, she blends with the lover's affectivity]" (Jad Hatem, *Travaux et Jours*, p. 17).

his former self. The "exaltation" that he experiences is intimately dependent upon a spiritual death in love, and it may therefore be understood in the sense in which "permanence" or "subsistence" (*baqā*) proceeds from extinction (*fanā'*). When the contemplation of God has extinguished man and reduced his individuality to ashes, God "restores" him to his original form as it was "intended" from all eternity. Man knows himself in his most profound reality only when he has accepted to be no more, in the sense of no longer being "independently" (and therefore illusorily) apart from God.

Considering this spiritual process from the point of view of Majnūn and Laylā's love story, one may say that the reason why Laylā appears to be annihilated in Majnūn's experience flows from the fact that the real Laylā is actually none other than the inner essence of Majnūn. In this process of spiritual self-realization, poetry functions as a kind of mediation. Having found a retreat far from the world of men, Majnūn is "severed from his tribe and soon from the commerce of men, and even from language except for the purpose of evoking and poeticizing his beloved."[46] As Rūmī puts it in one of his poems: woman is not created, she is creative, not so much *natura naturata* as *natura naturans*. She is also by the same token transformative. It is through her contemplation that poetry is set in motion and that it culminates in the realization of the inner Self. As Jad Hatem has noted in a most cogent way:

> If the absence of Laylā provokes the interiorization of Laylā, her name opens up an avenue without which poetry would have been impossible.[47]

Poetry may henceforth be the means through which the bridging of the gap between the lover and the beloved results in an interiorization of the name, or the word, that ultimately unveils the identity between the name, the named, and the one uttering the name. In Sufism, this triad is nothing but an exteriorization and a polarization of the only Reality that is. In his *Mathnawī*, Rūmī expresses this mystery by reference to the symbolism of a lover's relationship with her beloved's name:

> Zuleikha applied to Joseph the name of every single thing.
> From a grain of celery to a branch of aloe.

---

[46] *Ibid.*, p. 7: "Qui déraisonne est retranché de sa tribu et bientôt du commerce des hommes, et même du langage sinon pour évoquer et poétiser sa bien-aimée."

[47] *Ibid.*, p. 8: "Si l'absence de Laylā provoque l'intériorisation de Laylā, son nom ménage une issue sans laquelle la poésie eût été impossible."

She hid his name under all other names, and only let
Her special confidantes into the secret....
This is what the name of the Beloved can do
When you are truly and finally lost in love.
When the soul has truly been united to God
To speak of God is to speak of the soul
And to speak of the soul is to speak of God.[48]

The one who invokes (*dhākir*) becomes so infused with the presence of the beloved who is invoked (*madhkūr*) that everything becomes an invocation (*dhikr*) of the name of the beloved. Perceived in this sense, and as a prolongation of the "invocation" of the One through the multiple "names" of the many, poetry can be considered a kind of ruse through which multiplicity, or duality, is give access to unity. Laylā is the theophany, and at the same time the autophany, that reveals the unity which precedes all dualities, this unity being both objective and subjective, or rather, situated beyond the level on which this polarity functions. As Henry Corbin has remarkably commented, in his exegesis of Rūzbehān al-Baqlī's *Jasmine of Fedeli d'Amore*: the contemplation of human beauty must be founded upon *iltibās* or double meaning. Corbin uses the term "amphiboly" to translate this difficult concept of *iltibās*. In English the terms "amphiboly" and "amphibolic" denote ambiguity and uncertainty, and there is little doubt that the contemplative experience which Corbin has in mind presents an element of ambiguity that is actually the sign of its depth and also its pitfalls. As Frithjof Schuon puts it when evoking the mystery of the contemplation of God in formal and erotic beauty:

> The ambiguity of earthly pleasure—above all sexual pleasure—is that on the one hand it is concupiscence or animality in the sense that it implies the desire for what we do not have, and on the other hand it is an angelic and quasi-divine awareness of what we are, of what we are in our ontological and paradisiacal substance. All moral and mystical oscillations and tensions are explained by this; and the ambiguity is not in the experience only, it is in the subject as well as in the object. Man oscillates between sacraments and idols, objectively and subjectively.[49]

This ambiguity is so to speak situated at the point of juncture between extremes: the divine and the corporeal; and it is what accounts for the powerful

---

[48] Rūmī, cited in Andrew Harvey, *Teachings of Rumi*, p. 77.

[49] Frithjof Schuon, *Christianity/Islam: Essays on Esoteric Ecumenicism*, p. 113.

contemplative potentialities of love and eroticism. In this connection, the concept of "amphiboly" that Corbin has used to refer to this theophanic experience must be understood in light of the etymological meaning of the symbol. If the latter, through the Greek prefix *sym-* (or rather *syn-*) implies the "togetherness" of two elements that are conveyed in a kind of *syn*thetic unity, the concept of "amphiboly" or *iltibās* can then be understood to refer to the co-presence of two "sides" at one and the same time. The contemplative experience of *iltibās* corresponds neither to a situation of exclusiveness—which would retain a dualistic form—nor to one of mere synthesis—which would reduce that duality to unity—but points rather to a situation in which both sides of the same reality are contemplated at the same time, i.e., the physical and aesthetic phenomenon *and* the spiritual meaning or presence. This inner situation is one in which, as Corbin says, the contemplative soul enjoys the "coincidence of reaching and missing the inaccessible, that of the vision refused through the vision that is granted, absence tasted in presence, disquietude of a still beyond in the quietude that is sometimes tasted here below."[50] The ebb and flow of reality is so to speak instantaneously present in the message of beauty since that message is simultaneously an encounter with limitless beatitude and constraining limitation. Poetry is particularly apt at suggesting this most paradoxical state of the contemplative experience of God in theophanic beauty, since it is predicated upon a double-sided and subtle relationship with the word: on the one hand poetic expression may be considered under the aspect of its outer perfection—i.e., as both source of contemplative inspiration and limitation—while on the other hand it can be seen to open onto the infinite silence of blissful plenitude.

The "amphibolic" character of poetry—and of beauty in general—also finds an expression, quite paradoxically, in the poetic acknowledgment of the necessity of absence or void as the center of spiritual contemplation. The word is a means of alluding to the heart of all spiritual life, which is beyond form. In "One-Handed Basket Weaving," Rūmī suggests that the creative core of all arts is emptiness, and that the search for this essential emptiness is actually the main aspect of contemplative and artistic endeavors:

> I've said before that every craftsman
> Searches for what's not there
> To practice his craft.[51]

---

[50] Henry Corbin, *En Islam iranien III*, p. 28 (my translation).

[51] Rūmī, "One-Handed Basket Weaving," cited at www.armory.com/~thrace/sufi/poems.html.

In poetry, this empty center is none other than silence. In this respect, poetry might be defined as a circle of words dancing around silence. The central importance of silence in mystical poetry finds an expression in the fact that early Sufi poets tended to favor a shorter form of expression, that of the quatrain or *rubāʿī*, a form that was most appropriate to express flashes of intuition or emotion independently from a specifically didactic purpose. The brevity of the quatrain is particularly apt to suggest the limits of expression and the meaningful background of silence. Independent of this aspect of brevity, the rhyme scheme—three of the four verses of the quatrain must rhyme, while in the *ghazal* and the *mathnawī* consecutive or alternate pairs of hemistich must also rhyme—introduces an element of harmony that suggests a unity to the whole composition, therefore subtly leading back to silence. This harmonic principle of unity finds a correspondent element in the thematic unity that characterizes the unfolding verses; for, as Laleh Bakhtiar puts it, "each verse corresponds to the primary image of the arabesque in its continuous repetition of a single theme."[52] As with the void in the graphic art of the arabesque, silence—functioning as an allusion to the unity transcending multiplicity—is suggested by the harmonic and thematic texture of the poem.[53]

In this sense, poetry symbolically reduplicates the contemplative process; but it does so by abolishing in some ways its own reality. The contemplative inversion at the core of all mysticism—the passage from multiplicity to unity, in which the initial allure of multiplicity is ultimately superseded by unity—is presented by Rūmī in a most expressive way that implies, in a certain sense, a self-abolishment of language and poetry. The images are strikingly powerful:

> God has allowed some magical reversal to occur,
> So that you see the scorpion pit
> As an object of desire,
> And all the beautiful expanse around it,
> As dangerous and swarming with snakes.[54]

---

[52] Laleh Bakhtiar, *Sufi: Expressions of the Mystic Quest*, p. 112.

[53] One could apply, *mutatis mutandis*, what Seyyed Hossein Nasr says about the arabesque and the void to the relationship between poetry and silence: "The arabesque enables the void to enter into the very heart of matter, to remove its opacity and to make it transparent before the Divine Light. Through the use of the arabesque in its many forms, the void enters into the different facets of Islamic art, lifting from material objects their suffocating heaviness and enabling the spirit to breathe and expand" (*Islamic Art and Spirituality*, p. 186).

[54] Rūmī, cited in *The Essential Rumi*, trans. Coleman Barks, p. 24.

The fundamental mystery of the contemplative *opus* amounts to an inversion that only God can bring about through the "magic" of His grace. The image of the "scorpion pit" is evocative of a dark depth, but also of a sense of death and resurrection, a sense of transformation. It also entails an element of "ugliness" that is to be transfigured by the spiritual process. To choose a contemplative life amounts to a kind of jumping into this scorpion pit, a "letting go" of all fear and attachment that is the precondition for spiritual awakening or resurrection. The most luminous light is hidden in the very depth of obscurity, and it is there that it has to be found. It is moreover by virtue of this finding that the soul will be able to free itself from the "beautiful expanse around it." Poetry becomes an invitation to plunge into that "pit" of contemplation and to find in it the plenitude of emptiness. The possibility of this paradox—that of a form calling to the overcoming of all forms—is actually founded upon the very secret of creation: the metaphysical enigma of existence as a consequence of the desire for the essential emptiness:

> Praise to the emptiness that blanks out existence. Existence:
> This place made from our love for that emptiness![55]

The human love for emptiness is the essence of a desire that can be satisfied only by the emptiness of the Supreme, an emptiness that is also fullness, depending upon the standpoint from which one wishes to consider it: a void with respect to the false plenitude of indefinite multiplicity; a fullness by contrast with the vain illusion of reality, which is truly "nothingness." When trying to account for this supreme paradox, poetry reaches a summit and a limit in the sense that it "condemns" itself to disappear in its very utterance; whence the conclusive notes of the poem, which are marked by a kind of contradictory resolution, a *coincidentia oppositorum* in which discourse affirms its own failure:

> These words I'm saying so much begin to lose meaning:
> Existence, emptiness, mountain, straw:
> Words and what they try to say swept
> Out the window, down the slant of the roof.[56]

---

[55] *Ibid.*, p. 21.
[56] *Ibid.*, p. 22.

The image of the window evokes the relationship between an inner and an outer meaning, or conversely the contrast between a confinement and a liberation. As for the image of the roof, it connotes both the idea of a peak or a top, and that of a covering: extreme limits of poetic language—touching the infiniteness of the sky—and linguistic "envelopment" of reality. In all respects, poetic language cannot fulfill its mission in complete permanence: it is marked by tension, discontinuity, and disappearance. It springs forth to bear witness to the One, but it can never uphold its testimony to the point of securing an unfailing access to the Source. In a sense, the instability and insufficiency of words have also something to do with their abuse ("these words I'm saying *so much*"): words, especially poetical words, tend to lose their freshness and therefore their evocative power. Rūmī is particularly keen on stressing this very inability of words, while at the same time indicating that poetry constitutes the best means of gaining access to Love, understood here in the sense of an actualization of the Divine Presence.

The relationship between poetry and contemplation may therefore be understood from two standpoints: one that conveys a sense of continuity between words and experience; the other, on the contrary, pointing to the apophatic dimension of contemplation. In the latter perspective, Rūmī highlights the limits of language when it comes to conveying a sense of contemplative fulfillment:

> Whatever I say to explain or describe Love
> When I arrive at Love itself, I'm ashamed of my word.
> The commentary of words can make things clear—
> But Love without words has more clarity.
> My pen was rushing to write its thoughts down;
> When it came to Love, the intellect is impotent,
> Like a donkey trapped in a bog.[57]

Poetry, insofar as it is dependent upon language, can only obscure the contemplative experience while yet trying to convey it: on the highest level, unity can only be obscured by multiplicity. More precisely, and more paradoxically, as principles of clarifying obscurity—or of obscuring clarification—words have a function to play in the economy of contemplation. The acceleration of writing that would suggest an attempt at remaining as close as possible to the very source of the experience, by "keeping up" with

---

[57] Rūmī, cited in Andrew Harvey, *Teachings of Rumi*, p. 77.

it, cannot in the least equate with the reality of the experience. Rūmī does not repudiate poetic discourse in that it is a way of "translating" the experience of mystical love into the language of human commonality. However, such an attempt presupposes a tension between two poles: that of the identity of words with presence—or the mysterious ability of inspired words to be channels of presence—and that of the region of dissimilitude, to make use of a Neoplatonic concept.

The polarity we have just mentioned actually amounts to a question of perspective. Words, and consequently poetry, are both divine and human realities, and this double nature accounts for the highs-and-lows of a contemplative practice of poetry. This dual nature of language, which leads us back to the mystery of *iltibās*, is to be understood in terms of a distinction between informal essence and formal substance, a distinction that is moreover parallel to that of inward nature and outward manifestation. Rūmī explains this "amphiboly" in the following terms:

> With us, the name of everything
> Is its outward appearance;
> With the Creator,
> The name of each thing is its inward reality.
> In the eye of Moses, the name of his rod was "staff;"
> In the eye of the Creator, its name was "dragon."
> In brief, that which we are in the end
> Is our real name with God.[58]

The ontological and spiritual nature of language is rooted in archetypes, i.e., in realities as they are contained in God's intelligence and "willed" by Him. However, in "normal"—or should one say "abnormal"?—everyday circumstances we have access only to the outer shells of things, which are symbolically designated by their outer and conventional names. To name somebody or something amounts, in a real sense, to knowing their nature, and it ultimately amounts to perceiving that nature from the standpoint of the archetypical reality. The reference to Moses' staff that becomes "dragon" in God's eye suggestively indicates that realities are always much more "real" from the latter standpoint than they may appear to be from the former. "Real" names correspond to higher realities and, consequently, "real" poetry, as a "real" language, reaches the domain of archetypes. However, poetry is not

---

[58] Rūmī, cited in *Rumi Daylight*, trans. Camille and Kabir Helminski, p. 38.

Revelation, it is still "on our side" of things; it may rather, therefore, be defined as the realm of the extreme formal limits of human language, the point at which human language may so to speak "invert" itself to reveal its hidden "reverse" side. When al-Hallāj writes, "and my words if I wish are inverted," he most likely alludes to these boundaries of expression where opposites meet, when wisdom is folly and vision blindness.[59] When poetry comes close to its ultimate possibility and function, it tends to defy the laws of conventional reality and logic because it has to conjugate extremes in order to capture the formless in a single form. On this level, poetry transcends the realm of distinction and logical exclusiveness. In his *qasida*, al-Hallāj points to this mystery when he juxtaposes in a striking contrast the dualities and distinctions that are entailed by common human arts and endeavors on the one hand and, on the other hand, the literally absurd expressions that "make sense" of the categories of mystical experience. The poet is first intent on emphasizing the dichotomies of terrestrial knowing and being:

> Science is double, rejects, accepts
> The oceans are two: navigable, dreadful
> Time is two days: blamed and praised
> Men are double: endowed and plundered ...[60]

Human knowledge is the epitome of a distinctive apprehension of reality since it is founded on discriminating truth from error. As for the two oceans, they probably refer to the two seas of the Sūrah of the Cave, one sweet and the other salty, which may be interpreted as two different planes of reality. Time and mankind are also submitted to this law of exclusion which alternates between highs and lows. However, the supreme contemplative experience, the "foolish wisdom" that al-Hallāj tries to convey in words, reunites contradictions, making the impossible possible. The symbols of the spiritual experience that are evoked are abruptly deprived of their formal and human features to suggest the coincidence of *tanzīh* and *tashbīh*, transcendence and immanence:

> I climbed a peak without any feet
> Its scaling was hard for others than I

---

[59] "Blindly seeing and wisely foolish. And my words if I wish are inverted" (Al-Hallāj, *Selections from the Poems of Zuhair ibn Abi Sulma and Husain ibn Mansur al Hallaj*, trans. Arthur Wormhoudt, p. 83).

[60] Al-Hallāj, *Selections from the Poems of Zuhair ibn Abi Sulma and Husain ibn Mansur al Hallaj*, trans. Arthur Wormhoudt, p. 82.

I dived in a sea without setting foot
My soul waded in it, my heart wanted it,
Its pebbles pearls no hand touched
But the mind's hand had plundered them.
I drank its water without a mouth
Much water that mouths often drank from,
For my soul of old thirsted for it
And my body felt it before creation.[61]

Three basic motions or actions recapitulate a symbolic path in which the formal analogies of imagery are as if reintegrated into their supreme *analogon* "before creation": ascent of a mountain (transcendence), descent into a sea (immanence as inclusion), and absorption of its water (immanence as assimilation). The ternary "without any feet … without setting foot … without a mouth" resounds as a rhythmic pattern of apophatic abstraction that quite suggestively illustrates the "reversal" of words and images that characterizes the limits of contemplative poetry. To walk without feet, to drink without a mouth: this is the razor's edge of contemplation, insofar as the linguistic means of poetry can suggest it. Let us note in this respect that the body is characterized as most directly aware of reality: the "soul of old" has nostalgia for what it has lost but the body apprehends most immediately what it experienced "before creation." The immediate spontaneity of the Self is reflected in that of the body, while the soul that lies in the intermediary zone of reality appears as if "torn" between the conflicting objects of its desires.

It follows from what we have said above—just as it also appears in the various works that we have been commenting upon in the context of Sufism—that, set on the confines of expression, mystical poetry may take three different paths: symbolic and imaginal suggestion, paradoxical and self-reversing expression, and extinction into silence. The first mode of expression is primarily akin to *tashbīh* and ultimately proceeds from the crystallization of spiritual insights in the imaginal world. The process of crystallization we are alluding to is analogous to that of theophanic realities in general and it therefore conforms, *mutatis mutandis*, to Henry Corbin's definition of the entrance of spiritual realities into forms:

Just as a divine Name can be known only in the concrete form of which it is theophany, so a divine archetypical Figure can be contemplated only in

---

[61] *Ibid.*, pp. 82-3.

a concrete Figure—sensible or imagined—which renders it outwardly or mentally visible.[62]

By contrast with this theophanic modality, the second and third modes of poetic expression of the ineffable, in conformity with *tanzīh*, are chiefly characterized by an attempt to suggest the distance that separates their own expressions from reality. In the first case, this is effected through a sort of immanent subversion of common language, a disarticulation of the syntax of horizontal coherence that may take on the mode of a kind of bursting apart of language and reason. This type of poetry is akin to the social behavior of *qalandars* and *malāmat*, the type of mystics who display an often eccentric disdain for normative conventions of conduct and thrive on systematic reversal. The idea is to open up cracks in the world of appearances in order to give way to the perception of Reality. This is the way proposed by Sa'di when he suggests that, "With a sweet tongue and kindness and silence, Can you catch an elephant by a hair."[63] Such a dynamic and negative approach runs parallel with the apophatic language of "unsaying" that has been analyzed by Michael A. Sells in his study of Ibn 'Arabī's "Garden among the Flames": in this connection, to cohere with concepts and images amounts to stopping "at a particular station or experience, however exalted, and bind the real to it." Inasmuch as language involves a "reification" of itself it must "correct" and "negate" itself in order to convey the Real.[64]

As for the choice of silence, it obviously corresponds to a limit that cannot be reached without abolishing poetry and language; however, this extreme tendency can find a suitable outlet through either a semantic or a prosodic strategy of intimation of silence. The poem may enunciate or suggest the primacy of contemplative silence through its meaning—either explicitly or implicitly—or it may more obliquely allude to this primacy through its rhythmical and harmonic patterns and practices. The regularity of rhythm and harmony introduces a sense of unity that suggests the experience of single-pointed concentration through a prosodic centering of the multiplicity

---

[62] Henry Corbin, *Creative Imagination in the Sufism of Ibn 'Arabī*, p. 138.

[63] Sa'di, *Gulistān*, ch. 3, p. 108, cited in Anne-Marie Schimmel, *As Through a Veil*, p. 273, note 135.

[64] "The habits of language pull the writer and reader toward reifying the last proposition as a meaningful utterance. To prevent such reification, ever-new correcting propositions must be advanced" (Michael A. Sells, *Mystical Languages of Unsaying*, p. 207).

of linguistic forms. Whether it be through "musical" techniques or through the suggestiveness of meaning, words must in any case undergo a kind of "transfiguration"—i.e., both a "reduction" and an "elation" of their form and meaning—in order to serve as pure witnesses of Reality; so it is that they may be both blurred and fixed (*fi'l fanā' wa'l baqā*, as it were) in the integral and suggestive meaning that "silently" radiates through them, in the image of Rūmī's candle that becomes a "sign without signs":

> Place before the sun a burning candle,
> See how its shining disappears before those lights:
> The candle exists no longer, is transfigured into light.
> There are no more signs of it; it itself becomes a sign.[65]

---

[65] Rūmī, cited in Andrew Harvey *Teachings of Rumi*, p. 91.

III. *Poem of the Hall of Pines and Wind*
Huang T'ing-chien (1045-1105)
Sung Dynasty, cursive script

3. LU CHI'S *WEN FU*
Poetry as Contemplation in the
Chinese Classical Tradition

Lu Chi's *Wen Fu* (*The Art of Writing* or *The Poetic Exposition on Literature*) is a most important text to consider if one wishes to gain some insight into the relationship between spiritual contemplation and poetic creation in the context of Chinese classical culture. Lu Chi lived in the third century of the Christian era, during a time of political instability and warring factions; he came from a renowned family of military leaders. He was himself an important military figure of the Wu Empire, but the fickleness of military and political fortune led him to withdraw from the official world into scholarly retreat for a period of about ten years. This period of his life allowed him to devote himself to the study of the classics of the Confucian and Taoist traditions, which are the spiritual backbone of his *Wen Fu*. He returned to military command during the last years of his life at the service of Prince Yin, but soon thereafter a severe defeat in 303 resulted in his execution for high treason at the age of forty-two. His considerable literary production gives evidence of a man exceptionally gifted for both the world of action and that of contemplation and writing; a man who was deeply engaged in the most important political and cultural events of his time, but who was also profoundly molded by the high religious and literary culture of the Chinese tradition. The considerable influence of his *Wen Fu* on later literary history in China, and more recently in the West, is probably due to the coalescence within him of profound and subtle literary insights with a fundamental contemplative disposition sustained by Confucian and Taoist models and practices. Lu Chi's poetic exposition might not be the work of a full-fledged contemplative or mystic, but it is certainly suffused with an awareness of the contemplative dimension of poetic creation.

*   *   *

He stands in the very center, observes in the darkness,
Nourishes feeling (*ch'ing*) and intent (*chih*) in the ancient canons.[1]

[1] Lu Chi, *Wen Fu*, cited in Stephen Owen, *Readings in Chinese Literary Thought*, p. 87.

83

The poet enjoys a central metaphysical position. Barnstone and Pou Ching translate this first verse of the *Wen Fu* as "a poet stands between heaven and earth,"[2] whereas Sam Hamill, literally closer to the original and to Owen's translation, renders it as "the poet stands at the center of the universe."[3] The Chinese *chung-ch'ü* refers to the idea of the center of the world or the cosmos. This central position is in a sense a general privilege of mankind, and it is no doubt what Barnstone has in mind in his translation, since it probably refers, if only through association, to the character *wang* which symbolically represents the median situation of man between Heaven (*tien*) and Earth (*ti*). Marcel Granet suggests that the notion of axis is antecedent to that of center,[4] but the two are difficult to separate, as indicated by the aforementioned ideogram, which includes a central vertical axis. The privilege of cosmic centrality is in a definite sense the concomitant aspect of the intermediary situation of man between Heaven and Earth. It is by virtue of his mediation between the two that man is able to enjoy a central position in the second of these realms.

The imperial connotations of this central position of the poet are not to be neglected. Like the emperor within his empire the poet stands at the center of the universe and exercises power from this center, which is actually the only real source of power. Be that as it may, the fact that the initial situation of the poet is defined as central indicates that poetry is connected to a metaphysical position which is a precondition for its production. François Cheng has convincingly shown that the status of Chinese poetry has to be understood as metaphysically and cosmologically grounded, and as related to two axes that are complementary: the "Taoist" axis that relates Vacuity and Fullness—or the Tao and the Ten Thousand Things—and the "Confucian" axis that articulates Heaven and Earth. The terms "Taoist" and "Confucian" are quite approximate in this context, but they have the methodical merit of contrasting what could be considered as a metaphysical perspective and a cosmological one. Cheng shows that these two axes do not imply a duality, but that they actually refer in both cases to a triad. It is on the first axis that Cheng situates the "Median Vacuity," which is like the necessary interplay between Void and Fullness, and is also—on the side of Fullness—the principle of alternation between Yin and Yang. On the "Confucian" axis, *homo*

---

[2] Lu Chi, *Wen Fu*, cited in *The Art of Writing: Teachings of the Chinese Masters*, trans. and ed. Tony Barnstone and Chou Ping, p. 6.

[3] Lu Chi, *Wen Fu*, cited in *The Art of Writing*, trans. Sam Hamill, p. 10.

[4] Marcel Granet, *La pensée chinoise*, p. 104.

occupies an intermediary position between Heaven and Earth: "Man is raised to an exceptional dignity since he participates as a third actor in the work of Creation; his role is by no means passive."[5]

In the wake of the preceding considerations, it is important to note that the contemplative principle that presides over the poetic experience reveals definite Taoist implications. As an illustration of Cheng's point, it should in particular be emphasized that Lao-tzu's center does not so much refer to man as cosmological mediator as it does to the metaphysical Mystery that is the principle of the Ten Thousand Things. In the *Tao Te Ching*, the symbol of the hub of the wheel points to this necessary but elusive Center:

> Thirty spokes on a cartwheel
> Go towards the hub that is the center
> —but look, there is nothing at the center
> and that is precisely why it works![6]

In Lu Chi's text, the emphatic reference to this central metaphysical position, which is the principle of all perfect productions, is confirmed and developed by reference to the poet's ability to "observe in darkness." As Owen explains in his edition of the *Wen Fu*, the term *hsüan-lan* (which he translates as "observes in the darkness") is a fundamental term belonging to the vocabulary of spiritual experience. The dark and the mysterious refer to the Taoist principle that Lao-tzu posits in the opening chapter of the *Tao Te Ching* as the first Reality that transcends both the "named" and the "without name." The duality of being and non-being, presence and absence (which is "epistemologically" duplicated by that of the "named" and the "without name") implies a kind of reciprocal relativity that is transcended only in the one "ground" of ultimate darkness.[7]

The deepest and most real dimension of reality is associated with darkness, and this association highlights its character of mystery as well as its transcendence of conceptual and linguistic categories. This second aspect of the supreme Mystery is clearly suggested by Hamill when he chooses to translate Lu Chi's initial verse as "contemplating the Enigma." The Supreme

---

[5] My translation. See François Cheng, *L'Ecriture poétique chinoise*, p. 7.

[6] Lao-tzu, *Tao Te Ching*, ch. 11, trans. Man-Ho Kwok, Martin Palmer, and Jay Ramsay, p. 46.

[7] Paraphrasing the French translation of the *Tao Te Ching* by Liou Kia-Hway and Etiemble, p. 3, we could write that "These two (the named and the unnamed) come from a same ground, are distinct only through their names. This same ground is called darkness. To darken this darkness is the door of all subtleties."

Reality is not approached in cataphatic terms through multiple attempts at defining it; rather, it is considered as the ultimate *koan*, the riddle *par excellence* that defies all concepts and words with which one would claim to capture it. Poetic contemplation is therefore primarily a concentration on the very mystery of being; it consists in situating oneself at the central point from which all things flows. This is the most substantial sap of poetic "inspiration" to which the poet must be fundamentally receptive. Poetic contemplation is therefore envisaged, as a prelude to "production," as a kind of emptying of the mind and soul.

As Owen suggests, this vision of poetical experience as a kind of eviction of all preconceived forms is strikingly different from that which has prevailed in the Western poetical tradition, which was primarily initiated by Aristotle's *Poetics*.[8] The Western concept is predicated upon the pattern of an "idea" or an "image" that is the principle of poetic creation, in the sense that it serves as the point of reference for the "shaping" of the poetic object. In this view, art—and poetry in particular—is to be understood as *mimesis*, whether it be imitation of nature or representation of a mental image. Such an understanding of the poetic act seems to give more functional importance to the individual agency of the poet as the "producer" of poetry. In the Aristotelian tradition, the Western poet's work is utterly dependent upon representation as its starting point and normative reference. Poetry is fundamentally imitation:

> Epic poetry and Tragedy, Comedy also and Dithyrambic poetry, and the music of the flute and of the lyre in most of their forms, are all in their general conception modes of imitation.... Poetry in general seems to have sprung from two causes, each of them lying deep in our nature. First, the instinct of imitation is implanted in man from childhood, one difference between him and other animals being that he is the most imitative of living creatures, and through imitation learns his earliest lessons; and no less universal is the pleasure felt in things imitated.[9]

In this context, representation is often understood on the model of plastic arts, particularly painting. The "eidetic" (referring to the *eidos* or the ideal form of the work to be produced) and the visual are profoundly associated. The role of the poet is in a sense actively passive in that he must imitate nature

---

[8] "From Aristotle on, the long and complex history of the theory of the imagination in the West is based on the metaphor of forming pictures in the mind" (Stephen Owen, *Readings in Chinese Literary Thought*, p. 88).

[9] Aristotle, *Theory of Poetry and Fine Art*, p. 7 (I) and p. 15 (IV), trans. S.H. Butcher.

and forms through "imagination" and "production." In the Chinese model, the role of the poet seems to be, at least initially, more receptive than creative, more passive than active, since being, as "passive" participation, supersedes imitation as "active" creation. We are tempted, however, to say that for the Chinese poet what matters is to be passively active in the sense of Lao-tzu's *wu wei* (action without action). Following the contemplative emphasis of Taoist and Buddhist themes of meditation, the point is to eliminate all that could be an obstacle to a perfect and single-minded focus on the Abyss from which all things proceed and which is the very "act" of nature.

Given its very central metaphysical status, the poet's source of "inspiration"—here we use the term in the very general sense of creative influence—would however be too abruptly "non-formal" if it were not complemented by two other sources of sustenance from a more relative order: that of the literary tradition, and that of nature. The poet cannot just stand in contemplation of the Abyss or Enigma. On the one hand, by contrast with the mystic, the poet's contemplation is not his only or ultimate end. He must re-enter at some point into the world of forms. In a sense, his initial exclusive contemplation of the supreme Darkness is, in his case, only a means of access to numerous realms of light and motion. The exclusion of outer forms is a prelude to the exploration of the inner world. One may well speak in this respect of a genuine poetic voyage, a voyage that will be treated in more detail in the second part of the Lu Chi's treatise, in verses 15 to 30.

In addition, the poet is not an island. Poetry is not only a matter of personal creativity; it is also the result of a complex interplay between the self and the natural and cultural ambience in which he lives. In both cases, the poet learns and is enriched by identifying with his milieu. This is the reason why the Chinese poet never severed himself from his literary tradition, or from the natural environment of which he is an integral part. Far-Eastern art, in general, is acutely aware of nature and shows a strong reticence towards any kind of sentimental or humanistic aggrandizement of man, which could only result from a disconnection of man from his cosmic ambience. It is also keen to prevent an excessive individualization of poetry by situating it in the ever-flowing presence of the "ancient canons."

Furthermore, the correspondence between signs and nature is one of the chief concerns of Chinese poetry. Ideograms already point in that direction in so far as they proceed toward a kind of correlation between natural objects and signs. However, we would be mistaken to interpret this orientation in the sense of an outwardly mimetic or naturalistic tendency. Chinese ideograms aim at a kind of secret cosmic "number" or "essence" of things; they do not "represent" in a superficial sense. François Cheng has suggested that a concern for such a correlation constitutes, in fact, the primary character of Chinese semantics and poetics, which is insistent on avoiding any "rupture between signs and the world."[10] As a methodical preparation for the cultivation of that concern, the "identification" to which we referred above could be compared to a kind of "saturation" through participation. The multiplicity and diversity of the "poetical" and emotional interactions of the poet with both nature and literature are brought to such a degree of intensity and refinement that they must ultimately result in a work of poetry. In verses 3 to 8 and then 9 to 14, Lu Chi considers respectively "participation" in the cycle of nature and "participation" in the literary tradition.

In the context of Lu Chi's poetics, nature is not merely envisaged as an external milieu that provides the poet with images and forms of inspiration. In fact, it is difficult to distinguish the outer reality of leaves, trees, and seasons from the inner realities that echo them. On the one hand, the poet reacts emotionally to the array of natural phenomena embraced by the seasonal cycles of the year; on the other hand a close correspondence between inner microcosm and outer macrocosm seems to transform these responses into participatory modes of being. We must not forget that the initial "observation in darkness" or "contemplation of the Enigma" leads us toward the interior realm. We would actually like to suggest that this contemplation in darkness introduces us to a dimension of reality in which the very distinction between inner and outer is abolished or suspended.

This suspension is what is referred to by Chuang-tzu as the "fasting of the mind" (*hsin chai*). The Taoist sage characterizes this "fasting"—which is also envisaged by him as "sitting in oblivion" (*tso wang*)—in the following passage:

> You must, first of all, unify the movements of your mind. Do not listen with your ears, but listen with the mind (thus unified and concentrated). (Then proceed further and) stop listening with the mind. Listen with the pure spirit. The ear (or more generally, sense perception) is confined to listening (i.e., each sense grasps only a particular kind of physical quality).

---

[10] "To suppress the gratuitous and the arbitrary on all levels of a semiotic system founded on an intimate relationship with the real, in such a way that there would not be any rupture between signs and the world, and therefore between man and the universe: such appears to be that toward which the Chinese have always tended" (François Cheng, *L'Ecriture poétique chinoise*, p. 13 [my translation]).

The mind is confined to (forming) images corresponding to their external objects. The pure spirit on the contrary is itself "void" (having no proper objects of its own), and goes on transforming limitlessly in accordance with (the universal Transmutation of) things. And the Way in its entirety comes into this "void." Making the mind "void" (in this way) is what I mean by the "purification of the mind."[11]

It appears that this contemplation in darkness may well be interpreted, in Lu Chi's context, as a transcending of the individual mind, resulting in a pouring forth of "the Way," i.e., of the "thousand beings" as they flow from their intrinsic nature. If, as Toshihiko Izutsu puts it, "(the Perfect Man) is completely one with the ten thousand things as so many manifestations of the Way,"[12] we may infer that Lu Chi's poet participates, through *hsüan-lan*, in a state of ecstatic unity with all things. This participatory unity which mingles natural phenomena and inner feelings is not to be equated with Romantic emotional and sentimental projections into nature; it is rather a "moving along" with the very flow of nature by virtue of a suspension of the individual animic identity. François Cheng expresses this contemplative dimension of poetry in a most cogent way:

The poet aims at suggesting that, by dint of contemplating the tree, he ends up by being one with it and that he lives from "within" the tree the very experience of its *eclosion*.[13]

The shamanistic roots of this Taoist contemplative orientation are hardly doubtful since shamanism can be precisely characterized as the psycho-spiritual science of inner contact with the powers of nature.[14] Taoism is indebted to this shamanistic spirituality of harmony and consonance with the natural

---

[11] Chuang-tzu, *Inner Chapters*, IV, cited byToshihiko Izutsu, "The Absolute and the Perfect Man in Taoism," in *The Unanimous Tradition*, ed. Ranjit Fernando, p. 52.

[12] *Ibid.*, p. 52.

[13] François Cheng, *L'Ecriture poétique chinoise*, p. 17 (my translation).

[14] "One of the most ancient strands of Taoism is shamanism.... The role of the shaman, the key figure in this faith, is to be able to contact the other world, to be in touch with the forces which affect the world and to either pacify them or to call upon their aid. The shaman goes in a trance whereby he or she is able to move between the worlds and to answer questions or seek help. This idea of the shaman being in touch with the world of the spirit is what lies behind the Taoist notion of the sage being able to flow with the true natural forces of the universe" (Jay Ramsay, cited in the introduction to Lao-tzu, *Tao Te Ching*, p. 9, Kwok, Palmer, and Ramsey trans.).

forces and spirits. Chuang-tzu describes this anthropocosmic participative harmony in his *Inner Chapters* when characterizing the true man:

> He is as cool as autumn and as mild as spring. His joy and anger flow like changing seasons. He is in harmony with all things and has no limitations.[15]

The consonance of Lu Chi's poet with the diachronic unfolding of "natural" time through qualitative phases is no doubt indebted to the Taoist concept of the Perfect Man. However, as we have suggested above, the very capacity for "peering" at all things, "sighing" at the passing of seasons, and "brooding" on the richness of things seems to presuppose a certain tendency toward reflection that is perhaps the precondition for the dynamics of creation. Poetry cannot simply be a participation in nature: the poet must manifest an intention to act toward the production of a poem, thereby introducing an almost imperceptible distance from the beings of nature, which is the condition for his bringing forth words. We do not think however that this "productive" goal of poetry must necessarily be understood as an essential element that would radically distinguish Lu Chi's poetic statement from Taoist contemplative practices. Arguing in favor of this distinction, Owen writes that "it is important to distinguish between a useful, attractive model for the operations of the mind in literary composition and true Taoist values," and suggests that "Lu Chi is simply transferring the Taoist spiritual model to the writer's quest for words and ideas."[16]

The two main arguments for this claim are, first, that the *shou-shih fan-t'ing* ("retraction of vision, reversion of listening") in question is to be sharply distinguished from a suspension or "cutting off" of sensory perceptions, and secondly, that Lu Chi—contrary to Taoist principles—does not dismiss "knowledge."[17] The first argument is closely connected to the idea of production as goal since it implies that the subject not close himself to all perceptions whatsoever, but that he focus exclusively on the inner perceptions that are the *materia* for his work. Now this line of argument seems to be considerably weakened by the implications of several important occurrences

---

[15] Chuang-tzu, *Inner Chapters*, trans. Gia-fu Feng and Jane English, p. 117.

[16] Stephen Owen, *Readings in Chinese Literary Thought*, p. 97.

[17] "We might note that Lu Chi never rejects knowledge, that rejection being essential to the Taoist spiritual project" (Stephen Owen, *Readings in Chinese Literary Thought*, p. 97).

in Taoist classics. One of them is Chuang-tzu's apologue about Prince Wen Hui's cook:

> Prince Wen Hui remarked, "How wonderfully you have mastered your art." The cook laid down his knife and said, "What your servant really cares for is Tao, which goes beyond mere art. When I first began to cut up oxen, I saw nothing but oxen. After three years of practicing, I no longer saw the ox as a whole. I now work with my spirit, not with my eyes. My senses stop functioning and my spirit takes over. I follow the natural grain, letting the knife find its way through the many hidden openings, taking advantage of what is there, never touching a ligament or tendon, much less a main joint.[18]

This passage is highly instructive in that it illustrates the intimate connection between the contemplative dimension and the "poietic" realm, taking here "poietic" in the etymological sense of a "making." The explicit emphasis on the primacy of the Tao, far from being exclusive of a perception of forms, conveys to this perception a sense of metaphysical wholeness and immediacy which is the key for the perfect accomplishment of the "artistic" act. Now the "reversion" and "retraction" of senses that is recommended by Lu Chi is a necessary condition for an "absorption" in spirit that opens up the vigilant receptivity of the subject and makes him able to perform his task in a most effective way. Chuang-tzu's distinction between outer and inner ears and eyes actually suggests that the "cutting off" which is referred to by Owen might very well be the contrary of a total suspension of sensory perceptions, i.e., a deeper inward looking mode of perception:

> What I mean by the expression "having good ears" does not concern the faculty of hearing the external objects (*t'a*). It concerns only hearing one's own "self" (*tzŭ*). What I mean by the expression "having good eyes" does not concern seeing the external objects. It concerns only seeing one's own "self."[19]

Notwithstanding the commonality of this fundamental method of interiorization, we will grant that poetic art might appear as more sophisticated than the butcher's work since it entails both a more complex inner percep-

---

[18] Chuang-tzu, *Inner Chapters*, p. 55.

[19] Chuang-tzu, *Outer Chapters*, cited in Izutsu, "The Absolute and the Perfect Man in Taoism," p. 51.

tion of objects and a manifold outer rendering of these objects into words. However, the higher degree of sophistication that this art implies does not substantially alter the methodical principle that is involved. The perfect rhythm and harmony of the cook's work presupposes perfect spiritual concentration as a principle for perfect outer execution. These remarks are also related to the question of the purported opposition of Taoism to knowledge: according to Taoist principles, knowledge—whatever may be its level and mode—must necessarily rely on a way of being. Knowledge as such is not dismissed, it is simply seen in a metaphysical and existential context that makes it part of being a "true man": "First, there must be a true man; then there can be true knowledge."[20] Chuang-tzu's joking dismissal of a knowledge that is not rooted in a knowledge of Tao seems to echo Socrates' irony toward the knowledge of Sophists and rhapsodists who do not even know what knowing is. Now a "true man" is precisely one who stands at the center and "observes in darkness."

Notwithstanding the major import of Taoist principles for Lu Chi's description of the poet's participation in natural rhythms, the dynamics of the passage that illustrates this participation ("He is as cool as autumn and as mild as spring. His joy and anger flow like changing seasons. He is in harmony with all things and has no limitations") are quite revealing in mapping out the dual aspect of the experience: a kind of all-embracing expansion that encompasses, through parallelism, the whole spectrum of the four seasons, is followed by a vertical soaring that abruptly signals a change of focus.

We think it plausible to read in the juxtaposition of the aforementioned ample "horizontal" movement and the final "flight" over the clouds, a symbolic expression of the complementarity between *ch'ing* and *chih* that is highlighted in Owen's analysis of *Wen Fu*.[21] "Feelings" (*ch'ing*) are envisaged as a full range of emotional responses: they measure the whole spectrum of the receptive soul. The four seasons are the standards of these responses. The "profusion" upon which the mind "broods" most likely refers to the summer: Barnstone and Chou Ping's rendering as "the swarm of living things" seems to reinforce this interpretation by highlighting the phase in which nature is in its fullest state of unfolding and development. As complements to this allu-

[20] Chuang-tzu, *Inner Chapters*, p. 113.

[21] "*Ch'ing* 'feeling,' tends to be the passive and receptive aspect of 'mind,' *hsin*; here it has a capacity to be nourished or fed, and in this sense is perhaps closest to English 'sensitivity.' Although also stirred by things, *chih* is an active component of mind, that which 'goes out' or 'goes toward' something" (Stephen Owen, *Readings in Chinese Literary Thought*, p. 89).

sion, the references to the "grief" of "autumn" and the "rejoicing" of spring are more explicit references to other moments of the yearly cycle, as is also finally the verse "his mind shivers, taking the frost to heart." This cycle of *ch'ing* culminates in the drive or the "poetic ambition" (*chih*) that is like the axis of the four directions of feeling. Hamill proposes to read the verse as "summer clouds can make his spirit soar," the somewhat unwarranted reference to summer providing for a seasonal fourth element that his very general translation of verse 4 as "the many ways of the world," had left unmentioned; whereas both Barnstone/Ping and Owen also allude to the verticality of *chih*, but in a manner that is more suggestive of a towering overview than of ascending flight: "My ambition floats with high clouds" and "His intent is remote, looking down on the clouds." This implication reinforces the sense of poetic reflectiveness, a reflectiveness that was already suggested, as Owen pointed out, in the "brooding" over the wealth of forms of nature. The sense of "going out" that is conveyed by *chih* suggests a kind of resolution of the cosmic journey of *ch'ing*. The sense of "floating" still implies a lack of stability and direction, whereas that of "remoteness"—favored by Owen—present in the "modal descriptive *miao-miao* … (describes) the quality of something that is tiny and faint in the distance,"[22] thus the purely potential status of the poem. Both translations therefore suggest that the intent is like a seed which still needs to grow, or like a triggering motion that has not yet seen its effects. The mention of the clouds probably reinforces this aspect of being *in potentia*: the clouds (*yün*) being a symbol of the fertilization to be, that is of the upcoming production of the poem. "Looking down on the clouds," the remote intent of creation is about to precipitate the poetical act.

By contact with the literary tradition, the poet is also sustained in *ch'ing* and *chih*. These two key-notions, which Owen translates as "feeling" and "intent," express respectively the passive and active connotations of these two states of mind. In other words, the sensibility of the poet is opened up by his reading of the classics, but it is also stimulated by this contact, which becomes in its own right a new source of creation. There is a very expressive complementarity between the kind of aesthetic inebriation that results from repeated cultivation of the classics and the final outcome of this whole frequentation of the masters of the past:

> He sings of the blazing splendor of moral power (*tě*) inherited by this
> age,

[22] Stephen Owen, *Readings in Chinese Literary Thought*, p. 91.

Chants of pure fragrance (or "reputation") of predecessors,
Roams in the groves and treasure houses of literary works,
Admires the perfect balance of their intricate and lovely craft.
With strong feelings he puts aside the book and takes his writing brush
To make it manifest in literature.[23]

As in the case of nature, in a clear parallelism of structure, the exploration of the world of literary tradition is the precondition for the final resolve while at the same time remaining still sharply distinguished from it. The "making manifest" (*hsüan chih*) is so to speak the final outcome of the "contemplation in darkness" (*hsüan-lan*): what was hidden in the darkness of inner contemplation must come into the light of literature. Parallel to the sudden and abrupt volitive "breakthrough" of *chih* emerging from an extensive participation in the rhythms and colors of nature, the "taking of the brush" has in a sense no direct and definite causal relationship with what precedes it: it is self-assertive and can be related to no other agency than the poet's will as it has been shaped and nourished by nature and culture. Owen seems therefore to be correct in asserting that there is no such thing as "inspiration" in Chinese poetry; if, i.e., one understands the latter as a kind of "possession" by a divine entity such as one of the Muses. However, if by "inspiration" we refer to an influence or a sort of "breathing in" of natural qualities and poetic "perfumes," then there is no reason to deny the validity of this term in Lu Chi's poetics.

*   *   *

Thus it begins: retraction of vision, reversion of listening,
Absorbed in thought, seeking all around,
My essence galloping to the world's eight bounds,
My mind roaming ten thousand yards, up and down.[24]

The fourteen opening verses of *Wen Fu* have merely set the prerequisites of the poetic voyage. Now this creative periplus begins: and this beginning takes the form of the most extreme contraction of sensory faculties. However explicitly principal this focusing reduction is, a distinct shift of emphasis separates Owen's translation from both Hamill's and Barnstone/Ping's: while the latter focus on spiritual concentration as the exclusion of all outer

---

[23] Lu Chi, *Wen Fu*, cited in Stephen Owen, *Readings in Chinese Literary Thought*, p. 92.
[24] *Ibid.*, p. 96.

determinations ("eyes closed, he hears an inner music"[25] and "at first, I close my eyes. I hear nothing"[26]), the former stresses that this exclusively inward concentration is subordinated to an inner expansion that it actually fosters. The choice of words, "reversion" and "retraction," as opposed to Hamill's "closing" of the eyes, points to a change of direction rather than to a complete suspension of faculties. The discovery of the objects of poetry occurs within and not without.

This opening of the second section of the text may be interpreted as an analogous reduplication of the centering and contemplation of darkness that opened the piece; the difference between the two remains clear however: what was a kind of ontological participation in the whole of reality by means of a concentration on its Mysterious Center is now followed by a process of interiorization through which the actual creative process may take place. The receptive and creative faculties have been sharpened by an ecstatic dilation before they can be launched into an exploration of the inner realm. In a sense the surprising discrepancy between Hamill's "inner music" and Barnstone/Ping's "nothing" is not as shocking as it might at first seem if one assumes that the "nothing" can be taken as the extrinsic face of the intrinsic flow of "inner music." What is non-existent when perceived from outside is all-existent when envisaged from inside. To speak of "retraction" and "reversion" implies some kind of modification of the perceptions, which are as if "returned" to their original place of focus. The mind is now in search of internal objects and this search knows no boundaries.

We should note that this unbounded travel to the confines of the inner kingdom can be considered as a kind of "heating up" of the "essence" or "spirit" (*ching*) of the poet, and it is not by chance that this "enstatic" and quasi-shamanistic voyage ends in kindling a light that gradually enlightens poetic objects. As Isabelle Robinet has shown,[27] Taoist alchemy considers *ching* to be the primordial nature or essence that "contains" the ultimate void, *wu*: this essential nature must be activated by changing the usual direction of one's "gaze" and desire, turning them inward. It is through this "change of heart" or this conversion of *ching* that the alchemical process may be accomplished. More specifically, Taoist alchemy represents the inner fire that

---

[25] Lu Chi, *Wen Fu*, cited in Sam Hamill, *The Art of Writing*, p. 11.

[26] Lu Chi, *Wen Fu*, cited in Tony Barnstone and Chou Ping, *The Art of Writing: Teachings of the Chinese Masters*, p. 9.

[27] Cf. Isabelle Robinet, "*Xin Fa*, l'art du coeur et de la connaissance dans le Taoïsme," *Connaissance des Religions* nos. 57/58/59 (January-September 1999):246-65.

is contained in the waters of the loins with the pre-cosmic yang—a full line—that is situated between two yin or broken lines, as indicated by the trigram *kan*, thunder or tiger. One of the principles of Chinese alchemy consists in heating up the watery fire, which then ascends from the loins as a tiger, while its complement, the fire "enclosing" waters (*li*), as the dragon, descends to unite with it. In this symbolic and transformative context, fire springs forth from water and light from darkness; and this is also the fundamental pattern of the ignition of the primordial nature—which is as if dormant—by the concentration of the heart. In Lu Chi's poetical alchemy, the connotations of "images igniting images" and that of "things become luminous" similarly function as a symbolic response to the initial contemplation in darkness. Accordingly, the characterization of the whole Chinese alchemical process that is proposed by Isabelle Robinet seems to us to apply to Lu Chi's poetical contemplation: "within quietude, motion is born, its activation, its manifestation ... but within this awakening quietude remains present."[28] In other words, the darkness must be "brought out" by light while being at the same time the "substance" of light: both are interconnected, like two sides of the same reality; but the appearance of one amounts to the disappearance of the other.

It may be necessary to add, in this metaphysical and poetic context, that we should not conclude from what has just been said that darkness and brightness (*ming*) must be considered as opposites. On the highest level of reality they may not even be considered as complements. The very fact that Chuang-tzu and other Taoist writers refer to the supreme state of contemplation both as "darkness" and "brightness" already implies that the opposition—or complementarity—is valid only up to a point. We are tempted here—at the risk of relating spiritual contexts that are formally worlds apart—to call on Dionysius the Areopagite's "hyperluminous darkness" as an expression of the Divine Essence for an analogy. As we have suggested above in another context, what is dark from an outer standpoint may be bright from an inner perspective and vice-versa. In Lu Chi's *Wen Fu*, darkness is in any case the *conditio sine qua non* of brightness.

The images associated with this brightness that makes "things" visible to the poet's inner eye, refer to five parallel registers: savoring, flowing, hunting, fishing, and gathering. These images are all connected to the modes

---

[28] "Au sein de la quiétude, naît le mouvement, sa mise en exercice, sa manifestation. Mais au sein de cette mise en branle, reste présente la quiétude" (*Ibid.*, p. 257 [my translation]).

of appearance of poetic "objects" in the zone of consciousness. There is an expressive contrast between the growing accuracy of the "objects," their precision, and the cosmic expansion, galloping and roaming, that precedes them. From the moment of their inner perception, the whole process is very much akin to that of a gradual focusing of the attention of the mind upon them. The objects that become the *materia* of the poetry are not only discovered in the sense of their being found, but they are also dis-covered in so far as their potential poetic meaningfulness is unleashed.

However, the question to be raised is that of the ontological status of these "objects." The term used by Lu Chi is *wu*, which can refer to a very wide spectrum of realities but seems to have in all cases a meaning of phenomenal objectivity.[29] They appear to refer mostly to words, images, sentences, and harmonies, and can therefore be defined as poetic and linguistic "objects." They are probably to be understood as "poetic entities" that associate semantic, sonoral, and even graphic elements. It may be relevant to note, in this respect, that the graphic and phonetic characters of written and oral Chinese are akin to such an understanding of poetic objects. As Paul Claudel has suggested in his *Knowledge of the East*, the Chinese ideogram is like an independent being endowed with life and evocative of a divine nature. The character is akin to the *I Ching* hexagrams in terms of its spiritual, magical, and divinatory effectiveness. Its graphic self-containment and its freedom from syntactical bonds contribute to asserting this independence. One should not try to understand the Chinese character as one would understand a written word in Indo-European languages. The latter cannot be isolated from its etymological, declensional, and syntactical aspects: it is always part of a wider structure, which denies its ontological singularity. Analogically, the monosyllabic structure of the spoken language gives a kind of objective identity and singularity to Chinese words. It also lends to each character a "great mobility with regard to its ability to combine with other ideograms."[30]

Be that as it may, one of the implications of this search for "objects" seems to bring us back to Hamill's idea of an "inner music" since we may infer that the inner microcosm resounds with a "music of words" that has

---

[29] "*Wu*: 'thing,' 'phenomenon,' and eventually 'other' (as in Liu Yi-tsai's use of the term in identifying with another person). *Wu* varies in usage from an 'animal' to a 'physical thing' to any 'object of consciousness.' The term 'object' is perhaps the English term with the closest semantic range (excluding the meaning of 'animal')" (Stephen Owen, *Readings in Chinese Literary Thought*, p. 594).

[30] François Cheng, *L'Ecriture poétique chinoise*, p. 14 (my translation).

to be brought from potentiality to full manifestation. On the other hand, Lu Chi also uses the term *ch'ing* (mood or feeling) to refer to objects of the poet's inner exploration. Now as Owen has pointed out, *"ch'ing* is usually … a condition of perception rather than an object of perception."[31] Hamill's translation, through its continued use of musical images ("the inner voice grows clearer as objects become defined") implies a sort of "subjectification" of the "inner music," which becomes the "organ" for the manifestation of the "objects." This translation has the merit of suggesting the ambiguous status of poetical perception, which is neither exclusively subjective nor objective but both at the same time.

The "subjective objects" we have just mentioned are apprehended in various modes. The image of savoring refers to the first of these modes. In this context, essentiality and aesthetic pleasure are intimately connected, as expressed in both Hamill's and Barnstone/Ping's translation ("he pours forth the essence of words, savoring their sweetness" and "I drink the wine of words"). The "savor" of words flows from their innermost reality as a delightful quintessence. The surface of words is tasteless because it concerns only the least common denominator of communication: on this level, language is merely instrumental—a tool in view of human "commerce." It is "used up" and as if desecrated by this reductive use. Accordingly, the function of the poet is both "conservative" and "revolutionary." He attends to the most permanent, ontologically grounded dimension of language, but in so doing he breaks away from the profane commonality of daily, worn-out words. The ideas of conservation and new creation are in a sense captured together in Owen's translation, "the sweet moisture of the Classics," the term *jun* (moisture) implying a fertilization of the new by a pleasurable absorption of the old. This aesthetic contact which distils the inner substance of words is then amplified by a reverse absorption of the poet into the "moisture" of streams, lakes, and oceans: "I drift between Heaven and the abyss, at rest in the current, I bathe in the falling stream, immersed in its waters."[32] The active search has reached a point where it is superseded by a passive abandonment. Moreover, through a kind of inversion of the relationship between subject and object, the line of demarcation between the latter and the former is as if blurred once again. We could also say that the absorption of the "object" by the "subject" must be the prelude to an absorption of the "subject" in the "object," the second movement implying a more intense and profound loss

---

[31] Stephen Owen, *Readings in Chinese Literary Thought*, p. 99.

[32] Lu Chi, *Wen Fu*, cited in Stephen Owen, *Readings in Chinese Literary Thought*, p. 98.

of ordinary consciousness. The final "immersion" and "flooding" ("diving" in the two other translations) constitutes the culmination of this movement of loss of self.

In the wake of this increasing "liquefaction" in the poet's modes of perception, the three metaphoric modalities of fishing, hunting, and gathering appear both in a continuous and discontinuous sequence. The continuity is implied by the juxtaposition of images of immersion and fishing that Hamill highlights by making the poet the subject of both the diving and the catching of fishes, "he dives to the depths of seas ... and he brings up living words like fishes hooked in their gills, leaping from the deep."[33] The symbolic cohesiveness of the sequence is moreover fostered by conjuring up images of hunting and gathering, "intricacies of craft ... caught by stringed arrow"[34] and rhymes being "picked" like flowers. However, the continuous line of metaphors should not veil us to the shift in emphasis that has taken place from passive receptivity to active search. This subtle interplay between contemplation and "production" is a hallmark of Lu Chi's poetics and it may in fact appear as another aspect of the indistinction between subject and object that is part and parcel of contemplative Far Eastern practices and disciplines of art and mysticism.

The active dimension of poetical work is most importantly brought out in verses 27 and 28: the poet "gathers in writing omitted by a hundred generations,"[35] or he summons "words and images from those unused by previous generations" (Hamill),[36] i.e., words which are more truly defined as "forgotten" than as "new." Should one read in these lines a mere concern for originality in the ordinary sense? We would rather understand these expressions as indicating a creative preservation of the original (in the sense of the origin) richness of language. The present is in this sense an attentive cultivation of the past. Receptivity and creativity join in this "giving of a purer meaning to the words of the tribe" (Mallarmé) that constitutes one of the poet's major functions. The origin is not lacking anything; actually everything is contained in it *in potentia*, but this potentiality is virtually unlimited and provides unending avenues for new poetic formulations.

The conservative originality we have here in mind is fully and beautifully expressed in verses 29 and 30: "It falls away—that splendid

---

[33] Lu Chi, *Wen Fu*, cited in Sam Hamill, *The Art of Writing*, p. 11.

[34] Stephen Owen, *Readings in Chinese Literary Thought*, p. 101.

[35] *Ibid.*, p. 102.

[36] Tony Barnstone and Chou Ping prefer the expression "neglected for a hundred generations" (*The Art of Writing: Teachings of the Chinese Masters*, p. 9).

flowering of dawn, already unfurled, but there opens the unblown budding of the evening."[37] If one is to understand dawn and evening as poetic references to moments in literary history, one will also appreciate the implications of a kind of alternation in the form of a yin-yang graphic symbol: the beginning is in the end as the end is in the beginning. In other words the fully unfolded masterpieces of the past, if not dismissed (as some commentators would have it), are in any event subject to a kind of aging while the late comers of poetry are full of promise. Authentic poetry always conveys a sense of perpetual renewal and "originality" or "freshness." It is also twice over an "original" contribution in that it actualizes an "unexpressed" component or a "blank space" of cultural language as "origin" while doing so by virtue of a personal resonance with the transmitting line of that language. Tradition is not a museum of bygone fossilized beauties but an ever-flowing river of creation. Tu Wei-ming's characterization of the poetic vision of Confucianism seems to us to apply most pertinently to this concept of tradition:

> The first vision (of the classical Confucian Way) is poetic (and by inference artistic and musical) whereby a human being is conceived as one who is constantly involved in an internal resonance between the self and other human beings, and between the self and transmitted culture. Poetry refines human feelings and sentiments into artistic expressions of humanity.[38]

To speak of "internal resonances" amounts to saying that tradition is above all an "object"—or rather a multiplicity of objects—within. This implicitly Confucian way of envisaging poetic creation as an interiorization of the self-transforming chain of cultural interactions does not however constitute the final word of what could be called the investigative phase of creation. The two final lines of the second part of the text bring us back to a sense of contemplative unity and instantaneity that is like a concluding echo of the opening "standing in the very center" and "observing in the darkness":

> He observes all past and present in a single moment,
> Touches all the world in the blink of an eye.[39]

The synthetic perception that brings the whole movement to a close transcends the linear polarity of new versus old and situates the poet in the

---

[37] Lu Chi, *Wen Fu*, cited in Stephen Owen, *Readings in Chinese Literary Thought*, p. 102.

[38] Tu Wei-ming, "Confucianism," in *Our Religions*, Arvind Sharma (ed.), p. 195.

[39] Lu Chi, *Wen Fu*, cited in Stephen Owen, *Readings in Chinese Literary Thought*, p. 104.

immediacy of a metaphysical consciousness. From the opening eye observing in the darkness to the blink of the eye that concludes the second movement of the text, vision has reached the two ultimate limits of its scope: innermost Mystery and outermost expanse of manifestation. The aspect of immediacy that is conveyed by the contact with the latter is most expressively strengthened by the term *fu*, which is translated as "touch," and therefore implies a "concrete" contact[40] that radically takes us beyond the element of duality and distance still present in the ordinary idea of "vision." The instantaneity of this direct "contact" with the whole of manifestation confers an anthropocosmic and "mystical" quality upon the poetic gaze. Poetic contemplation does not merely amount to observing an object in order to imitate and represent it; it is a vibrant unity with the whole spectrum of existence. It is as if the original contemplation in the darkness had become objectified and actualized in the outward dimension of reality, thereby reducing the latter to a central point of consciousness that "touches" "all the world," since "extremes meet."

To summarize the movement we have just analyzed: the dynamics of poetic creation set in motion by the initial "reversion" or "closing" of the eyes and by a focus on inner silence or music can be described as a three-fold process that evokes a cyclical structure. From "eyes closed" to the "single blink of an eye," through the inner odyssey of moods, images, and word searching, it is as if three phases are to be envisaged: (1) A contraction or withdrawal from the external world and from all reference to external images as well as to the words of men; (2) An expansion that encompasses the most extreme limits of the cosmos (from "depths of seas" to "passing clouds") in a symbolic and inward mode of "enstatic" fusion; (3) A final coincidence of opposites (both spatial and temporal) that synthesizes the whole of space and time in the pure consciousness and vision of an instant. We have returned to the central point after having departed from it while trodding and galloping through the unlimited space of outer and inner realities.

This vast and intense voyage forms a cycle that can be understood as the inner preparation for the actual craft of poetry. So far, it has not been a question of painstakingly working on words but of "tuning" the spiritual instrument and "searching" for the ore or the "raw material" from which the work will be made. This is, properly speaking, the contemplative phase of the process of poetic creation. A central question must be raised at this juncture:

---

[40] Owen specifies that *fu* also means "caress" and often implies "care" (*Readings in Chinese Literary Thought*, p. 104).

what is the relation between the preparatory "work" of the Chinese poet and the inspiration that is the starting point of poetic creation in the Western tradition? It is clear, as we have already mentioned above, that one cannot equate Lu Chi's early motion with the divine possession of Plato's Ion or the Renaissance and Romantic influx of inspiration coming from the Muse. First of all, no divine or semi-divine personification of poetic power can be found: this, no doubt, is in keeping with the metaphysical language of the Taoists as well as that of the Confucian tradition. Second, the poet is not the passive receptacle of a divine manna. Third, and correlatively, his creative vigilance is called forth.

With these undeniable qualifications and differences in mind, it seems quite plausible to establish a parallel between the Bacchic or Dionysiac sources of the Western poetic reliance upon inspiration and the shamanistic underpinnings of the Taoist principles and values that are at work in Lu Chi's work. Both spiritual traditions refer to a transcending of ordinary individual consciousness through expansive fusion with powers and forces of nature. Both entail a kind of effusion and multiplication of that consciousness and an ability to enter various living forms by "magic" or "manic" imitation and identification. Just as the Dionysian current informs the Platonic understanding of poetry as *mania* ("inspired" madness), so shamanistic practice makes reference to an "alienation" of the personality of the shaman. Both worldviews, with their attendant ecstatic practices, are predicated upon the ontological principle of a dyad, symbolized by the pairs "above and below," or "inner and outer," while evoking the possibility of a fusional interplay of the two. According to this path, Unity is to be reached in and through multiplicity, and the latter so to speak produces an energy that is the fuel for a return to the former.

*   *   *

> Only afterward he selects ideas, setting out categories,
> Tests phrases, putting them in their ranks.[41]

The next section of *Wen Fu* is more directly concerned with the technical process of composition. It may be considered therefore as having a less direct relationship with contemplative practice. It comes "only afterward," being

---

[41] Lu Chi, *Wen Fu*, cited in Stephen Owen, *Readings in Chinese Literary Thought*, p. 104.

both diachronically posterior and methodically subordinate: knowledge of the craft can manifest its full effectiveness only once the contemplative situation has been set. This is not to say, however, that the technical dimension of composition does not touch upon our primary concern; it actually does so in several respects. First of all, there is an element of attention involved in the classification, ordering, and pruning of the poetic *materia*. Hamill's translation is particularly sensitive to this contemplative dimension of attention: "he considers his words with great care and fits them with a sense of defined proportion."[42] Care and a sense of harmony are like extrinsic aspects of the poetical contemplative practice. In this connection, Owen has also emphasized the pregnancy of the metaphors of political ordering: "setting out categories, test[ing] phrases, putting them in their ranks."[43] This is so to speak the Confucian phase of the poetic work. As Confucian wisdom entails a path of finding and expressing "transcendence in immanence" (Tu Wei-ming's phrase),[44] poetic composition may appear as a kind of rational[45] and organic ordering of the gifts unveiled in the mysterious and supernal realm of the inner self.

This attention is also very much connected to the sense of the organic nature of the composition. Words and images have been found, their creative power has been unveiled, but they still need to be envisaged from the standpoint of their reciprocal relationship and their organic rapport with the whole. In other words, the intention is not simply to reproduce the order of nature, as with *mimesis*, but to produce objects as nature does. Natural metaphors suggest the diverse and complex strategies that this concern entails: these multiple and contrasting aspects of his work invite a wealth of pairs and antitheses (branches and leaves, waves and source, hidden and manifested, simple and difficult, tiger and beasts, dragon and birds, agony and ease). These dual structures may express a refined awareness of syntagmatic relationships between words: "[relying] on the branches to shake the leaves"

---

[42] Lu Chi, *Wen Fu*, cited in Sam Hamill, *The Art of Writing*, p. 12.

[43] "*Hsüan-yi … k'ao-tz'u*: Placed in parallel construction, 'select' and 'test' are the language of evaluating the qualifications of aspirants to government service…. *an-pu … chiu-pan*: These phrases also belong to the language of political judgment, making assignments that match a particular talent to an office" (Stephen Owen, *Readings in Chinese Literary Thought*, p. 105).

[44] "The Confucian project has a transcendent dimension. The idea that the human Way is sanctioned by Heaven implies that Confucian this-worldliness is profoundly religious" (Tu Wei-ming, "Confucianism," p. 203).

[45] Hamill stresses this new rational dimension in his translation: "Shadowy thoughts are brought into the light of reason" (*The Art of Writing*, p. 12).

and "follow[ing] the waves upstream to find the source" are thus metaphors of a "natural" way to deal with meaningful sequences. On the one hand, words derive from other words in a harmonious chain of meaning; on the other hand, a given term may bring the poet back to a seminal image by virtue of a kind of poetic inference.

Another type of dual structure refers to the aforementioned interplay between potential and hidden simplicity and expansive or intricate manifestation. Barnstone and Chou Ping prefer to refer, in a more explicit way, to the poet's privilege of "[bringing] the hidden into light." Here again the poet may proceed from the simple to the difficult or he may choose the reverse. In a certain sense these strategies of composition reproduce on their level the dialectic of exclusive unity and inclusive complexity that animates the first two sections of the treatise. The whole movement of *Wen Fu* is a kind of pulsation or breathing that contracts in order to expand and expands in order to contract. There is an alchemically creative virtue in this kind of cyclical motion that makes the poet participate in a self-transforming experience of the Way (Tao).

In addition to dual associations marking continuity or progression, others seem to highlight sharp contrast and structural rupture. This is particularly the case with the metaphor of the tiger and that of the dragon: "It may be that the tiger shows its stripes and beasts are thrown into agitation, or a dragon may appear and birds fly off in waves around it."[46] The first animal is a traditional symbol of Earth and the material world while the second points to Heaven and spirit. Must one infer that the tiger refers to the "material substance" or *chih* while the dragon indicates the "spiritual principle" or *li*? In so far as *li* corresponds, *mutatis mutandis*, to the Sanskrit *dharma* and to the Greek *ethos*, it is the universal principle that particularizes itself as a specific "law" or "nature" for a given individual being, and that is both its "quiddity" and its "entelechy," or again, its "essence" and its "self-transforming motion"; one can make it a quasi-synonym of "meaning" or "content" in the poetic realm. As for *chih*, it seems to refer to the more factual "objects" that are the prime matter of poetic composition, or else to the style of the poet. The parallelism between the tiger metaphor and the dragon metaphor appears to us therefore as a duplication—on two different levels of literary production, one more "factual" and "formal," the other more "meaningful"—of a same structure of contrast or opposition between poetic utterances that are so aesthetically

---

[46] Lu Chi, *Wen Fu*, cited in Stephen Owen, *Readings in Chinese Literary Thought*, p. 107.

powerful that they may obliterate by their effect the other syntagmata that precede or follow them. On a paradigmatic level, which has more to do with the process of "vertical" choice between competing terms, it may also be that the "tiger" and the "dragon" represent the most expressive and pleasing possibilities that supersede all others.

The last significant dual pattern is that which alternates ease and difficulty in the process of writing. The poetic production is either gradual and painstaking ("at first he hesitates on his dry lips … he may have held the brush in his lips, [his mind] far in the distance") or, on the contrary, immediate, spontaneous, and flowing ("it flows freely through the moist pen … each mutation is right on the face").[47] Beyond its disappointing surface of truism, the distinction between these two types of creative moments may lead us to the key of the composition that is at stake. How are we to account for this abrupt contrast between times of "dryness" and times of "moisture"? It seems that the principle of this duality stems from the present efficiency of *li* or lack thereof:

> Natural principle (*li*) supports the substance (*chih*), a tree's trunk;
> Pattern (*wen*) hangs down in the branches, a net of lushness.[48]

In other words, as in terms of organic growth, *li* is the fundamental basis for the poetic work. We have already discussed *chih* as "factual substance," whereas *wen* refers to style (Hamill) or pattern (Owen and Barnstone/Ping). Now *li* is to be understood as the "cause" of the poetic work—both a "formal" and "efficient" cause. It is that which makes it what it is as a transformative or creative process and as a quiddity. If, as Owen puts it, "*li* is the universal structure that inheres in any living, formative process,"[49] then we may infer that *li* is fundamentally what makes the poem come into being. It is the formative idea without which there is no real poetry, the intellective sap that sustains the growth and harmonic unfolding of the conceptual and formal whole. Poetic contemplation is therefore, on the level of composition, a heightened receptivity to the flow of *li*.

If we are not entitled to interpret this process in terms of "inspiration" in the ordinary sense, we can certainly understand it in the sense of an immanent flux that also inherently unfolds as a principle of happiness ("in this event

---

[47] *Ibid.*, p. 110.

[48] Lu Chi, *Wen Fu*, cited in Stephen Owen, *Readings in Chinese Literary Thought*, p. 113.

[49] Stephen Owen, *Readings in Chinese Literary Thought*, p. 113.

[the event of creation, when *li* 'flows'] can be found joy, firmly held in honor by sages and men of honor"). The association of writing and joy is much more than a psychological cliché; it points to a profound congruence between creation or manifestation as an expression of *li* and existential elation or exhilaration. We may trace the evidence for this congruence in cultural history, and note, with Owen, that "in China literature is associated with play, or rather a liberty of ease and movement."[50] Literature is not only transmission; it is also creation, and this second characteristic opens up a space of freedom and alacrity in a cultural world that relies strongly on the immutability of the cultural structures of duty and obedience. We may also remark, on more profound grounds, that the outburst of laughter that welcomes poetic creation is a most direct expression of the freedom of *li* and of its "budding" forth and expanding through and beyond limitations and obstacles:

> Language gives its breadth, expanding and expanding
> Thought pursues it, growing deeper and deeper.[51]

We notice that both "form" and "idea" undergo an exponential process of opening up to the ever-expanding space of creation, each one in its own right. "Form" has organically to do with complexity, multiplication, and extension whereas "idea" refers back to the inward-looking process of searching for more and more profound resonances. In this expansive progression, both in breadth and depth, laughter is like a victory over tension and dryness; we might even say that it proceeds from tension and dryness in the sense of being a response to them. Manifestation, or creation, is joy and laughter: the very process of ontological and poetic unfolding is a kind of divine laughter. This is precisely what Lu Chi stresses by associating the joy "held in honor by Sages" with the passage from non-being to being. The cosmogonic character of the poet is to be understood along Taoist paradigms; it emphasizes both the spontaneous springing forth of reality in constant transformation, but also the demiurgic role of the poet which makes this springing forth possible in certain circumstances:

> A trial of void and nothing to demand of it being,
> A knock upon silence, seeking sound.[52]

---

[50] *Ibid.*, p. 118.

[51] Lu Chi, *Wen Fu*, cited in Stephen Owen, *Readings in Chinese Literary Thought*, p. 120.

[52] *Ibid.*, p. 118.

The interrelation between void and phenomenal existence is one of the central themes in Chinese art. Through the use of void, Chinese art—as inspired by Taoism—aims at suggesting the immanent presence of the "supra-formal reverse" of reality, its very essence. Let us note that we have here three terms: void/silence, being/sound, and a third element that mediates between them: trial/knock. Poetry appears to echo the role of what François Cheng calls the "median Void," which "resides at the heart of all things, inspiring breath and life into them, keeping all things in relation with the supreme Void, allowing them to access transformation and unity."[53]

From a methodical and creative standpoint, we have here defined the essence of the relationship between contemplation and creation in Lu Chi's poetics. The poet is not totally passive, he "does" something, but what he does might very well be understood in the terms of Lao-tzu's *wu wei*, "non-doing doing." Several key passages of the *Tao Te Ching* express this fundamental principle of Taoist metaphysics and spirituality by referring to various levels of its application, for instance, government: "the highest form of government is what people hardly even realize is there."[54] There is, in a sense, an unbridgeable distance or an irreconcilable disproportion between what is done and what flows from what is done. The idea here is rather that of triggering a process, or that of removing the obstacles which prevent *li* from expressing itself in and through the work. Such a capacity stems from an understanding of the universal process of transformation, and therefore from a vigilant and peaceful attention to it.

In the context of the treatment of the harmony of sounds, the strictly musical side of poetry, Lu Chi asserts this important character of the truly contemplative poet: "if one grasps mutation and understands succession, it is like opening a channel to receive a stream."[55] It is quite clear, again, that the poet does not "create" the stream; he opens the channel by making himself aware of the immanent harmonics that preside over sequential changes. The type of awareness required pertains to an intuitive and contemplative dimension that cannot be reduced to the general principles that may guide it. It expresses itself through the immediate responses called forth by a given context and a given occurrence. Man is less an imitator of a divine act, or a collaborator in it, than a subtle, attentive, and self-effaced initiator of its

---

[53] François Cheng, *L'Ecriture poétique chinoise*, p. 7 (my translation).

[54] Lao-tzu, *Tao Te Ching*, chapter 17 in Kwok, Palmer, Ramsey trans., p. 58.

[55] Lu Chi, *Wen Fu*, cited in Stephen Owen, *Readings in Chinese Literary Thought*, p. 139.

unfolding. Expressions such as "trial of void" and "knocking upon silence" are highly suggestive in this respect for they convey the sense of a Japanese *koan*—that seemingly senseless riddle, the gnawing meditation upon which "prompts" but does not "produce" *satori* or illumination—which characterizes poetic creation. On the most literal level of rational cohesiveness you cannot try nothing, just as you cannot knock upon silence. So the paradox here is a way to refer to this incommensurable gap between cause and effect. We think it is precisely this disproportion that is, in part, at the root of the Western tradition of "poetic inspiration" or "poetic *mania*": this hyperbolic symbolization is a way of accounting for the mystery of creation that does not come from the poet but rather through the poet.

In a sense, the lack of art and lack of understanding of his own nature and capacity, which Socrates reveals through his maieutics with the rhapsode Ion in Plato's dialogue, is analogous, *mutatis mutandis*, to the minimizing images chosen by Lu Chi to express the strictly "material" side of the creative process: "He contains remote distances on a sheet of writing silk, emits a boundless torrent from the speck of mind."[56] The contrast between contracted and unlimited space that is described is of a different import than the one which paired—in the first sections of the text—the contemplative preparatory concentration of the poet and the expansive flight of his participatory encounter with numerous elements in the infinite stretches of his inner world. In the latter case, expansion was so to speak in the fist of contraction; there was a kind of discontinuous continuity between the two, since the first was the necessary preparatory stage for the second. Here, the idea symbolically highlighted is rather one of a continuous discontinuity between the "material cause" and the poetic effect. We would like to suggest that the "sheet of writing silk" and the "speck of mind" are nothing but quantitative means of intimation of the qualitative discontinuity between the demiurgic role of the poet and the overflow of *li*. In fact, the two perspectives are opposite: the first one considers the flow of the river from the point of view of the source, if one may say so, whence the sense of continuity that predominates—notwithstanding the suggestive contrastive play between "retraction" and "flight," whereas the second contemplates the tiny point of departure from the perspective of the ocean of poetic manifestation, a perspective that accounts for a sense of discontinuity. We must add that the two points of view can also be situated within the context of the creative phase in which they participate,

[56] *Ibid.*, p. 119.

that of the introspective search for poetic "objects" and that of composition. The aspect of discontinuity appears in full light in the course of the second phase because it concerns the production of an "otherness," and not only the exploration of the self.

The dimension of discontinuity we have just considered is both a riddle and a source of awe. It is the mystery of the relationship between man and the ever-flowing manifestation of Reality. The act of writing is a central occurrence of this mystery, precisely because it entails not only receptivity but also production, not only intuition of "sameness" but also creation of "otherness." As Barnstone and Chou Ping express it in their translation: "Writing is a struggle between presence and absence."[57] This "striving between being and nothing"[58] is not only an image of the moment of writing that painstakingly bridges the gap between a blank page and the appearance of words, it is also, and above all, a contemplative experience of the rhythms that are intricately connected with the flow of Being. These rhythms do not result from the universal principle but are rather a consequence of the individual limitations that impede the free manifestation of the latter. In other words, rhythms are concomitant with the fact that the Ten Thousand Things are not the One. Lu Chi's injunction not to "give up" ("in deep or shallow, not giving up") most profoundly refers to the idea that the *li*—or the Tao as universal principle of formation and transformation—is in a sense always available and can be expressed in any circumstance, even though its manifestations are *de facto* contingent upon the "quality" of a given circumstance. The struggle takes place on the side of the poet, or of man, not on the side of Reality. Man is in search of what could be designated as the ultimate secret of nature, whence Tu Fu's verse, "when the poem has been completed, gods and demons are stupefied!"[59] A major consequence of this principle lies in the fact that poetic expression is ultimately dependent on the "coming forth" of the universal principle, or the intellective essence, for its perfection:

> Require that your words attain their ends, that the principle (*li*) come
> forth;
> Have nothing at all to do with long-winded excess.[60]

[57] Lu Chi, *Wen Fu*, cited in Tony Barnstone and Chou Ping, *The Art of Writing: Teachings of the Chinese Masters*, p. 11.

[58] Lu Chi, *Wen Fu*, cited in Stephen Owen, *Readings in Chinese Literary Thought*, p. 125.

[59] Tu Fu, cited in François Cheng, *L'Ecriture poétique chinoise*, p. 17 (my translation).

[60] Lu Chi, *Wen Fu*, cited in Stephen Owen, *Readings in Chinese Literary Thought*, p. 135.

This important passage is in perfect consonance with the often-quoted aphorism from the *Analects* of Confucius' philosophy of language: "words should attain their ends and that's all."[61] It is quite clear that the "substantial" aspect of poetry must be subordinate to its "essential" intent, which means that there is a point at which the former reaches its perfection by "manifesting" the latter. The European neo-classical principle enjoining a transparency of the "enunciation" vis-à-vis the "concept" is to some extent a distant echo of this principle: "what is distinctly conceived is clearly enunciated."[62] Hamill's translation appears to go along these lines: "language speaks from its essence, from its reason."[63]

In this way of thinking, some contemporary neo-Confucian scholars (like the Vietnamese Pham Quynh) have attempted to draw a parallel between French seventeenth-century poetics and Confucian aesthetic principles. One should, however, take note of the sharp divergence between the Classical idea of utter transparency of stylistic form vis-à-vis the idea conceived by the mind, and the Chinese "coming forth" of the intellective principle through words, the making manifest of that which is occult and which remains occult in itself. In other words, the neo-classical ideal may be thought of as a kind of translation: on one side lies a clear and distinct set of concepts that may be skillfully "transferred" onto the other side by virtue of their clarity and distinction, that of unambiguous words and expressions. The epistemological and aesthetic background for such a transparent view is none other than *mimesis*. Lu Chi's Confucian model is not to be understood along the lines of the same hierarchical parallelism, i.e., from ideas to words, but rather as a coming into the light of what is by definition implicit and ineffable ("the Tao that can be named is not the real Tao").

This distinction seems to us fundamentally akin to Gilbert Durand's analysis of the semantic distinction between allegory and symbol. According to this understanding, which illuminates the contrast we are pursuing, "the allegory is the concrete translation of an idea that is difficult to grasp or to express simply,"[64] not because of its unfathomable depth or its conceptual vagueness but merely because of the multiplicity or complexity of its aspects. The affinity of Western Classical art and literature with allegorical

---

[61] *Ibid.*, p. 136.

[62] "*Ce qui se conçoit bien s'énonce clairement*" (Boileau, *Art Poétique* [my translation]).

[63] Lu Chi, *Wen Fu*, cited in *The Art of Writing*, trans. Sam Hamill, p. 16.

[64] "L'allégorie est traduction concrète d'une idée difficile à saisir ou à exprimer simplement" (Gilbert Durand, *L'imagination symbolique*, p. 10 [my translation]).

representations is therefore by no means coincidental. By contrast, the symbol can be defined as follows: "a sign referring to an ineffable and invisible signified and that is therefore obliged to embody concretely this adequation which escapes it."[65] The relative inadequacy of the symbol is not necessarily to be opposed to the "attainment of their ends" that is required of words in Lu Chi's poetics. In fact, as we have suggested, this attainment is never presented as perfect transparence or as a "naming" of the "thing itself." The symbol "attains its end," that of manifesting what is unmanifested without in the least abolishing the gap that separates this manifestation from what it manifests. If one is to accept this general distinction and apply it to the two kinds of literary models that we have in view, one will most likely be led to acknowledge that the Chinese model cannot be reduced to the Classical Western discourse of reason and *mimesis*. Actually, the Chinese model, as exemplified by Lu Chi's poetic essay, affirms its affinity with contemplative practice in and through its distance vis-à-vis that discourse. The conclusion of *Wen Fu* allows us to take a more precise measure of that distance:

> The functioning of literature lies in being
> The means for all natural principle.
> It spreads across ten thousand leagues, nothing bars it;
> It passes through a million years, a ford across.[66]

Beyond the separative and abstracting mode of the operating of reason, literature —in the widest sense—is accordingly the instrument of an all-pervading expression of the principle. The images of irresistibleness and overarching relatedness may *prima facie* appear as hyperbolic and apologetic statements whose function is to extol the moral and political eminence of poetry. Such are the most immediate implications of expressions referring to the role of letters in providing "models for coming generations," the "contemplation (of) images in the ancients," the "succor" of "the Way of the ancient Kings" and the "manifestation of reputations."[67]

Beyond this order of consideration, however, we would be mistaken to neglect the fact that the function of poetry is elevated to a metaphysical and contemplative status that makes it the vehicle of ontological continuity

---

[65] "… signe renvoyant à un indicible et invisible signifié et par là étant obligé d'incarner concrètement cette adéquation qui lui échappe …" (*Ibid.*, p. 18 [my translation]).

[66] Lu Chi, *Wen Fu*, cited in Stephen Owen, *Readings in Chinese Literary Thought*, p. 179.

[67] *Ibid.*, p. 179.

and spiritual consciousness in the world of forms. Symbols of hieratic permanence (metal and stone) and effluent transformation (music and moisture), alternating absoluteness and infinitude, Yang and Yin, complement each other to emphasize the power of universal manifestation that is vested in poetry: it is presence in absence but also absence in presence (the witnessing of steles bridging all temporal gaps but also the instantaneous evanescence of melodies opening a void into the fullness of the present), it is the rationally unsolvable enigma of being in non-being and non-being in being, the "hide-and-seek" of uniting love and dispersing time. This "semblance of divinity in transformation" achieved by poetry is like the perfection of the art that unveils the unmanifested to bring us back into its fold. Fullness becomes a perfect expression of the Void that mysteriously informs it. Drawing on the profound kinship and analogy that the Chinese classical tradition perceives in the relationship between poetry and painting (painting is "silent poetry," *wu-sheng-shih*), we would like to conclude that such is the major lesson of the story of the painter Wu Tao-tzu, reinterpreted by Marguerite Yourcenar in her *Nouvelles orientales*,[68] who, after having accomplished his task in painting a perfect image of mountains, forests, and clouds, invited the Emperor to follow him in the painting and disappeared into it forever.[69]

[68] Marguerite Yourcenar, "Comment Wang-Fō fut sauvé," in *Nouvelles orientales*, pp. 11-25.
[69] Cf. Ananda Coomaraswamy, *The Transformation of Nature in Art*, p. 22.

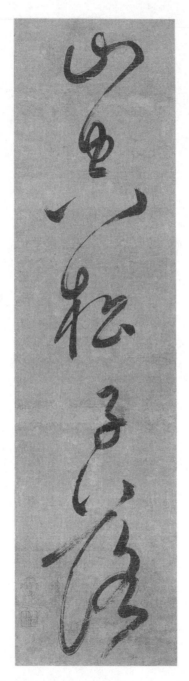

IV. "There is no one in the mountain ..."
Muromachi period (1392-1573)

4. JAPANESE POETRY
The Sketch of Metaphysical Perception[1]

At the outset, when referring to Japanese art and poetry, it is methodologically useful to stress the two aesthetic dimensions of form and simplicity. These two dimensions seem to be fundamental premises that account for more circumstantially determined definitions of Japanese aesthetic ideals. Donald Keene, using the writings of the fourteenth-century Shintō priest Kenkō as interpretative keys,[2] proposes the four fundamental principles of suggestion, irregularity, simplicity, and perishability as defining criteria of Japanese aesthetics.[3] It can be argued that suggestion, irregularity, and perishability all pertain to a sense of simplicity in that they leave something to be "perfected" or "perceived," echoing an unassuming simplicity that is the hallmark of Japanese beauty. If suggestion is akin to a love for beginnings and endings, the aesthetic idea presiding over the sense of ephemerality and a taste for asymmetrical "aeration" stems from the same principle: an intuition of the Void that is genuine fullness.

The cultivation of an ideal for perfection of form, whether it be manifested through artistic works, practical arts, or social conduct, is so pervasive in the whole of Japanese traditional life that some Western analysts have gone so far as to interpret Japan as a pure "empire of signs" in which forms do not refer to anything else than themselves, thereby functioning independently of any "meaning" that could be attached to them.[4] The Buddhist metaphysical identification of form and emptiness, or *samsāra* and *nirvāna*, indicates that this line of interpretation is, however, fundamentally flawed because it considers formal emphasis to be intrinsically exclusive of an essence. A contemporary semiotic paradigm is, in other words, abusively substituted for

---

[1] The English word "sketch" derives from the Latin *schedium*, which refers to an extemporaneous poem. The term should not, therefore, be understood in a negative sense in our current context. It is above all not to be understood as implying the idea of an incomplete or preparatory stage preceding the full development of poetry.

[2] Cf. *Tsurezuregusa* ("Essays in Idleness"), in Donald Keene, "Japanese Aesthetics," in *Japanese Aesthetics and Culture*, ed. Nancy G. Hume, pp. 27-41.

[3] Donald Keene, "Japanese Aesthetics," pp. 27-41.

[4] This is the approach fostered by the contemporary critic Roland Barthes in his semiotic "travelogue" *L'empire des signes*.

the symbolic vision that presides over the crystallization and elaboration of traditional forms.

One of the primary causes—and this may be an "extenuating circumstance"—of such a misreading lies in the tendency of many European and North American analysts to project a concept of "essence" as a hidden and purely transcendent reality on their Japanese object, whereas Japanese spiritual artists would rather understand the essence as manifested in the very "appearance" of the form. In this seemingly paradoxical sense, the emphasis on form that is at the very core of Japanese culture can be understood as the language of essentiality: perfection of form becomes in itself a way to hint at the essence that is, so to speak, inseparable from it.[5] In other words, form is essence and essence is form. There is little doubt that this perspective is organically bound up with what Masao Abe translates as "dependent coorigination" (*pratītya-samutpāda*), i.e., a view of reality according to which emptiness is the very "ground" of all existents, not in the sense of a self-perpetuated substance, but in that of a reality transcending all dualities and causality. In the first chapter of Nāgārjuna's *Mūlamadhyamakakārikā*, entitled "Analysis of Conditioning," we read that "wherever and whatever they are, things are never produced from themselves, from others, from both or from no cause."[6] This classic statement of Mādhyamika metaphysics, which is at the basis of Buddhist understanding, indicates a kind of universal relativity since no independent or absolute reality is posited. This amounts to saying that *nirvāna* lies outside of the realm of causation. We find a similar expression of this subtle metaphysical principle of "dependent coorigination" and "non-affirmative negation"[7] in the works of certain Christian mystics like Meister Eckhart and

---

[5] This predominance of form over "content" has been interpreted by Frithjof Schuon as a manifestation of the Shintoist emphasis on the "style of action": "The Shintoist ethic, which claims for the *yamato* race the attribute 'divine,' is perhaps essentially a style of action; it is in fact possible to conceive of a perspective in which style would take precedence over contents by largely neutralizing the imperfections of the latter, for a noble form is necessarily opposed to base actions" (*Treasures of Buddhism*, pp. 181-82).

[6] Nāgārjuna, *Mūlamadhyamakakārikā*, cited in Georges Driessen and Yonten Gyatso, *Traité du Milieu*, p. 29 (my translation).

[7] Mādhyamika epistemology establishes a distinction between "affirmative negation" and "non-affirmative negation": the first kind of negation, in denying one reality, implies the existence of another, as in the sentence, "the fat Devadatta does not eat during the day," which implies—as indicated by his fatness—that he does eat at night.

Angelus Silesius for whom "before I was, God was not." Referring to the *grunt* (ground) or *strik* (ring) that is the essence of the Trinity, Meister Eckhart can thus write:

> God himself never glimpses it and never has glimpsed it, as long as he has himself in the manner and according to the quality (*eigenschaft*) of his persons.... Therefore, if God is ever to glimpse it, it must cost God all his godly names and the quality of his persons.[8]

The fundamental essence of the Deity is therefore situated by Eckhart beyond any procession, spiration, and causation, in a "silent desert," a "little castle" or a "spark." The fundamental spiritual consequence of this metaphysical understanding of the Supreme Reality is that "He who does not want to decline, even in Paradise, must be eternally empty, even empty of God."[9] *Nirvāna* is situated beyond all relationships and all "self-substantiated origination," including that of a self-consciousness of *Nirvāna* that would remain "centered" upon its own "realization." As Masao Abe points out:

> ... throughout its long history,... Mahāyāna Buddhism has always emphasized "Do not abide in *Nirvāna*" as much as "Do not abide in *samsāra*".... if one abides in so-called *Nirvāna* by transcending *samsāra*, it must be said that one is not yet free from attachment, an attachment to *Nirvāna*, and is confined by the discrimination between *Nirvāna* and *samsāra*.[10]

Discrimination must therefore be subsumed under a concrete consciousness of the principle that form is essential emptiness and essential emptiness is form.

*   *   *

With regard to simplicity, it is primarily understood in Japan as a view of art that fosters a close relationship between aesthetics and nature. D.T. Suzuki has repeatedly emphasized, in the wake of Kakuzo Okakura's works,

---

[8] Meister Eckhart, Predigt 2, DW 1:43, cited in Michael Sells, *Mystical Languages of Unsaying*, p. 162.

[9] "Wer auch im Paradiss nicht noch sol untergehn, Der Mensch muss ewiglich, auch Gottes, ledig stehn" (*Cherubinischer Wandersmann*, ed. H. Plard, p. 142 [my translation]).

[10] Masao Abe, "Buddhism," in *Our Religions*, ed. Arvind Sharma, p. 124.

that the Japanese love of nature is founded upon a sense of respect that is ultimately grounded in a vision of nature as being "destined like ourselves for Buddhahood."[11] There is no radical epistemological and ontological chasm between the world of man and that of nature; in fact they are one. A major dimension of this vision lies in the fact that the "Buddhahood" of nature accounts for both its being and its mode of operation. Like nirvanic Buddhahood in its relationship with the samsaric flow, Nature is "simple" in its manner of operation in a sense that does not exclude a complexity of forms: the main point to emphasize is that nature "works" toward its end with a kind of spontaneous directness and immediacy, a way that precludes the inordinate complexities of a deliberate search for "effects."

For the Japanese artist, the point is not to copy nature in a representational manner, but it is rather to make use of nature both as a "material" and as an aesthetic and creative principle. The very artistic "form" is therefore conceived as an expression of nature itself. As for the *materia prima* of the art, it also appears as closely associated with nature: it proceeds from it in a very direct manner, to such an extent that it could be said that nature is both the object and the material substance of art. As a case in point, Japanese architecture does not emphasize a distinction of art from nature, in contrast to European neo-classical architecture; it tends, on the contrary, to work as a prolongation, or perhaps a mere refinement, of nature.[12]

This idea of "naturalness," so pervasive in much of Japanese art, may seem to be contradicted by what could easily be interpreted—from a Western standpoint—as a "formalistic" tendency characteristic of Japanese cultural productions. In other words, the "perfection" of forms may appear somewhat "artificial" in their refinement or daintiness. To this it must be answered first of all that formal "perfection" is in no way excluded from nature; quite the contrary, since the natural realm, whether it be in the mineral, vegetal, or animal domain, is characterized by instances of aesthetic and functional "perfection"—i.e., occurrences of a self-sufficient wholeness in a set of constitutive

---

[11] "What is the most specific characteristic of Zen asceticism in connection with the Japanese love of Nature? It consists in paying Nature the fullest respect it deserves. By this it is meant that we may treat Nature not as an object to conquer and turn wantonly to our human service, but as a friend, as a fellow being, who is destined like ourselves for Buddhahood" (D.T. Suzuki, *Zen and Japanese Culture*, p. 351).

[12] As a most typical manifestation of this contrast, Kakuzo Okakura has rightly noted how to "European architects, brought up on the traditions of stone and brick construction, our Japanese method of building with wood and bamboo seems scarcely worthy to be ranked as architecture" (*The Book of Tea*, p. 30).

features. It must be added that the perfection which is the aim of Japanese art is always comprised of an element of imperfection; it must never be confused with a kind of geometric and so to speak planimetric flawlessness. This "imperfection" may in a certain sense already be apprehended in the "minimalistic" tendencies of Zen poetry. The brevity and matter-of-factness of most of Zen production is evocative of an aesthetic approach that suggests the maximum in and through the minimum. According to D. T. Suzuki the love for the "small" and even the "down-to-earth," which is so characteristic of Japanese culture, is in a certain respect a manifestation of this sense for "imperfect perfection." Considered from such a perspective, this type of apprehension of reality is yet centered on "perfection" in that it focuses on a very definite and actual occurrence and thereby fosters an attention to its purest phenomenal integrity. All the same, this "perfection" must also be considered from the standpoint of its "imperfection" since it must needs suggest the whole that can be reached in and through—while also lying "beyond"—it. In this context, a concern with formal integrity presupposes that the form be envisaged as an appearance of the Void and that, as such, it bespeak the coincidence of fullness and emptiness, presence and absence, plenitude and privation. It is precisely in this coincidence that form and simplicity meet.

Japanese contemplative poetry brings these ideals to the fore. This is primarily exemplified by the *haiku*, undoubtedly the best-known form of Japanese poetry. R.H. Blyth has insisted upon the fact that *haiku* is primarily a poetry of sensation, but a poetry in which the sensation is so to speak the catalyst of a union of opposite, or at least of quite distinct, realities:

> In *haiku*, the two entirely different things that are joined in sameness are poetry and sensation, spirit and matter, the Creator and the Created.[13]

The fundamentally non-dualistic—as well as non-monistic—character of Japanese Zen poetry transcends both qualitative differences and epistemological scission between subject and object, which does not mean, however, that it negates these differences and this scission on the plane upon which they are undoubtedly meaningful. In a similar way, *waka*, which consists of just five rhymeless verses of five, seven, five, seven, and seven syllables each, is characterized, according to Toshihiko and Toyo Izutsu, by its "unusual short-

---

[13] R.H. Blyth, *A History of Haiku*, Vol. I, p. 7.

ness" and a "global view of a whole, in which the words used are observable all at once" in a kind of "poetic-linguistic 'field.'"[14]

One of the ways in which both *haiku* and *waka* may bring about this ontological and epistemological unity resides in the extreme reduction of their field of expression. This "minimalist" aspect of *haiku* and *waka*, however, is not only related to their form (in the case of *haiku*, a combination of three verses of five, seven, and five syllables respectively, with no rhyme and no emphasis), it is also—and even more importantly—connected with their theme or object, and its treatment. As far as the dimension of brevity is concerned, and as we have mentioned above, D.T. Suzuki has commented upon the Japanese liking for small things in the context of their lack of affinity with any grandiosity. Suzuki relates this aspect of Japanese culture to a distrust of abstraction and idealistic constructs.[15] Consequently, the term "philosophical," when used with reference to Zen, must be understood in a way that does not connote any mere ratiocination in view of "solving" this or that conceptual riddle: it actually entails a genuine "love of wisdom" in the sense of a concrete and integral apprehension of reality *hic et nunc*.

An awareness of this emphasis on the concrete and the most present may lead us to understand why there is something bordering on the trivial, or at least on the commonplace, in most *haiku*. Whether it be a question of nature or human activities, Zen *haiku* reveals affinities with the type of unassuming realities that might easily go unnoticed or even be disdained as unpoetical. Actually, Zen *haiku* will not even systematically shun the unpleasant or the ugly. Everything has its role to play in the economy of the Whole, and the various spiritual modes in which the negation of negation can manifest

---

[14] "The formal structure of *waka* is rather peculiar in its unusual shortness. A *waka* is a rhymeless poem consisting of 31 syllables in the form of an alternation of five- and seven-syllable words.... The *waka*-poet seems to go against the intrinsic nature of language, for, by means of words, he tries to create a synchronic 'field,' a spatial expanse. Instead of a temporal succession of words, in which each succeeding word goes on obliterating, as it were, the foregoing word, *waka* aims at bringing into being a global view of the whole, in which the words used are observable all at once.... Such a global view of a whole constitutes what we mean by a 'field.' In a 'field' thus constituted, time may be said to be standing still or even annihilated in the sense that the meanings of all words are simultaneously present in one single sphere" (Toshihiko and Toyo Izutsu, *The Theory of Beauty in the Classical Aesthetics of Japan*, pp. 2-4).

[15] "Perhaps one most egregiously Japanese characteristic is to take notice of the small things of nature and tenderly take care of them. Instead of talking about great ideals or highly abstract thoughts, they cultivate chrysanthemums or morning-glories, and when the season comes they delight to see them bloom beautifully as they planned" (D.T. Suzuki, *Zen and Japanese Culture*, p. 231).

itself are nowhere else more cultivated than in the matter-of-fact realism of Japanese contemplative practice. The point is obviously not to defile the grand, the dignified and the beautiful—if they really are what they claim to be and are not a mere masquerading of self-importance—but rather to inject a healthy and sometimes quite humbling sense of proportion into the realm of thirst for truth.

Let us consider, as an example of this tendency, the Japanese poetic treatment of the discomfort brought about by summer heat. In the second volume of his classical anthology *A History of Haiku*, R.H. Blyth has gathered ninety *haiku* devoted to heat. What is most striking about this collection is the fact that such a theme, apparently uninspiring and somewhat bothersome, could constitute the motif of a great diversity of poems, from the quasi-lyrical to the trivial. An analysis of a few of these pieces will be instructive. Let us first mention Sōseki's poem:

> The red sun
> Sinking down into the sea,
> Heat!

Contrast Kyorai's evocation:

> So many maids
> Serving at table
> In this heat!

Taigi's version:

> The voice of flies
> Heard in a wine-cellar,—
> The heat!

And Tōsei's piece as a conclusion:

> I made up my mind
> To become a monk,
> This hot day.[16]

---

[16] R.H. Blyth, *A History of Haiku*, vol. II, pp. xxxiii, xxxiv, xxxv, and xxxviii.

The first piece is representative of the "cosmic" dimension of Zen poetry, and it is probably in this connection that we can detect the closest affinity of Zen with the autochthonous way of the *kami*, or god-spirits. *Haiku* is fundamentally—although not exclusively—a poetry of nature and Blyth has very plausibly referred to the "animistic" dimension of Shintō to account for this dimension.[17] The "elemental" simplicity of Sōseki's *haiku* could only be matched by that of Sokuchi's, "Clouds, yes; / Rain, no: / The heat!"[18] In both cases the heat is set against the background of contrasted realities, sun and sea, clouds and rain, but the contrast is ultimately dismissed by the "annulment" of one of the terms. In the first case, the image is that of a paradox: the sinking of the sun does not seem to result in any immediate relief. Rather, it is suggested as a profound penetration, as if the heat of the sun, like a burning center, will also enter the depths of the sea, leaving nothing out of its reach and power. So the disappearance of the sun is rather a kind of "neutralization" of what the freshening moisture of the sea could have felt like. The heat is perceived as an all-pervasive presence which suggests that "enlightenment and enheatenment are the same," to use Blyth's suggestive phrase.[19] Whether it be a matter of mist, sun, clouds, or heat, the all-pervading character of climatic conditions is a direct image—and even more than that, the manifestation on a cosmic plane—of the omnipresence of the Buddha-nature or Emptiness. The visible principle of the heat may well disappear to the eye: there remains its deepest reality, the heat as a pervasive ambience.

Inasmuch as Sokuchi's piece points to the self-same realization of the inescapable presence of the "heat," it is also founded on the sensation of an absence of "relief" from it, with a sense of condensed directness and tension that gives it a much more suggestive impact than Sōseki's. The alternation of the affirmative and negative forms ("Clouds, yes; / Rain, no") functions as a kind of suspension of the expectation of the soul: i.e., a relief from the heat through the freshening effect of rain. It is in this suspension, and the tension that it triggers, that the whole enlightening effect of the poem resides: the tension of the soul expecting to be relieved at the sight of the clouds is only resolved by the abrupt recognition of the "illusory" character of the "desire"

---

[17] "The animism of *haiku* is hardly ever explicit. There is little personification. But the Shintō belief that the sea is 'a mighty Being,' that the mountain is a god, is not far from Vaughan's stones that are 'deep in contemplation.' Unlike the stones of Jerusalem, however, they would never go so far as to 'cry out.' So with Bashō's animism, as when Homer says the sun rises or the moon sets, 'we can hardly detect the enthusiasm of the bard'" (*Ibid.*, p. 10).

[18] *Ibid.*, p. xi.

[19] *Ibid.*, p. 32.

for enlightenment itself, since the latter cannot result from any desire but only from the sudden transcendence of the egoic tension that desires foster and manifest.

Besides the immediate language of nature, Zen-suffused *haiku* also makes use of the great variety of skits or sketches borrowed from daily life and ordinary human interactions in order to bring home a deeper consciousness of Reality. Kyorai's allusion to a scene that may have happened in a tavern, that of many maids serving at table, is interesting in highlighting the affinity of Zen with all that unsettles and "annoys" in the experience of the world. There is however nothing either dramatic or sacrificial in the treatment of this aspect of reality, as opposed to the apprehension that some Christian mystics may have of similar instances. Kyorai was one of the disciples of Bashō and he lived most of his life in the 17th century. The existential "annoyance" alluded to in this poem appears to be connected with both the teeming presence of mankind and the sexual undertone of the busying service of the maids. The contact with many people and the interaction with women may at first appear as antithetical vis-à-vis the usual modes of contemplative life for monks, which necessitate solitude and chastity. For an ascetic male, the presence of a large number of women constitutes a challenge on the way to the ideal of concentration on the unity of the whole that is the central tenet of mystical contemplation. However, it seems that the *haiku* may be grounded upon a particular kind of Buddhist contemplation that consists in making use of the object of the "annoyance" by "welcoming" it into the field of one's contemplative awareness. What may therefore be considered at first sight as a mere association between the presence of a large quantity of women and the unease that results from the heat—and possibly also by association with the "heat" of desire—must be understood in fact as a kind of liberation resulting from the oversaturation induced by the ambience. The "overheating" of the latter could be compared to an acceleration of the round of *samsāra* that ultimately results in its flowing into emptiness.

The "gadfly" effect that is at work in Kyorai's poetry—through the distracting business of the many maids—finds a symbolic and revelatory expression in the relatively frequent use of the fly in the contemplative staging of *haiku*, as found in Taigi's rendition of heat. This insect is small, easily "annoying," and may even be associated with impressions of dirtiness and disgust. The fly tends to disturb the well-ordered, carefully tended and "perfectly" cleansed ambience that the ego would like to build for and around itself. The persistent fly "buzzes" in our ears and flies around us as a somewhat irritating reminder of relativity; it can upset even the most serious and the most dignified pose. When flies are many, and when they are moreover buzzing in the enclosed and stifling space of a wine cellar, like in Taigi's poem, their power of nuisance is all the more affirmed and potentially all the more enlightening. It may even be assumed that their power of exasperating and producing mental discomfort becomes such that it "turns on" the "heat" of *satori*, as in the case of a saturated chemical solution. The last poem of our summer florilegium, "I made up my mind / To become a monk, / This hot day!" is most explicit about the saturating and liberating effect of unbearable heat. It conjures up Buddhist images and references of the world in flame while unambiguously pointing to the sole refuge of the *Dharma*.

In a tradition that is characterized by a kind of formal supersaturation, Zen *haiku* can be considered—notwithstanding its formal rigor and the strictness of its linguistic conventions—as a "form-less" and quasi-subversive reaction against the possibility of an idolatry of form. This aspect of Zen is particularly emphasized in the poetry of Ikkyū, a Zen monk and master from the 15th century who has come to be known, in Lucien Stryk's words, as "an extremely independent (figure) … and something of a gadfly."[20] It is said that Ikkyū attained *satori* or enlightenment upon hearing a crow shriek as he was meditating on a boat on Lake Biwa. In his edition of free renditions of a series of poems by Ikkyū, Stephen Berg has judiciously chosen to place an English translation from *A Zen Harvest* by Sōiko Shigematsu as an epigraph to his collection:

Hearing a crow with no mouth
Cry in the deep
Darkness of the night,
I feel a longing for
My father before he was born.[21]

This piece is extremely suggestive of the spirit of Zen poetry, in that it blends natural sensation, subjective intuition, and metaphysical consciousness. Hearing a crow is a keen, sharp perception that awakens a profound zone of consciousness situated beyond the realm of rational and dualistic awareness. If one can imagine the monk plunged in a long and profound meditation, one can understand how this sudden and spontaneous shriek is like a sharp and

---

[20] Lucien Stryk, cited in Ikkyū, *Crow With No Mouth, Ikkyū, 15ᵗʰ Century Zen Master*, trans. Stephen Berg, p. 8.

[21] Cited in Ikkyū, *Crow With No Mouth*, trans. Stephen Berg, p. 17.

swift rending of the veil of ordinary consciousness. Moreover, it is an unlikely occurrence to hear the call of a crow during the night: this diurnal bird returns to his nest without a detour—"as the crow flies"—at twilight and no echo of his call is usually heard in the "deep darkness of the night." A crow with no mouth is a crow that cannot be seen, either because it is heard in the "deep night" of contemplation when the eyes of the *zazen* practitioner are shut, or more profoundly—and concomitantly—because the crow's call comes from beyond all forms, from beyond any uttering "mouth" that can be seen or described. The abrupt reference to "my father before he was born" points in the same directionless direction; it also obliquely alludes to the famous *koan*, "What was your original face like before you were born?" D.T. Suzuki has suggestively referred to this state of consciousness, which presupposes a going beyond the self-reflected sense of separate identity: before he was born, "my father" was none other than the Pure Subject that precedes all subsequent individual determination. My "true" father is "in Heaven" in this very sense. Here Suzuki refers quite interestingly to the Gospel saying of Christ, "Before Abraham was I am," a sentence that highlights—notwithstanding its theological implications in a specifically Christian context—the ontological primacy of the Divine over any human individual determination. It also implies transcending the plane upon which the perception of time as anteriority-and-posteriority is the primary focus. The "nostalgia" triggered by the crow's call is not simply a retrospective longing for the past: the time before "my father was born" is not really a "time"; it is rather a beginning that "precedes" all beginning, in the sense of not being "situated" within the chain of time as a sequence of moments. Time opens onto "non-time"; the instant in its most concrete "suchness" transcends the subjective "knitting together" of ordinary consciousness.[22]

Ikkyū's poem exemplifies the way in which sensory perception and metaphysical insight are connected in the Zen spiritual experience as it is crystallized in poetry: the starting point is a concrete occurrence, often characterized by its brevity and sharpness, an occurrence that triggers a psycho-spiritual reaction within the Zen practitioner. The end result of that reaction is a modification of ordinary, self-centered consciousness and a

[22] An interesting poem by the contemporary Zen poet Shinkishi Takahashi provides us with this image of "knitting" in respect of time. In its translation by Lucien Stryk, we read: "My wife is always knitting, knitting,… / With that bamboo needle / She knits all space, piece by piece, / Hastily hauling time in. / Brass-cold, exhausted, / She drops into bed and, / Breathing calmly, falls asleep./ Her dream must be deepening, / Her knitting coming loose" (*Triumph of the Sparrow*, p. 81).

perception of reality in its objective grounding. The object of poetry is both to express and to transmit an intuition of reality as it is, i.e., independently of egoic biases and distortions. In this context a contemplative practice of poetry consists in preventing any individual psychic interference from obscuring the mirror of the Self. This guarding of oneself against the ripples of self-mirroring, in order to keep one's attention directed toward "what is," ultimately amounts to an unveiling of that which we truly are.

Ikkyū's poetry is often centered upon this experience of the unveiling of the true Subject, that subjective reality which in Buddhism can be referred to almost only as a question. Let us first mention Stephen Berg's version of a most direct example of this self-investigative modality of Zen poetry:

> This ink painting of wind blowing through pines
> Who hears it?[23]

The remarkable feature of this poem undoubtedly lies in the subtle way in which it intertwines the mystery of spiritual expression through art and the fundamental *koan* "who am I?" The poem suggestively refers to the ability of truly contemplative art to capture the very essence of a given moment in our natural ambience. This essence as it is "rendered" by the painter obviously cannot be heard with ears of flesh. Here again, true "audition," as true "vision," refers to a "pre-existential" state of Buddhahood. The most profound layer of the "exterior" realm coincides with the most profound layer of the "interior" kingdom. In a way that is quite characteristic of Buddhism, this fundamental Selfhood is not approached or defined in an affirmative way—as is *Ātman*, the transcendent Subject, in Hindu *Vedānta*—but rather in the interrogative mode characteristic of the *koan*.

Other pieces by Ikkyū refer to the self-same question of identity in paradoxical ways. "Night after night after night stay up all night / Nothing but your own night":[24] this poem is founded upon a suggestive contrast between the repetitive sequence of the nights and the final affirmation of the "only" night that is, the night that "I" am. There is an interesting intimation of the disproportion between human effort and the ultimate outcome of the path. The multiplicity of ascetic practices finds its "truth" or its "resolution" in the final darkness of Buddhahood. The real "night" is the only night—in spite of the apparent endless sequence of nights—and it is at the same time

---

[23] Ikkyū, *Crow With No Mouth*, trans. Stephen Berg, p. 19.
[24] *Ibid.*, p. 21.

the "night" from which the "I" proceeds. This "negative" apprehension of the true Self is at times complemented by a more affirmative way, as when Ikkyū asserts the unmovable eternity of Buddhahood or the real "I":

> I won't die I won't go away I'll always be here
> No good asking me I won't speak.[25]

The contrast between the permanent "I"—that fundamental being-consciousness which cannot be uprooted—and the utmost silence that concludes the poem is profoundly evocative of the tension between being and language which is central in much of Japanese Buddhist poetry: the "I" that remains and will remain cannot speak. All that language can do is to remind one that the real "I" is always accessible; it can never give direct access to it:

> Don't worry please please how many times do I have to say it
> There's no way not to be who you are and where.[26]

If language tries to convey a sense of the ultimate identity of Reality, it will do so "apophatically" by referring to the emptiness that is at the core of the subject. Ikkyū refers to this emptiness in terms that suggest the transcendence of all names and forms:

> Sometimes all I am is a dark emptiness
> That I can't hide in the sleeves of my own robes.[27]

The real "I" is the only one that cannot be hidden because it is one with the Whole. There is nobody to hide anymore. This lack of self-substantiality (*anatta*) may also be spelled out by the sounds and images of nature. For example, the crow's shrieking may lead to *satori* by being the catalyst of a perception of the emptiness (*shunya*) that is the "background" of the formal and limited self:

> One pause between each crow's
> Reckless shriek Ikkyū Ikkyū Ikkyū.[28]

[25] *Ibid.*, p. 26.
[26] *Ibid.*, p. 33.
[27] *Ibid.*, p. 34.
[28] *Ibid.*, p. 51.

The alternation of pause and the crow's shrieking evokes the pulsation of manifestation and reabsorption, or the phases of breathing. The calls of "Ikkyū" function as a principle of egoic identification, which is not the real "I" or the Buddha-nature.

Ikkyū's poetry does not shun contrasting the unveiling of the real Subject with the limitations of the egoic nucleus. The "scandalous" and maverick aspect of Ikkyū's perspective is precisely characterized by a candid voicing of the distance separating the self-conscious ego—torn between its ideal and its reality—and the actual Self:

> I try to be a good man but all that comes
> Of trying is I feel more guilty.[29]

This kind of poem is certainly not to be interpreted as an expression of cynical despair, for it would otherwise be quite difficult to understand, to say the least, how Ikkyū came to be abbot of Daitokuji at the age of eighty-two. Zen is obviously compatible with an awareness of the "small" self's miseries but it is certainly not an advocate of moral failure. By connecting this poem with another piece like "I'm pure shame / What I do and what I say never the same,"[30] one may get a clearer sense of the contemplative implications of this method of self-deprecation. The point is not primarily to humiliate the ego by stressing its chronic inability to live in conformity with Reality—which is the perspective of much of Christian mystical life—but rather to free it from the illusions of a "self-improvement" that could stem only from itself, and which would comfort it with the image of its own "goodness" and control. In fact, Ikkyū's poetry aims at uncovering the fallacy of these pretensions of control. Truth does not appear before the eyes of the ego that strives for it and seeks it as an ornament. It springs forth at a time of perfect "*gelassenheit*" or self-abandonment, when the soul has confronted the reality of its "shame," i.e., its incapacity to be other than what it is.

At this juncture we would like to suggest that the way of Zen converges with that of Jōdo Shin—the latter being based on the methodical practice of the invocation of the name of Amida. According to Hōnen, the great 12th century patriarch of Jōdo, the practice of the invocation must be founded on perfect faith in Amida's vow to lead those who invoke his Name into the Pure Land of the hereafter; and this faith implies sincerity, steadfastness, and

[29] *Ibid.*, p. 31.
[30] *Ibid.*, p. 29.

trust.[31] In the wake of Hōnen, Shinran emphasized that the whole path of Pure Land Buddhism lies in "trusting the Other's power and in renouncing one's own power," which amounts to saying that "the invocation to Amida is for the practitioner neither a practice nor a good action."[32] It is "neither a practice nor a good action" because it is not based on any human or individual excellence or decision: it is purely dependent on Amida's grace. Ikkyū's emphasis on the self's incapacity amounts to implying a similar perspective, and this similarity raises the question of the relationship between invocatory utterance and *koan* meditation. D.T. Suzuki has shown how the practice of *koan* meditation and that of the systematic invocation of the Buddha Amida (*nembutsu*) are far from being opposed. Some Western admirers of Zen have asserted an irreducible opposition between them out of a negative bias against devotional practices—this bias itself quite often being an understandable reaction against the flatly anti-intellectual and even anti-mystical mainstream of post-Medieval Christianity.

Actually, these two spiritual approaches represent two methodical poles that are present—with very different emphases and at very uneven degrees— in all forms of spirituality. Japanese Buddhists designate these two poles as the "power of oneself" (*jiriki*) and the "power of the other" (*tariki*). Zen is akin to the first of these paths, given its emphasis on relentless mental effort and "ascetic" meditation, and Amidism or Pure Land Buddhism is akin to the second, by relying on Amida's vow to save all sentient beings before entering *Parinirvāna*.[33] As it stands however, Zen opens onto Jōdo by its "destruction" of all self-assurance, while Jōdo opens onto Zen through the question, "Who invokes?" If the invocation is not a practice stemming from the individual—as Hōnen and Shinran stress—its very practice must raise the question of its origin, and it is through this question that Jōdo meets with Zen. D.T. Suzuki has shown how the practice of *nembutsu* was often combined with *koan* meditation. Chinese Masters of Ch'an from the fifteenth century such as Tu-

---

[31] Cf. *Ichi mai kishōmon*, in *Le Bouddhisme japonais, textes fondamentaux*, ed. G. Renondeau, p. 19.

[32] Shinran, *Tannishō*, cited in *Le Bouddhisme japonais, textes fondamentaux*, ed. G. Renondeau, p. 31.

[33] The Bodhisattva's vow is synthesized as follows: "O *Bhagavat*, if the beings of the innumerable and incommensurable Buddha-lands, who have heard my name after I have attained Buddhahood, should turn their thoughts towards birth into my Buddha-land, and to this end bring their merit to maturity; if these beings should not be born into my Buddha-land, even those who will have repeated this thought no more than ten times—always with the exception of beings who have obstructed the Good Law or abused it—then may I not attain to supreme Knowledge!" (Cf. Frithjof Schuon, *Treasures of Buddhism*, p. 155).

fēn Chi-shan and Ch'u-shan Shao-chi insisted on the question of knowing *who* invoked the Buddha and from *whence* the invocation came:

> See into the *whence* of your thought which makes you utter the name of the Buddha; where does it originate? But you must go even farther than this and make inquiries as to the *who* of this person who wants to see into the *whence* of a thought. Is it mind, or Buddha, or matter? No, it is none of these, say the masters. What is it then?[34]

Such questions led Suzuki to the typically Buddhist conclusion that "Zen and *Nembutsu* are not the same and yet are the same."[35] This identity in difference seems to us to be at the core of the relationship between utterance and silence, poetry and contemplation. Poetry "is" and "is not" contemplation; finding where it stems from, finding its *whence* is the only way of fully and concretely understanding what it is all about. As Frithjof Schuon has insightfully suggested, the function of a *koan*—and the same could be said here of a *haiku mutatis mutandis*—is not merely that of an absurd statement intended to bring about a mental change; it consists in expressing "the spiritual experience of a given master in a symbolical—and intentionally paradoxical—form, the significance of which is verifiable only by undergoing the same experience."[36] Now such an experience can occur only beyond the level of discursive thinking, whence the paradoxical and "mind-boggling" character of most of Zen expressions.

If we refer back, in this context, to Ikkyū's poem on the crow's shriek, "Ikkyū Ikkyū Ikkyū" and the pause in between each call, we can suggest that "access" to Reality is to be found—in the "pause" or the "void" from which the shriek of affirmation stems—at the "interstices" of relative and formal existence, which is the principle of "void in form" that Ikkyū has also expressed in his poem on the Heart Sutra:

> Void in form
> When, just as they are,
> White dewdrops gather
> On scarlet maple leaves,
> Regard the scarlet beads![37]

[34] D.T. Suzuki, *Essays in Zen Buddhism*, p. 116.

[35] *Ibid.*, p. 117.

[36] Frithjof Schuon, *Treasures of Buddhism*, p. 78.

[37] Ikkyū, *Crow With No Mouth*, trans. Stephen Berg, p. 11.

In this classic piece, the discontinuity and emptiness of *samsāra* is apprehended in and through the separate substances represented by dewdrops, whereas the continuity of the Whole—to be understood as the Buddha-nature—may be suggested by the background of maple leaves. The complement of this metaphysical perception of the void in form is expressed by Ikkyū in the poem entitled "Form in void":

> The tree is stripped,
> All color, fragrance gone,
> Yet already on the bough,
> Uncaring spring.[38]

As D.T. Suzuki has indicated: "according to Chinese philosophy, winter symbolizes the limit of the feminine principle when the universe, shorn of all its outward showiness, holds within itself all the creativity needed for the coming season."[39] Fullness is "already" present in emptiness in the form of a bud. Moreover, it could even be said, from a certain point of view, that emptiness is fuller than fullness. In this connection, Suzuki's allusion to the feminine principle is most likely to be referred to the Taoist notion of the Great Darkness associated with the Mother, in the sense that the feminine principle is no different from Buddhahood. It is the "formless" Mystery from which emerges each and every formal reality.

Ikkyū is not only keen on crystallizing approaches to the Buddhahood of the real "I," he is also interested in suggestively and reflectively evoking the way in which the insightful brevity of the *koan* may give access to the dark mystery of the "I":

> Inside the *koan* clear mind
> Gashes the great darkness.[40]

The *koan* opens a cut into the fundamental substance of being after the mind has been sharpened by the relentless practice of meditation. Poetry is the art of "cutting" through phenomena to reach Reality. The sudden contact between the *koan* and the purified mind in a state of perfect and active

---

[38] Ikkyū, cited in *Zen Poems of China and Japan*, ed. Lucien Stryk, trans. Takashi Ikemoto, p. 135.

[39] D.T. Suzuki, *Zen and Japanese Culture*, p. 232.

[40] Ikkyū, *Crow With No Mouth*, trans. Stephen Berg, p. 57.

receptivity produces a spark of enlightenment. The poem is a crystallization of this enlightenment and it may function as such in the form of a *koan* for those who become involved in meditating upon it. When this happens, the sense of individual separateness disappears and a profound connection with the whole of being is established:

> The mind is exactly this tree that grass
> Without thought or feeling both disappear.[41]

This is the fundamental point of the Zen contemplative experience and it is also consequently the very key to the production of a truly suggestive poem. This experience of both extinction and fusion profoundly modifies the relationship between subject and object as well as the interaction between two subjects. In the absence of egoic projections, two human beings in a state of enlightenment become mirrors of each other:

> Mirror facing a mirror
> Nowhere else.[42]

The encounter takes place here and now, and nowhere else, each person being totally present in the instant, and totally receptive.

As we have suggested above, the relationship between words or utterances and illumination is highly ambiguous in that the former may be conceived either as an obstacle to understanding that must be subverted and transcended—this is the usual perspective of the Zen *koan*—or as a manifestation of the Void in the world of sonoral and linguistic forms. The second of these perspectives is highlighted in the works of the 13th century founder of the Sōtō school of Zen Buddhism, the illustrious Dōgen, who—in stark contrast to most previous Zen masters—deplores the fact that the latter "do not know that thought is words and phrases, or that words and phrases release thought."[43] Steven Heine has suggested that Dōgen's use of *waka* is a way to convey *yojō*, or "overflow of feeling," by using the most concise types of expression. In other words, the contemplative experience of poetry proposed by Dōgen is not one in which language proceeds as a kind of negation of itself in order to hint at what lies beyond the realm of discursive

---

[41] *Ibid.*, p. 30.

[42] Dōgen, cited in *Crow With No Mouth*, trans. Stephen Berg, p. 30.

[43] Dōgen, cited in Steven Heine, *The Zen Poetry of Dōgen*, p. 3.

expression; it is rather one which evokes a plenitude of meanings and implications that are so to speak condensed in the concise field of the poem. The polysemic nature of language, through a variety of strategies such as a playing with puns, cultural and religious connotations, and *double entendre*, is used as a fundamental tool in order to foster the highest contemplative potentialities of poetry. Obviously, language in itself is unable to convey a full experience of Reality; it is only a marker, but one which should not be disregarded since it has a dharmic function to play in the spiritual economy of the world. The *waka Furyū monji* ("No reliance on words or letters") expresses this trust in the manifesting power of language within the confines of formal limitations:

> Not limited
> By language,
> It is ceaselessly expressed;
> So, too, the way of letters
> Can display but not exhaust it.[44]

Heine acknowledges that his rendition of *Furyū monji* is at odds with the "strictly literal" translation which would rather indicate that "words and letters also leave no trace on it."[45] It seems however that the two renditions are not necessarily mutually exclusive since language may express the *Dharma* without affecting in the least its intrinsic integrity, therefore "leaving no trace on it." If all beings continuously manifest the Buddha-nature there is obviously no valid reason, to say the least, to exclude linguistic forms from such a manifesting function. Commenting upon Dōgen's *Kyōge betsuden* ("Special transmission outside the teaching"),[46] Steven Heine thoughtfully asserts:

> The Dharma must be expressed. It cannot escape the necessity of discourse, yet the affirmation of the role of language contains the admonition not to use up or exhaust the Dharma through unedifying discussion.[47]

[44] *Ibid.*, p. 103.

[45] *Ibid.*, p. 171

[46] "The Dharma, like an oyster
  Washed atop a high cliff:
  Even waves crashing against
  The reefy coast, like words,
  May reach but cannot wash it away" (*Ibid.*, pp. 63-4).

[47] Steven Heine, *The Zen Poetry of Dōgen*, p. 64.

We are thus entitled to distinguish between two types of language whose respective relationships with *Dharma* are diametrically opposed: there is an "unedifying" and vain talk that is a veil upon Reality because it does not proceed from its source; but there is also a "primordial language" which is of the very substance of the whole of Reality:

> Traveling the six realms,
> Seeking the primordial words
> Of the seven Buddhas of Nara,
> Which are ceaselessly
> Pervading all paths.[48]

The problem is not with language as such, but with an abuse of language that originates in a limited perception of Reality. Language, just as any form, "is" the Buddha-nature or *Nirvāna* when it is grasped in the co-origination that is Emptiness.

As an example of Dōgen's integrating use of language, a *waka* such as *Jinjippōkai shinjitsunintai* ("True person manifest throughout the ten quarters of the world") is characterized by the fact that the didactic intention is manifested in a symbolic fashion that is highly suggestive but in no way puzzling or mysteriously ordinary as in many Zen *haiku*:

> The true person is
> Not anyone in particular;
> But, like the deep blue color
> Of the limitless sky,
> It is everyone, everywhere in the world.[49]

In such a poem, the semantic unity of the whole is guaranteed by the dialectic interrelation between individuality and universality, a dialectic that is mediated by the symbolic coincidence of the two dimensions of depth and limitlessness as conveyed by the color blue. The central imaginal presence of the deep blue sky suggests the immanence of Buddhahood as well as the interiorizing orientation that is the key to its unveiling. Another example of this correlation between natural and spiritual realities is to be found in the *waka Fubo shoshō no manako* ("True seeing received at birth"):

---

[48] Dōgen, cited in Steven Heine, *The Zen Poetry of Dōgen*, p. 110.
[49] *Ibid.*, p. 101.

Seeking the way
Amid the deepest mountain paths,
The retreat I find
None other than
My primordial home: *satori*![50]

In his commentary upon this particular poem, Steven Heine points to the importance of the final pun on *satori* meaning both illumination and village. This pun articulates the interplay between outer and inner journeying, thus providing a most telling example of the *waka*'s tension toward a plenitude of meaning. The imaginal and linguistic universe of *waka* appears as one of correspondences and correlations, one in which *Dharma* and the many *dharma* are fundamentally connected along an axis of ontological continuity.

As appears clearly from an examination of Dōgen's poetry, one must emphasize the sharp contrast between *waka* and *haiku*, the first form fostering linguistic and semantic articulation in order to convey a metaphysical meaning and the second relying upon an abrupt "short circuit" of language and ordinary representation. The relative brevity of the *haiku*, in comparison with the *waka*, is not without relationship to the latter characteristic. Originally, the *haiku* was a part of a longer piece, the *renga*:

> *Haiku* was originally called *hokku*, meaning the starting verse of *renga* (the linked poem), which was historically the forerunner of *haiku*, serving as a connecting bridge between *waka* and the latter. *Haiku* was born when the starting verse (*hokku*) of linked poem (*renga*) was given independence.[51]

This "independence" of the *haiku* is highly suggestive of a "disconnection" that fosters what Izutsu calls "the formation of a non-temporal, poetic-linguistic field."[52] *Haiku* is not primarily characterized by a syntagmatic structure; it is not to be understood in the perspective of a meaning stemming from sequential elements, but rather as a "vertical," paradigmatic coincidence whose meaning issues forth from the "collapse" of diverse, uneven or opposite realities. *Haiku* aims at suggesting the ultimate Emptiness from which everything flows through a contemplative disarticulation of reality. In *waka*, the semantic structure informs the imaginal and linguistic structure by using

---

[50] *Ibid.*, p. 102.
[51] Toshihiko and Toyo Izutsu, *The Theory of Beauty in the Classical Aesthetics of Japan*, p. 62.
[52] *Ibid.*, p. 62.

it as an articulated support of expression, whereas in *haiku* it is the experience that informs language and meaning by illuminating their phenomenal and ordinary "substance" and by freeing them from a binding perception that had illusorily abstracted them from the Void. From a certain point of view, it could be said that *waka* stresses the continuity between essence and form by thriving on the full subordination of the latter to the former, whereas *haiku* could be considered as playing with the discontinuity between the two in order to unveil the unity that this discontinuity ordinarily obscures.

In *waka*, the verbal articulation tends to be secondary in reference to "mind" or "spirit." These two terms are possible translations of the Japanese key term *kokoro*. *Waka* is a form of poetry in which the images drawn from nature and their linguistic articulation constitute the means of an actualization of a state of subjective consciousness. *Kokoro* is defined by Fujiwara Teika, the great 12th century poet and theorist of *waka* as the "seed" of the "flower" which is the linguistic manifestation of the poem. *Kokoro* is the "intuitive idea" that presides over poetic creation and without which there is no *waka* properly so-called. However, *kokoro* should not be interpreted as a mere conceptual framework but rather as a "state of mind" that makes it possible for the poem to be manifested.[53] *Kokoro* is much more direct and immediate than any "idea." Actually, "ideas" or "images" refer to a domain that is intermediary between *kokoro* and verbal utterances: the realm of *omoi*, that is to say, thoughts or concepts. The latter must flow from *kokoro* and should not be controlled or corrected at their own level since their perfection stems only from the clarity of the *kokoro*.

A fourth element is constituted by "feeling" (*jō*): this element, as opposed to *omoi*, is never articulated; it is a kind of informal fullness of aesthetic energy that proceeds from *kokoro* but cannot in any way be "formalized" or "crystallized," whether it be in the domain of "internal language" (*omoi*) or "external language" (*kotoba*), to use the terms of Toyo Izutsu.[54] In fact, the notion of *jō* seems to be very similar, functionally speaking, to that of the Hindu *rasa*. It is therefore not surprising that the contemplative dimension

---

[53] "As mental concentration of the poet reaches the uttermost, out of the absolute serenity of his creative subjectivity showing no sign of vacillating this way and that—there, naturally and effortlessly, emerge, in spite of himself, poems, among which we would most probably find the 'exemplary' *waka*" (*Ibid.*, p. 87).

[54] "The *jō* as an immediate manifestation of *kokoro*, together with its semantically articulated counterpart, *omoi*, constitute not only the most important elements of creative awareness itself but also the aesthetic objective to be expressed and externalized into the poetic-linguistic 'field' of *waka*" (*Ibid.*, p. 14).

of poetry is primarily related to a cultivation of *kokoro*, and *waka* is in that respect akin to other modes of the *Gei-doh*, or the Way of Art, like flower arrangement, swordsmanship, and the tea ceremony. The technical aspects of the art function as formal vehicles of a mode of consciousness. This consciousness is essentially independent from them and yet is still linked to them insofar as it needs them in order to manifest forth and shine through. In such a contemplative perspective, the formal dimension of poetry should be understood as an exercise fostering the emergence of something that transcends it. The key to *Gei-doh* is a "non-seeking search" for that which cannot be attained but can only "be produced of its own accord." Through a regular repetition of the formal exercise of the art—though not as an inevitable and so to speak mechanical result of it—an "artless" point may be reached from which true creation flows. The fluidity resulting from a perfect "alignment" between "state of mind" and "words" is the peak of contemplative creation.

The possibility of reaching this peak, however, does not imply that there is in fact always a qualitative correspondence between *kokoro* and *kotoba*. The perfection of *kokoro* normally—or normatively—results in a perfection of form, but one must also allow for the paradoxical possibility of a "clear" state of mind that does not result in a perfect creation. The interplay between contemplative experience and formal creation is determined not only by factors pertaining to the former; it may also be affected by the contingencies and instruments of formal expression—in other words, the technical means may not be on a par with the spiritual intent. The possibility of such a disjunction accounts for the fact that in his treatise *Maigetsushō*, Fujiwara Teika clearly subordinates verbal composition to *kokoro* and unambiguously states that, should he choose between poems that fail with respect to verbal expression and others that are weak in regard to *kokoro*, his "choice would go to those poems which are awkward in verbal expression rather than to those deficient in *kokoro*."[55]

It is quite interesting to note that while discussing these two poles of *waka* poetry, Fujiwara Teika acknowledges a certain impoverishment of *waka* through successive generations, as manifested by the gradual decline of *kokoro* and the concurrent and growing importance of verbal forms. In other words, a technical mastery of forms may lead to an inordinate concern with the polished surface of the poem—probably connected with an excess

---

[55] Fujiwara Teika, cited in Toshihiko and Toyo Izutsu, *The Theory of Beauty in the Classical Aesthetics of Japan*, p. 85.

of aesthetic reflexivity—whereas the archaic and normative forms of *waka* were rather characterized by a "forceful and rugged realism"[56] in which the elemental aspect of poetic wording testified to "an immediate effusion from the *kokoro*."[57]

However, Fujiwara Teika does not advocate a return to archaic modes of expression because he does not consider the intimate relationship between *kokoro* and "forceful realism" or vigorous simplicity as the only possible means of conveying *kokoro*. For one thing, what is most simple is in a sense most difficult, and one cannot return to a state of "simplicity" by artificially overlooking the specific conditions that determine a definite creative endeavor. Time and history present a variety of qualitative modes of experience that cannot be reproduced at will and which therefore constitute a "given." When describing the ten modes that constitute the palette of *waka* poets, Fujiwara Teika is quick to stress the difficulties that are inherent in the Mode of Rugged Vigor by emphasizing "that this is a mode in dealing with which the beginner is liable to face difficulties and pitfalls."[58]

Although Fujiwara Teika does not specifically indicate the reason for these pitfalls, we may infer from his other comments upon archaic *waka* writing that they stem from the very evolution—or rather, devolution—of both mankind and language. Referring to the most ancient compilation of Japanese poetry known as *Manyō-shū* (8th century), Teika emphasizes both the excellence of the models that it includes and the risks involved in a premature attempt at imitating these models. These risks are related both to *kokoro* and to linguistic forms. A certain naivety, or else directness, in the mentalities of people from the past make it difficult—if not impossible—for contemporaries to enter into the psychic climate of ancient *waka*. The "purity and ingenuousness" of mind that was the hallmark of *Manyō* poets is out of reach to Teika's contemporaries: a certain level of civilizational refinement seems to be at odds with the "antique style." Poets, and humanity in general, cannot simply set aside certain of their experiences; they cannot artificially return to a state of "primordial purity" without having "digested," so to speak, the cultural and literary development that has ensued. In Teika's words, "one who is still at the initiatory stage should never indulge in trying to adopt the

---

[56] Toshihiko and Toyo Izutsu, *The Theory of Beauty in the Classical Aesthetics of Japan*, p. 85.

[57] *Ibid.*, p. 85.

[58] *Ibid.*, p. 82.

antique style."[59] In a certain sense, utter simplicity requires utter refinement, and the ability to use "rugged" words presupposes a command of "tenderness and delicate sensitivity." The consummate contemporary poet needs therefore to master the latter before he can claim to have developed a command of the former. It is so, not only because of the psychic differences that separate men of old from men of today, but also because language has become at the same time more complex and more "dilapidated," tending thereby to turn simplicity into triviality. The "crude and coarse" words that could be used by *Manyō* poets in a context of elementary simplicity should be avoided because they now "have associations much too close to the worldly affairs of those that sound crude and coarse."[60]

It is most likely that a certain social differentiation has contributed to a relative heterogeneity of cultural styles and registers so that "simplicity" and "nobility" unavoidably tend to become more and more disconnected. As a result, a return to simplicity is the most difficult challenge of all. In a certain sense, *waka* is a form that bears witness *par excellence* to this difficulty and to this heterogeneity, precisely because it relies on poetic associations that are to a large extent conventional and stereotyped. These associations, and the arrangement of words that are their means of conveyance, necessarily involve the actualization of *yo-jō* or "emotional plenitude" which is the creative principle of *waka*.[61] Toyo Izutsu suggests that the actualization of *yo-jō* is therefore interconnected with "a feeling of the cosmic amplitude of Nature"[62] as it is evoked by a wealth of poetic and cultural connotations or consonances. Izutsu also indicates that the verbal articulation, which provides the descriptive background for the *waka*, functions as a kind of mold for the projection of the creative energy and contemplative perception of the subject. This mold is however less limitative than informing and expansive: it provides an integral formal structure by which the creative power of the poet may "measure" itself and through which his contemplative awareness may resonate within the cosmic expanse and the poetic images that are inherited from the traditional

---

[59] *Ibid.*, pp. 80-81.

[60] *Ibid.*, p. 81.

[61] "Despite the fact that *yo-jō*—though it is essentially trans-linguistic—can be induced and actualized only as a concurrent phenomenon of linguistic expression, in the dimension of linguistic expression by the linguistic expression itself, the aspect of *yo-jō* in the poetic field of *waka* comes to be conceived as more and more distinctly independent of *kotoba*, the dimension of linguistic expression" (Toshihiko and Toyo Izutsu, *The Theory of Beauty in the Classical Aesthetics of Japan*, p. 16).

[62] *Ibid.*, p. 19.

genre and the cultural ambience. In other words, contemplation expresses itself in an imaginal and verbal language that "objectifies" its perception by "manifesting" them in a familiar and homogeneous world of meaning.

While in *waka* the coincidence between self and nature occurs through the complexity of an articulated whole, *haiku* can be primarily considered as a way of elemental simplicity; the way in which *haiku* reaches this simplicity, however, is not through suggesting an elemental congruence between a contemplative state and an imaginal and linguistic structure, but rather through the intimation of an emptiness or void lying at the heart of both being and language. The subject disappears in its confrontation with the object while the latter loses its ordinary and purely rational coherence. Toyo Izutsu proposes to illustrate the distance that separates *waka* from *haiku* by relying on a quotation of two representative poems from each genre whose English translations are placed in contradistinction—without providing any explicit commentary upon them:

Waka 1: Deep in the mountain
           As the stag is heard crying forlorn
        Treading on the tinted maple leaves fallen
           The autumn is felt
              Fraught with sorrow.

Waka 2: On a balmy spring day
           Under the ethereal rays of the sun,
        The ever-lasting and tranquil,
           How incessantly do they fall
              The cherry-petals, fluttering.

Haiku 1: Stillness
           Into the rocks, sinking
              The cries of cicadas.

Haiku 2: Above the surging sea waves
           Lies the Milky Way
              Toward the Island of Sado.[63]

On a semantic level, a contrasting analysis of these two pairs may reveal meaningful differences with regard to their respective articulation of words, ideas, and experiences. The two seasonal *wakas*—evoking autumn

[63] *Ibid.*, p. 75.

and spring—are characterized by a semantic homogeneity; in them, the series of images and allusions form a suggestive whole that is suffused with an appropriate contemplative mood. The deep recess of the mountain, the solitary deer, the fallen leaves on the ground: all contribute to suggest the approach of winter and a mood of contraction that blends nostalgia with detachment. The emotional "charge" that is condensed by these images characterizes the entire piece. In an analogous fashion, the spring *waka* calls into service the "consecrated" and conventional images of cherry blossoms on a warm and sunny afternoon in order to convey and expand a mood of peaceful detachment that may be considered as a gentle counterpart to the autumnal mode of the previous *waka*.

In contrast to these two pieces, Bashō's first *haiku* is crystallized by the coincidence of two sets of reality that are not fused together by a single emotional mood and a conventional tableau of nature, but which are collapsed as mere instances of the pure act of being. The stillness of the rocks and the persistent song of the cicadas evoke the intertwining of stillness and motion, silence and utterance, non-being and being. The song "sinks" into the rocks as if the two modes of reality were experienced in the unity of a single metaphysical perception. The outcome is not an allegorical representation of metaphysical concepts. More profoundly, the contemplative consciousness of the unity of being colors the experience, even in the most ordinary instances. It is so because consciousness is not only a mental phenomenon but an integral—physical, psychic, and spiritual—perception and mode of being. As a result, what remains here is the rock of pure being that "absorbs" the act of existence of the cicadas' song.

Bashō's second *haiku* is based upon a similar *coincidentia oppositorum*, that of moving waves and fixed stars, a coincidence that is perceived in the instantaneity of a visual and spiritual perception. The mention of the Island of Sado is an important indication, for it points to the immediate situation of the experience, making a purely conceptual or allegorical reading impossible. It also provides a context for the evocation by alluding to exile and loneliness, since Sado's island became the home of famous historical figures in exile from the Japanese mainland.[64] Accordingly, a sense of *sabi*, or lonesome poverty, pervades the evocation. This feeling is reinforced by the smallness of the island set under the vast expanses of the starry night.

---

[64] "Sado is an island on the Sea of Japan, some fifty miles off the mainland coast. Some eminent people, including Zeami, led a sorrowful life here after being banished from the Capital" (Makoto Ueda, "Bashō on the Art of the Haiku: Impersonality in Poetry," in *Japanese Aesthetics and Culture*, ed. Nancy G. Hume, p. 175, note 4).

Now, one may be tempted to identify the specific elements which, in this particular poem, allow for the expression of the contemplative experience; obviously, these cannot be the mere mention of stars and waves, nor even the opposition and paradoxical juxtaposition of images and words. The fundamental point is that these images, contrasts, or juxtapositions must be perceived from a certain inner perspective in order to reach a full understanding of the poem. In other words, a profound grasp of this *haiku* presupposes that one knows "what it is about," or that one has at least an intimation of the meaningless meaning of that uneventful event. It is also more than likely that the element of poverty, *sabi* or *wabi*,[65] which is part and parcel of the Japanese *haiku*, is intimately connected to the genius of the Japanese language—both syntactically and phonetically—since it conveys a particular sense of reality or a certain spiritual flavor. In English translation—or in other European languages—this "poverty" might be semantically or imaginally inferred, but not directly savored as in the original choice of words. It would seem, for example, that the strongly and clearly syllabic structure of Japanese phonetics tends to foster a sense of swiftness and instantaneousness—in consonance with the intuitive glimpse of perception—that may easily be diffused or weakened in English and most other European languages. Along similar lines, one could also mention, as a syntactic feature of the Japanese language that is conducive to *haiku*'s sharp and swift expressiveness, the frequent use of brief connectors like *no, ni* and *o* in the flow of the poetic sentence.[66]

Be that as it may, a further comparison of Dōgen's and Bashō's poetics would be most revealing in spelling out the profoundly different approaches to reality that are involved in the respective *waka* and *haiku* aesthetics. In Dōgen's *waka*, the convergence of poetics and contemplative practice is effected through what Steven Heine calls "an emotional attunement to impermanence."[67] The emotional plenitude that overflows from the choice of

---

[65] "... I have occasion to refer to what is known mostly among the tea-men as *wabi* or *sabi*, which really constitutes the spirit of tea. Now, this *wabi*, which literally means 'solitariness,' 'aloneness,' and more concretely, 'poverty,' is, we might say, what characterizes the entirety of Japanese culture reflecting the spirit of Zen" (D.T. Suzuki, *Zen and Japanese Culture*, p. 253).

[66] Referring to one of Bashō's most famous *haiku*, Theodore de Bary writes that this piece "depends a great deal for its effect on an exquisite choice of words that cannot be approximated in translation, there is suggested the correspondence between impressions of *sabi* received through different senses" ("The Vocabulary of Japanese Aesthetics," in *Japanese Aesthetics and Culture*, ed. Nancy G. Hume, p. 54).

[67] Steven Heine, *The Zen Poetry of Dōgen*, p. 22.

images and words plays a fundamental role in this convergence. In speaking of this mode of emotional plenitude, Toyo Izutsu refers to a network of centrifugal resonances that evoke the rippling effect of water. In this system of implications and resonances, the less must call forth the more in the sense that the potential of images, words, and prosodic patterns (pivot-words, seasonal words, puns) must be actualized in and by the poetic whole in order to foster the effusion of *yojō*, or intense feeling. This fundamental aspect of *waka* seems to be tellingly implied by an interesting remark of Fujiwara Teika in the conclusion to his *Maigetsushō*. The *waka* poet and theoretician recalls that his father, himself a master in the art of *waka* writing, used to choose "in the final stage the words which should be put at the head of a *waka* and wrote them down at the last phase of his composition."[68] If the first line comes last it is no doubt because it must seal, so to speak, the coming forth of *yojō*. This aspect corresponds to the ideal of brevity that is characterized by Chōmei when he writes that in *waka* "many meanings are compressed into a single word, (and) the depth of feeling are exhausted yet not expressed."[69] It could be said that in Dōgen's *waka*, what is sought and realized is the coincidence between linguistic elements, natural realities, and spiritualized sentiments by virtue of a communion with nature and a deep interiorization of the literary and cultural heritage. Dōgen's *waka*, and perhaps *waka* in general, seems to point to a poetic wisdom of integration through convergence and correspondence.

In contrast, *haiku* is akin to a form of art that aims at integration through a sort of disintegration or imbalance. A key to this characterization is provided by Bashō when he attributes to himself the quality of *fūrabō*. D.T. Suzuki explains that the term *fūrabō* is a compound of three different words that mean "wind" (*fū*), "thin fabric" (*ra*), and "monk" (*bō*). A thin piece of fabric floating in the wind is an excellent image that suggests the utter abandonment and simplicity which are the inner precondition for the actualization of *haiku*. The wind of the spirit carries away the individual who abandons himself to its command and forsakes any sense of ordinary coherence. The only coherence that results from this contemplative abandonment is that which results from being in congruence with the spirit of nature. The liberty of the wind is not in itself arbitrary, but it follows modes of being that cannot be understood from a merely rational—or even strictly traditional—standpoint: "the spirit

---

[68] Fujiwara Teika, cited in Toshihiko and Toyo Izutsu, *The Theory of Beauty in the Classical Aesthetics of Japan*, p. 94.

[69] Chōmei, cited in Steven Heine, *The Zen Poetry of Dōgen*, p. 62.

bloweth where it listeth" and the modes of its blowing cannot be fixed in exclusive patterns. Suzuki's translation of the term *fūrabō* as "lunatic"[70] also conveys a sense of a "non-rational" mode of being that defies the usual categories of experience. Bashō's poetry is particularly apt to convey this sense of "coherent incoherence" that results from a heightened receptivity to the universal presence of the Void.

Haiku draws its contemplative power from the poet's ability to convey a sense of the miracle of pure being through the most concrete and paradoxical of its occurrences, or to use D.T. Suzuki's expression "to make us recall the original intuition as vividly as possible."[71] Bashō's dual nature as a contemplative and a layman is no doubt in deep consonance with this dimension since it entails both a sense of the eternal and a receptivity to the temporal freshness of beings. In a sense, this ambiguous situation could be used as a defining characteristic for contemplative poetry since the latter presupposes a certain inner distance or "other-worldliness" as well as a gift of expressive creation in the world of forms, words, and motions, a certain "worldliness" so to speak. In Kyorai and Dohō's accounts of Bashō's teaching about poetry, we find the idea that the poetic spirit manifests itself in two different modes, one "that has qualities transcending time and place, and the other that is rooted in the taste of the time."[72]

However different they may appear, these two modes both pertain to the genuine poetic spirit of *haiku*. The "originality" of the poem may, therefore, be considered from two complementary standpoints; one is related to the metaphysical ground that is the unmoving pole of creative perceptions—originality in depth so to speak—and the other is akin to the freshness of the present moment as it expresses reality in its most immediate unveiling. A truly contemplative poetry in the tradition of *haiku* does not introduce a dichotomy between these two dimensions. Bashō is illustrative of this tradition, being both a monk and a sort of joker who manages to convey the limitless within and through the play of limitation itself:

---

[70] "Bashō ... classifies himself as belonging to the group of such artists as Saigyō (1118-90), Sōgi (1421-1502), Sesshū (1421-1506), and Rikyū (1521-91), who were all *fūrabō*, "lunatics," as far as their love of Nature went" (D.T. Suzuki, *Zen and Japanese Culture*, p. 258).

[71] *Ibid.*, p. 243.

[72] Cf. Makoto Ueda, "Bashō on the Art of the Haiku: Impersonality in Poetry," p. 152.

Under the trees
Soup, fish salad and all
In cherry blossoms.[73]

The dimension of humor that is apparent in quite a number of *haiku*—
and this was even the hallmark of the genre until Bashō gave *haiku* its "letters
of nobility"—is fundamentally connected with the coincidence between
a consciousness of Reality and a swift grasp and expression of relativity
within the context of this Reality. Just as the contemplative poet who is its
medium, the *haiku* is—to use Makoto Ueda's expression—"part of that life
and … not so."[74] It is precisely this dual ontological status that makes it a
particularly attractive form of expression in the modern world and accounts
for its relative popularity in the West. Ezra Pound and the Imagists even
attempted integrating the minimalistic and "objectivist" principles of *haiku*
into English poetry. It must be emphasized, however, that when considered
from its purely formal and phenomenal standpoint, the *haiku* can give rise to
facile misreadings and imitations. The tradition of *haiku* cannot be separated
from the Zen spiritual discipline of "no-mind" without being depleted of
what makes it alive and worthy of a profound interest. If one reduces *haiku*
aesthetics to an ideal of mere verbal simplicity bordering on the trivial or the
grotesque, one will most likely run the risk of missing its spirit, and this will
be a serious disregard for its contemplative foundations as an expression of
immediate insight into the nature of things; an insight that can occur only
through a full inner consonance with "naked" being in its most concrete
manifestations of nature and mankind.

As distinct manifestations of the spirit of Japanese poetry, both *waka* and
haiku are rooted in the creation of a poetic space that is as it were "abstracted"
from the temporal sequence.[75] However, while *waka*'s goal amounts to con-

---

[73] Bashō, cited in Makoto Ueda, "Bashō on the Art of the Haiku: Impersonality in Poetry," p.
169.

[74] "Life is constant suffering for those who have not attained enlightenment; it is something
to flee from for those who long for the life of a recluse. But those who have returned to the
earthly world after attaining a high stage of enlightenment can look at life with a smile, for
they are part of that life and are not so. Knowing what life ultimately is, they can take suffering
with a detached light-hearted attitude—with lightness" (Makoto Ueda, "Bashō on the Art of the
Haiku: Impersonality in Poetry," p. 171).

[75] "The *waka*-poet seems to go against the intrinsic nature of language, for, by means of words,
he tries to create a synchronic 'field,' a spatial expanse. Instead of a temporal succession of
words, in which each succeeding word goes on obliterating, as it were, the foregoing word, *waka*
aims at bringing into being a global view of a whole, in which the words used are observable all

stituting this space as the medium of an effluent feeling of identification with nature as a form of the Void, the aim of *haiku* is rather to catch the instant of intuition in its most immediate occurrence so as to convey the Void as in a lightning flash. In *waka*, the contact of self and nature fuels an emotional expansion that opens an entire space of resonances in which the self "drowns" in its own essence, in the Void. By contrast, the impersonal and objective ideal of *haiku* should rather be described as an extinction of the self, eclipsed by the contemplative intuition budding as the verbal event of the poem. In this connection, Bashō instructed his disciples to be wary of the least lapse that may interfere with poetic expression and obstruct the unity of experience and language: "If you get a flash of insight into an object record it before it fades away in your mind.... When you are composing a verse, let there not be a hair's breadth separating your mind from what you write."[76] Being—in the sense of experiencing by virtue of a metaphysical perception—must be one with writing. While it appears that in *waka*—which is informed by nature and language as culturally intertwined—writing crystallizes being, it could be said that in *haiku* it is being that spontaneously emerges in writing. Yet in both cases, the contemplative awareness of the poet remains the fundamental and animating principle of these few words that are worth saying.

at once—which is impossible except within the framework of an extremely short poem ... In a 'field' thus constituted, time may be said to be standing still or even annihilated in the sense that the meanings of all words are simultaneously present in one single sphere" (Toshihiko and Toyo Izutsu, *The Theory of Beauty in the Classical Aesthetics of Japan*, p. 5).

[76] Bashō, cited in Makoto Ueda, "Bashō on the Art of the Haiku: Impersonality in Poetry," p. 162.

V. Page from Proclus' *On Platonic Theology*
written by Stelianus Chumnus
Constantinople (1357/8)

5. Western Poetics
Inspiration, Self-knowledge, and Spiritual Presence

The relationship between poetry and contemplation constitutes, in the European context, a problematical, or at least paradoxical, reality. If, since the time of the Greeks, poetry has been synonymous with creation and production—*poiesis* referring to the making of things, in conjunction with *praxis* which relates to the world of doing or acting—contemplation appears to stand in opposition to these latter since it is usually understood to be a "seeing" or "gazing" that does not seem to entail any outward manifestation. The sharp Platonic contrast between *theoria*, or contemplation, and *poiesis*, or creation, brings this tension to the fore by highlighting two divergent ways of relating to reality. On the one hand, contemplation is a gazing of the eye of the *noūs* or intellect upon the intelligible forms that transcend the realm of physical reality; on the other hand, poetry is a mere imitation (*mimesis*) of the projected shadows of those forms as phenomena.

It is quite revealing to note, at the outset, that Plato does not primarily consider the case where poetry is the creative outcome of contemplation, or the "imitation" of the forms themselves within the domain of physical reality. This is all the more striking when one considers that in other similar domains, like that of music or *eros*, Plato is keen to bring out the highest contemplative possibilities of phenomena as means of ascension toward the realm of the intelligible. Whether his relative dismissal of poetry should be accounted for in terms of the *de facto* historical reality of his time, or in terms of a philosophic prejudice against poetry is not definitely clear; what remains true is that for the most part Plato does not *a priori* envisage poetry as a fully sapiential activity. One may wonder whether this somewhat reductive perception of poetry is not to be considered as a seminal manifestation of the relative uneasiness of the relationship between poetry and contemplation in a European context—as opposed to that which prevailed in China and India.

Another factor that has been somewhat detrimental to a harmonic integration of poetry and contemplation in the West may lie, as Octavio Paz has suggested, in the fact that Western thought has tended to focus—and rightly so in some respects—on the principle of distinction rather than on presence as the ontological foundation of identity. In such a context, both "mysticism and poetry have thus lived a subsidiary, clandestine and diminished life."[1] Being therefore of the world of "either or" and "this or that," the Western world has generally not been intent at exploring modes of apprehension of metaphysical and experiential unity. In a Christian context, contemplative poetry has at best reached heights of devotional and mystical intensity that are expressive—for example in Saint John of the Cross—of the intense joys and torments of the amorous intercourse. What is perhaps more striking in this context, and in the Western understanding of poetry in general, is the pregnancy of grace as a model for inspiration, and the supernatural pattern that it entails. However, this model of inspiration has also become highly suspect, and even the object of deriding skepticism, in post-Renaissance Europe. In the secularized, mechanistic, and materialist context of modern Europe, poetic inspiration may well appear as an obsolete if quaint fiction that cannot be seriously integrated into the scientific and quantitative mode of understanding peculiar to the world around us.

From this standpoint *Ion* is a seminal text in Western poetics in that it raises the central question of the origin of poetry as well as the correlative problem of the function of the poet. The way in which poetry is envisaged by Socrates and his interlocutor, the rhapsode[2] Ion, initially situates the definition of poetry within the context of its relationship with "art" and "science." These two terms are common translations of the Greek words *epistēmē* and *technē*, two concepts that both entail a knowledge of the general. After questioning Ion concerning the nature of his knowledge of Homer, and having concluded that this knowledge is both exclusive of that of other poets, as well as independent from that of sciences and activities that may be presented in Homer's works, Socrates is entitled to reach the following conclusion:

> No one can fail to see that you speak of Homer without any art or knowledge. If you were able to speak of him by rules of art, you would have been able to speak of all other poets; for poetry is a whole. [3]

Since the rhapsode's kind of knowledge is not one that would require a science and a technique of the general, it can be related to Homer and to

---

[1] Octavio Paz, *The Bow and the Lyre*, p. 87.

[2] In Ancient Greece, a rhapsode was a public reciter of epic poetry. Rhapsodes appear also to have added commentaries to their recitation.

[3] Plato, *Ion*, 532c, cited in Benjamin Jowett (trans.), *The Dialogues of Plato*, I, p. 287.

his poetry only by virtue of a direct transmission which Socrates refers to as *"theia dynamis,"* which literally means "divine power." Such a power cannot be taught, nor can it be learnt; it is a pure gift. Quite suggestively, Socrates identifies this kind of "power" with that of magnetic stones in the sense that the connection which exists between the Divine, the poet, and the rhapsode is comparable to that which binds a chain of rings to a strong magnet. The Divine, or the Muse, is compared to a magnetic stone, while the poet and the rhapsode are linked in a sequence of rings that are bound together by the power of the magnet, the one being able to transmit this power to the next as in a chain. The knowledge of the rhapsode is therefore analogous to that of the poet; it is pure gift from the Divine: "In like manner the Muse first of all inspires men herself; and from these inspired persons a chain of other persons is suspended, who take the inspiration."[4]

The main consequence of this understanding of poetry lies in the fact that "inspiration" constitutes the only real "qualification" of a poet. The term that is customarily translated by "inspired" is *entheos*, which literally means "god within." The adjective "enthusiastic" refers to such a case, one in which the extraordinary state of soul of the poet or interpreter is identified with a divine presence that moves the individual from within. The true agent of the poetic work is therefore not the poet, it is the god that "teach(es) ... by the mouth of the worst of poets."[5] In order to better illustrate this point, Socrates does not hesitate to state that the most beautiful poems are those in which the disproportion between the poet's skill and the actual result—a masterpiece— is the clearest. Mentioning the case in point of Tynnichos of Chalcis, Socrates asserts that "this (was) the lesson which the God intended to teach when by the mouth of the worst of poets he sang the best of songs."[6] Poetry can in no way be the result of an individual effort any more than it can be the outcome of a perfect command of technical skill: what defines it as poetry is its origin, its "inspiration," the "breathing in" of the words from the god.

What is the nature of the inspiration that is the essence of poetry? First, as with Bacchic and Dionysiac religious practices, the subject of the "inspiration" is said to be "possessed" by the god. The Greek terms used by Plato to refer to this extraordinary state are compounds of the verb *echein*, to have, to possess. We read that the poet is "possessed" (*katechetai*, 536b)

---

[4] Plato, *Ion*, 533e, cited in Benjamin Jowett (trans.), *The Dialogues of Plato*, I, p. 289.
[5] Plato, *Ion*, 535a, cited in Benjamin Jowett (trans.), *The Dialogues of Plato*, I, p. 290.
[6] *Ibid.*, p. 290.

and that he "belongs" to the Muse (*echetai,* 536b). In other words, he has been chosen as a *medium* by the god and he himself has no real control over the poetic process. It is interesting to note that another term which derives from *echein,* the noun *metexis,* constitutes a fundamental concept in the vocabulary of Platonic ontology. In *Politeia,* and particularly in the pages devoted to the allegory of the cave, Plato states that physical phenomena are only as projected shadows of ideas or archetypes in which they participate (participation, *metexis*). In other words, phenomena "are" only in so far as they participate in the "being" of their archetypes or intelligible forms. First of all, the sun is the highest reality (the supreme Good) without which ideal realities could not even be perceived. As for physical realities, they are only reflections of the latter. There is therefore a chain (*hormathos*) that relates all things from the Supreme Good down to physical realities. From the standpoint of epistemology, one must add that the higher realities can be known only in light of the Divine Sun, since they could not be visible without it. In several passages of his works, Plato indicates that this knowledge is akin to the vision of the eye, and he even alludes to the fact that there is in the soul of man an "eye" that is the seat of the contemplation of the Good. The physical eye is, in the lowest order, what the intellectual eye—the intellect (*noūs*) or organ of knowledge—is in the realm of ideas. In *Alcibiades,* self-knowledge is unambiguously identified with a knowledge of this mysterious point, which is "the seat of the specific virtue of the soul, that is to say its wisdom."[7] Socrates establishes that this point is in fact divine because it is that which defines most profoundly the very capacity of knowing in man.

An analogy should thus be drawn between Plato's ontology and the poetic chain of inspiration. In both cases, the unity of being results from an underlying principle that connects all levels of reality, as indicated by the very concept of the Great Chain of Being. In matters of ontology this continuity is constituted by the light of the sun or truth that binds together the world of reality and the realm of shadows. The doctrine of participation (*metexis*) presents us with a theophany: everything is in essence an appearance of the sun and, on a lower level, of the objects that it renders visible. In matters of poetry, it is less a matter of a chain of being than that of a chain of power (*dynamis*), less a matter of theophany than one of theurgy. Poetry is conceived by Plato as being akin to Dionysiac *mania* or madness. In *Phaedrus,* Plato defines poetic inspiration as a third kind of "madness," following love and

---

[7] Plato, *Alcibiades,* 133b, cited in Benjamin Jowett (trans.), *The Dialogues of Plato,* 2, p. 770.

prophecy. In all cases, the ordinary faculties of mankind are transported into a state of rapture that is induced by a divine presence; they are therefore states of heightened consciousness:

> The third kind is the madness of those who are possessed by the Muses; which taking hold of a delicate and virgin soul, and there inspiring frenzy, awakens lyrical and all other numbers; with these adorning the myriad actions of ancient heroes for the instruction of posterity. But he who, having no touch of the Muses' madness in his soul, comes to the door and thinks that he will get into the temple by the help of art—he, I say, and his poetry are not admitted; the sane man disappears and is nowhere when he enters into rivalry with the madman.[8]

This *mania* entails an ecstatic inebriation, a dismemberment of reality that is both the cause and the consequence of a traumatic experience of communication with the god. These modalities of sacred madness are not without analogy in the phenomena that surround the process of "election" in shamanistic traditions. Mircea Eliade has shown how shamanistic "madness" is to be understood as a prelude to divine gifts:

> The future shaman may sometimes be confused with a madman—as is often the case in Malaysia—but, in reality, his "madness" fulfills a mystical function: it reveals to him some aspects of reality that are inaccessible to other mortals, and it is only after he has experimented with and integrated these hidden dimensions of reality that the "madman" becomes a shaman.[9]

Madness is to be understood in this context as a disintegration of ordinary consciousness; it "opens up" the soul and makes it receptive to spiritual gifts. In a similar way, the inspired poets and rhapsodes are not "in their mind" (*emphrones*); they lose the faculty of prudential reason and become like puppets in the hands of the god. Accordingly, the poet, as the rhapsode, does not really "understand" what he conveys. In this respect, it is quite revealing that the words which define the epistemological status of the poet in the

[8] Plato, *Phaedrus* 245a, cited in Benjamin Jowett (trans.), *The Dialogues of Plato*, I, pp. 249-50.

[9] Mircea Eliade, "Expérience sensorielle et expérience mystique chez les primitif," in *Du corps à l'esprit*, p. 74 (my translation).

concluding page of the treatise, *mēden eidōs* ("knowing nothing"),[10] refer to the root verb *oida* ("to know, to see") which is also akin to *eidos* and *idea* ("form" or "archetype").

If we are mindful of the implications of these lexical indications, it would appear that, when envisaged from the standpoint of divine possession, poetry is indeed unrelated to eidetic contemplation. While the eye of the intellect is the organ of noetic knowledge, it is, however, not referred to as the organ of poetic consciousness. In fact, no such organ appears to be postulated by Plato, and the connotations of the term "possession" would rather lead us to infer that the poet, as the rhapsode, is "inspired" in his whole being, and not only through a given organ or faculty.[11] On the basis of such differences, it therefore seems methodologically useful to draw a distinction between a "mystical" and a properly "contemplative" dimension concerning contact with the divine in Plato's thought. By the adjective "mystical" we refer to an inner state that is not the direct result of an art or a method and which is experienced as coming from outside or from above. The term "participation" is thus more appropriate than "contemplation" since the latter is closely connected, in Plato's wisdom, to the idea of vision, as indicated by the central term *theōria*, from *theaō*, to gaze, to consider, to contemplate. Now, the importance of the visual pattern in the Platonic theory of intellective contemplation raises the question of its relationship with poetry.

In the *Republic* Plato severely criticizes poetry and even recommends its exclusion from the life of the ideal city. From this standpoint, poetry is conceived as an art of the "unreal" both in respect of its creations and of its goal. First of all, the reproduction of phenomena is only a copy of the external surface of things; it does not reach the essence. In this sense, poetry is not contemplative because contemplation (*theōria*) can refer only to the real, the realm of ideas. When Plato criticizes the "aesthetes" of his time, he refers to them as *philotheamones tas kalas phōnas kai chroas* ("amateurs of sounds and spectacles"), indicating that their vice is the "worship" of beauty; that is to say, the reduction of beauty to its lowest and most external mode of manifestation, and thus a losing sight of the archetypes that phenomenal

---

[10] "But if, as I believe, you have no art, but speak all these beautiful words about Homer unconsciously under his inspiring influence, then I acquit you of dishonesty, and shall only say that you are inspired" (Plato, *Ion*, 542a, cited in Benjamin Jowett, *The Dialogues of Plato*, 1, p. 296).

[11] From an integral standpoint, one could argue that Intellect and totality of being are one and the same. However, the "intellectualist" emphasis of the Greeks precludes such a clear identity while restricting the intellective dimension to the dialectical realm alone.

beauties reflect. Philosophers on the other hand are *philotheamones tēs alētheias* ("contemplators of truth"). Similarly, a true poet is characterized by his ability to choose subjects that are most real, and the finality of his art is never to be mere enjoyment but a higher participation in the true, the good, and the beautiful. This is the reason why the only kinds of poetry that Plato does not banish from his ideal city are those which praise the highest contemplative objects of man, i.e., divine beings or qualities and virtues:

> Hymns to the gods and praises of famous men are the only poetry which ought to be admitted into our State. For if you go beyond this and allow the honeyed muse to enter, either in epic or lyric verse, not law and the reason of mankind, which by common consent have ever been deemed best, but pleasure and pain will be the rulers in our State.[12]

All other kinds of poetry will lead to the rulership of "pleasure and pain," which amounts to saying that only the immediate emotional effects of phenomena will be involved in the practice of poetry. By contrast with this superficial, and ultimately dangerous understanding of the role of poets, Plato's contemplative practice of poetry is spelled out in the *Republic* where Socrates explains what constitutes true education:

> ... Just as the eye was unable to turn from darkness to light without the whole body, so too the instrument of knowledge can only by the movement of the whole soul be turned from the world of becoming into that of being, and learn by degrees to endure the sight of being, and of the brightest and best of being, or in other words, of the good.[13]

The very act of contemplation is, for Plato, an act of converting the gaze. It corresponds to an *epistrophē*, i.e., a change of orientation: the eyes of the soul must be directed toward the real world, that of the archetypes. If there is a place for poetry in such a view of contemplation it is mainly by virtue of the objects that are described by poets. Poetry in itself does not seem to lend itself to a contemplation of the higher realm, precisely because of its lack of intellective character. On the other hand, poetry may foster a more profound awareness of the divine, but in a way that is more existential than intellective.

---

[12] Plato, *Republic*, X, 607a, cited in Benjamin Jowett (trans.), *The Dialogues of Plato*, I, p. 865.

[13] Plato, *Republic*, VII, 518d, cited in Benjamin Jowett (trans.), *The Dialogues of Plato*, 1, p. 777.

It is interesting to note, in this respect, that *Ion* and *Menon*, the dialogues that deal respectively with poetry and virtue, end on a similar note. Just as Socrates finally conveys to Ion a sense of self-knowledge by making him aware of the divine origin of his gift, he also stresses the point, in engaging Menon, that virtue is neither a natural given nor a result of education: it is a "divine lot" (*theia moira*). The following are two conclusive statements that seem to echo each other:

> You have no art, but speak all these beautiful words about Homer unconsciously under his inspiring influence (*theiai moirai*).[14]

> Virtue is neither natural nor acquired, but an instinct given by God (*theiai moirai*) to the virtuous.[15]

Whereas common opinion (*doxa*) would tend to understand poetry and virtue as domains of human experience that are particularly connected with education and a mastery of rules and laws, Socrates refers both to a kind of supra-rational, gratuitous, and transcendent manifestation. It is worth noting that the absence of the "thinking process" is a hallmark of both "gifts": poetic contemplation, as moral contemplation, involves the totality of one's being; it is an existential participation in the divine that is not mediated by the intellective faculty. The term *theiai moira*, translated as "divine lot," refers to the concept of "part" or "destiny," not in that it connotes an innate ability but in that it refers to the unpredictable and unintelligible character of man's destiny and gifts.

In *Phaedrus*, Plato emphatically makes the point that the real poet is the one who is struck by poetic "madness" as opposed to one who relies solely upon his art. As we have seen, this state of altered consciousness appears to be totally independent of any possibility of human effort. In the context of this poetic inspiration or "possession" as defined by Plato in *Ion*, we would like to consider the Spanish notion of *duende* as a suggestive echo of the preceding lines. The concept of *duende* seems very close, in many respects, to that of divine *mania* as envisaged by Plato. Federico Garcia Lorca, one of the most penetrating analysts of *duende*, emphasizes two fundamental characteristics

---

[14] Plato, *Ion*, 542a, cited in Benjamin Jowett (trans.), *The Dialogues of Plato*, 1, p. 296.

[15] Plato, *Meno*, 100a, cited in Benjamin Jowett (trans.), *The Dialogues of Plato*, 1, p. 380.

of *duende*: the sense of totality that it entails; and the utterly spontaneous mode of its manifestations:

> The *duende*, then, is a power, not a work. It is a struggle, not a thought.
> I have heard an old maestro of the guitar say, "The *duende* is not in the throat; the *duende* climbs up inside you, from the soles of the feet." Meaning this: it is not a question of ability, but of true, living style, of blood, of the most ancient culture, of spontaneous creation.[16]

Duende, as poetic *mania*, is not a mental phenomenon: the mind separates, connects, analyzes, and compares, whereas *duende* entails an immediate sense of unity. Climbing up "from the soles of the feet," *duende* implies a Dionysiac and chthonian vital energy that has to do with breath ("the sage breathes from his heels" according to Chuang-tzu) and blood (the animic and all-pervasive substance of the body). More precisely, the *duende* appears (as in the case of Saint Teresa) on "the subtle bridge that unites the five senses with the raw wound, that living cloud, the stormy ocean of timeless Love."[17] The "totality" and integrity of *duende* has to do with its ability to recapitulate the whole of Reality in the flash of a synthetic perception: the self is as if "possessed" by Reality in a most immediate and non-mental way. It must be remembered in this respect that literally the *duende* is a kind of elf or goblin that may take "possession" of a soul, as Socrates' *daimon* or as Ion's Muse.[18] The latter is not Lorca's muse, who "awakens the intelligence, bringing a landscape of columns and a false taste of laurel"[19] since it has nothing to do with the *noūs* and should rather be understood as inducing poetic trance. If there is a difference between *mania* and *duende* it is that which allows us to draw a contrast between an inspiration from the outside and one coming from within. The *duende* is a sort of gift, but a gift that is so to speak already dormant in the soul and body and that needs only to be awakened: "one must awaken the *duende* in the remotest mansions of the blood."[20] Now the blood is the physical manifestation of the soul that is regenerated by the air of the

---

[16] Federico Garcia Lorca, *In Search of Duende*, ed. and trans. Christopher Maurer, p. 49.

[17] *Ibid.*, p. 58.

[18] Lorca strongly emphasizes the differences between the *duende* and the Muse, but it may be that the Muse he has in mind is more the conventional and academic allegory of poetry than its living spirit as in Plato.

[19] Federico Garcia Lorca, *In Search of Duende*, ed. and trans. Christopher Maurer, p. 51.

[20] *Ibid.*, p. 51.

spirit in order to energize the whole body. The *duende* possesses, as does *mania*, but it does so because it is already in a sense *duen de casa* ("master of the house")[21] and not because it comes from the outside to overtake us. Because of its supra-mental nature and the totality of its "possession," the *duende* is as spontaneous and unpredictable as can be. As Lorca demonstrates, to say that one "has" *duende* does not mean in the least that one can gain control over its manifestations. *Duende* cannot repeat itself either, precisely because it originates in a profound zone of reality that precludes any rational understanding or formal *mimesis*.

It would however be somewhat inaccurate to claim that there is no such thing as a preparation for the coming of *duende*. Indeed, *duende* is a kind of grace, and grace is by definition gratuitous; it is nonetheless well known that man can collaborate in the facilitation of grace. An anecdote allows Lorca to point out how this may be done: mentioning his attendance at a performance of the Andalusian singer Pastora Pavon, Lorca relates that the renowned singer failed to convey a sense of poetic excitement to her audience. All that she could obtain was a sarcastic, "Long live Paris!" which suggests that the "something else" transcending technical flair was absent from her singing. More than likely irritated by the critical allusion, the singer initiated a second round under the auspices of a glass of liquor; this time the *duende* came to the rendezvous. The conclusion that Lorca draws from this story is of the utmost importance for our understanding of the type of context that may favor the springing forth of *duende*:

> She had to rob herself of skill and security, send away the muse and become helpless, that her *duende* might come and deign to fight her hand-to-hand.[22]

We can perceive in this passage a situation that is not without analogy to the "madness" that is a prelude to inspiration. Madness and "helplessness" both refer to a loss of rational control, which seems to be the precondition for a surging of "grace." One could also speak of death, or the presence of

---

[21] "The notion of *duende* (from *duen de casa*, 'master of the house') came ... from popular Spanish culture, where the *duende* is a playful hobgoblin, a household spirit fond of hiding things, breaking plates, causing noise, and making a general nuisance of himself" (Christopher Maurer, *In Search of Duende*, p. ix).

[22] Federico Garcia Lorca, *In Search of Duende*, ed. and trans. Christopher Maurer, p. 53.

death, as a similar catalytic element for the coming on of *duende*. Jacques Maritain considered that such was also the paradoxical reason why surrealist poetry—which he rightly considered to be a profound deviation from spiritual consistency—could as if accidentally reach the level of true poetry by virtue of the "fortuitousness or the catastrophe of some singular disintegration" that it entails. The "arrows of being find an issue" because of the dissolution of the substance;[23] in other words, man must be deprived of all that prevents him from being a pure receptacle for the flow of *duende*.

At this juncture, we touch upon an important dimension of the contemplative implications of "living poetry": the emptying of self which is necessary for initiating the stage of creation. It is all the more interesting to note the fact that, as Lorca has profoundly suggested, the sudden appearance of *duende* coincides with a feeling of awe that is a response to a divine presence. As Lorca has noticed: "in all Arabic music, whether dance, song, or elegy, the *duende*'s arrival is greeted with energetic cries of Allah! Allah!, which is so close to the Olé of the bullfight that who knows if it is not the same thing?"[24] The coming forth of *duende* is an opportunity for a contemplative glimpse into the creative act of God, an act that is synthesized by the name of God. It is pure act emerging from emptiness, destruction, or disarray. Such is the reason why it cannot be followed by anything else than a prolonged and profound silence. In a sense this silence is that of extinction: nothing can compare, and therefore follow, what is pure affirmation of Reality. *Duende* lives between two deaths: the death of man to his own individuality, and the death of the world that is as if burnt down by lightning. *Duende* is that which appears when man cannot rely on anything else and accepts his emptiness and his utter helplessness before the abyss of death. Lorca tends to include in *duende* an element of dramatic and passionate struggle that he most likely perceives as the hallmark of the Spanish soul. There is undoubtedly in creative *mania* an element of suffering and discomfort that results from the disproportion between the soul and its divine content. Poetic contemplation is also in that sense a kind of laboring delivery: "inspiration" does not follow a

---

[23] Writing of the Surrealists, Maritain confines the rare areas of true poetry that they reach to the realm of spontaneous necessity: "Is it astonishing that these explorers fished up the larvae of a Freudianism already become a subject for textbooks and doctoral theses, and obsessions whose discouraging vulgarity could hardly be dissimulated by a very bourgeois refinement of aestheticism?... If an Eluard ... truly reaches in passing the savage heart of poetry, it is in spite of the surrealist system and procedure, and because through dissolution itself the arrows of being find an issue" (*Art and Poetry*, pp. 75-6).

[24] Federico Garcia Lorca, *In Search of Duende*, ed. and trans. Christopher Maurer, p. 53.

swift and smooth trajectory; its "ease" is that of the gods, but to man belongs the toil.

Such a reference to creative suffering should not be understood as a rendition of the clichéd hardships of poetic work. It also has much to do, as we have suggested, with the intrinsic demands of poetry as a contemplative discipline geared toward transcending the self. Rainer Maria Rilke has insisted upon the seriousness of those demands by highlighting the fact that a true poetic vocation must be grounded on certainty. In his *Letters to a Young Poet*, Rilke shows a remarkable awareness of the rigorously vocational character of poetry when he writes:

> This most of all: ask yourself in the most silent hour of the night: *must* I write? Dig into yourself for a deep answer. And if the answer rings out in assent, if you meet this solemn question with a strong, simple "I must," then build your life in accordance with this necessity.[25]

The imperative of essential commitment and self-transcendence that the poet must meet is also more generally incumbent upon others who deal with poetry, whether they be author, reader, or auditor.

In the history of Western poetics, Coleridge is probably one of those who expressed the highest awareness of that demanding necessity, whence—in his thoughts about poetry—his tendency to emphasize a close association between religion and poetry. For him, "religion is the poetry of mankind" because it "generalizes" the notions of men, taking them away from the narrow confines of their immediate personal interests. Poetry is "religious" in that it looks beyond the sphere of the constraining determinations of the here and now, beyond the limitations of human accidentality. Poetry also has in common with religion the fact that it situates "objects" at a "distance" from us; it obliges us to transcend the purely sensory dimension of our being, thereby fostering the practice of the virtues. The latter need to be cultivated as expressions of our inner freedom vis-à-vis the bondage of passions that absolutize the claims of our senses. Poetry, by virtue of its "ideal" horizon, directly contributes to an ennobling education of the soul: it forges an awareness of the universal norm that makes us human, or at least approximates that universality within the confines of a given civilization.

The function of "foundational" poetry, that of Homer or that of the Finnish *Kalevala*, is to provide a given sector of mankind with a normative

---

[25] Rainer Maria Rilke, *Letters to a Young Poet*, p. 6.

model of being and thinking. Accordingly, the most important common point between poetry and religion is that they both aim at a perfecting of the being. The aforementioned zones of convergence between the two domains reveal in fact a common root: self-transcendence. What is the meaning of perfecting the being if not a "generalization" of our sense of identity—a concrete consideration of a human norm that is more "real" than our own self-centered actions—and an "objectification" of ourselves, i.e., a degree of freedom and command in regard to our immediate desires, the vehicles of which are our senses? Poetry and religion therefore converge in helping us contemplate our true nature as it is defined by the full horizon of our destiny. If, according to Coleridge, "an undevout poet is an impossibility,"[26] it is only because poetry is by definition geared toward the universal and the supra-individual, and because there is no transcending of the self except in and by a relationship with the Divine. Here, one of the fundamental implications is that a true poet has infinite capacities and possibilities; he can therefore only look at a "distance" and at transcendence in order to express them. In fact the very existence of poetry, and the need that feeds it, is an evidence of God, the One. Poetry could not be explained if there were not in mankind a sense for transcendence; in the absence of such a sense, poetry becomes an inexplicable luxury. The practice of poetry, whether it be creative or merely receptive, requires a degree of contemplative attention. It is a kind of "ecstasy" that entails a moral and spiritual preparation.

Based on an understanding of its scope as both cosmic and universal, and with reference to the transcendence of its ends, poetry appeared to many Romantics as a mode of knowledge that reveals what is most essential in mankind. This universal essentiality may often be mediated by individual passions and experiences, but it claims to invoke supra-individual resonances that extol emotions to the level of fundamental signatures of mankind. Poetry aims at an expansion of the horizon of the individual to that which connects him with the all-encompassing space of nature and mankind. The idea of "connection" is especially important in Romantic poetics, in that it informs both the contemplative "style" of poets and the concept of imagination that presides over this practice. Poetry tends to the universal on the basis of its ability to reach the synthetic unity of all things.

We find a most interesting expression of this vision in Shelley's liminal distinction between the modes of operation of reason and those of imagination:

---

[26] Samuel Taylor Coleridge, "Poetry and Religion," in *The Portable Coleridge*, p. 397.

"Reason respects the difference, and Imagination the similitude of things."[27] Reason separates and distinguishes in so far as it introduces a structural and discursive order into things; its function cannot be "contemplative" because it does not "hold together" in a single glance the elements of its inquiry. By contrast, imagination, the organ of poetry, is that faculty in man which is able to perceive the unity of things and the subsequent analogies that confer a metaphysically meaningful cohesiveness to reality. Poetry is symbolic because it grasps the similitudes, which bind together phenomena of varying degrees and subsume them under the same essence. Poetic contemplation is a honing of the intuitive perception of those similitudes that enables man to "read" both macrocosm and microcosm in their metaphysical implications. Shelley can therefore posit imagination as a faculty that is by far higher in nature than reason, as well as more active in its function.[28] Only imagination can reach the level of the archetypes, given its participatory dimension. Reason can function only as a prolongation of imagination: it works on the intuitive data that are provided to it by imagination.

If it can be argued that there is room for thinking in poetry, the type of thinking that is involved is to be understood as an intuition and not as a discursive meditation; it is contemplative because it unveils connections rather than connects thoughts.[29] Poetry, as the primary language of imagination, is akin to a perception and an expression of the harmony that binds "sounds or motions ... to the impressions that excite them."[30] If melody can be compared to the ever-moving sequence of responses to the diversity of stimuli and transformations, harmony is an ability to accord the latter with the former, as well as the former with their expression. In poetry, the macrocosm, the human microcosm, and the poetic work as a cosmos meet according to the laws of harmony and similitude. The contemplative practice of poetry consists in a fine-tuning of our inner sense of harmony both with respect to the world and with respect to the flow of words. Accordingly, this vision is in a sense outward looking and expansive—it aims at the outermost shores of universal

---

[27] Percy Bysshe Shelley, *Defence of Poetry*, I.1.

[28] "Reason is to Imagination as the instrument to the agent, as the body to the spirit, as the shadow to the substance" (*Ibid.*, I.1).

[29] "We speak, for instance, of thought in poetry; but if poetry is pure and uncontaminated the thought it contains is of a different *kind* from what is ordinarily called thought: it is perception, not a cogitation, and in the finest kind of poetry it is a perception of the general in the particular" (John Middleton Murray, cited in Etienne Gilson, *Forms and Substances in the Arts*, p. 227).

[30] Percy Bysshe Shelley, *Defence of Poetry*, II, 8.

harmony—even though its underlying resonance is considered to be situated "within." The poet knows the world through the relations that link him to it and that are expressed by his words.

In this sense, the kind of Romantic understanding of poetic contemplation that we have just highlighted may be deemed as the analogical reversal of the neo-Scholastic understanding of poetry as a means of self-knowledge that is highlighted in Jacques Maritain's works on art and poetry. Among contemporary thinkers who consider themselves indebted to the Thomistic philosophical and theological tradition, Maritain is one who has repeatedly insisted upon the central role of human reflexivity in intellectual, moral, and artistic matters. Maritain considers this heightened reflexivity to be the chief characteristic of the "integral humanism" that he perceives as the culmination of contemporary endeavors in general, and of contemporary art in particular. Now, that reflexivity is totally absent from earlier practices of poetry since the latter do not entail a mode of discursive consciousness but rather a purely intuitive and immediate grasp of their objects. As Shelley puts it:

> In the infancy of the world, neither poets themselves nor their auditors are fully aware of the excellency of poetry: for it acts in a divine and unapprehended manner, beyond and above consciousness: and it is reserved for future generations to contemplate and measure the mighty cause and effect in all the strength and splendor of their union.[31]

This absence of reflexivity could certainly be interpreted as an eminence and a privilege since it presupposes a kind of substantial identification with language, and therefore a full savoring of its existential and theurgic efficiency. This is not, however, what Maritain has in mind: for him, traditional art and traditional man—the word tradition here referring to pre-Renaissance ways of being, seeing, and doing—lacks reflexivity in the sense that the individuality "is hidden" behind the normative forms that it inherits from the tradition.[32] This "hiding" does not prevent the artist from expressing his personal genius—in the sense of *ingenium* or inner gift—but it precludes, according

---

[31] *Ibid.*, I.12.

[32] "The art of China and India, like that of the Middle Ages, shelters itself in vain behind the rite or the simple duty of ornamenting life, it is as personal as, and more personal at times than that of the individualistic Occident. The more or less rigorous canonicity of art is here a secondary condition; in the days of old it was a condition favorable for hiding art from itself" (Jacques Maritain, *Art and Poetry*, pp. 88-9).

to Maritain, art becoming conscious of itself as art; and it is precisely this self-consciousness that Maritain welcomes, in modern times, as the source of the "fine dangers which mobilized poetry."[33] The dangers that Maritain has in mind most likely pertain to a hypertrophy of self-consciousness that can lead poets into the blind alleys of solipsist and idealist productions. But that is not of course what Maritain has in mind when he lauds the creative potential of modern reflexivity. In actuality, reflexivity cannot be separated from contact with the alterity of the world since by definition it involves an awareness of "otherness." For Maritain, there is no knowledge of oneself that is not predicated upon a relationship with the world. Outside of such a relationship, man remains a kind of obscure enigma to himself: he cannot grasp himself. Poetry, as a contemplative practice, can therefore be defined as an understanding of oneself through the mediation of the poem as it issues forth as a result of contact with the world. In Maritain's view, self-knowledge is possible only when the self is actualized in an act of creation: this act of creation itself presupposes that the subject encounters an object that resounds within him. This understanding of self-knowledge through poetic creation situates us at a distance from the Western Platonic tradition of self-knowledge, and the implications of that distance with respect to the contemplative function of poetry are of utmost importance.

In his *Alcibiades*, Plato answered the question of self-knowledge in a way that made it possible for the subject to grasp its essence through an interiorization of his contemplative gaze. The act of knowing and the capacity for knowledge being the highest characteristic of mankind, man can contemplate himself only when he directs his attention to the focal point of his contemplative ability. Self-knowledge is a knowledge of that through which everything else comes to be known. In order to expound this doctrine, Socrates makes use of an analogy with the eye: the eye can see itself only through the most central point in it, i.e., the pupil. The comparison is all the more striking in that the pupil is the only place where light can penetrate the eye. When one understands light as being a direct symbol of the Divine, one can grasp the full import of Plato's conclusion concerning the identification of the self with divinity:

> By directing our contemplation toward God, we would make use, with respect to the virtue of a soul, of what is most beautiful, that in which

---

[33] *Ibid.*, p. 89.

even human things could mirror themselves; and it is in such a way that we would see and know ourselves the best.[34]

Self-knowledge is therefore inward-looking and does not require the mediation of an "other": it simply consists in stripping the self of all extrinsic determinations so as to unveil its bare divinity. Man can know himself because he can objectify himself by situating himself at the standpoint of the divine substance that is the core of his being and the seat of wisdom. This fundamentally amounts to saying that man can fully understand himself only through the Divine that lies within him.

Now Maritain's concept of poetry seems precisely predicated on the impossibility of such a knowledge and such an objectification. Only the transcendent God may know man as he is. At the basis of Maritain's thought is the notion that man is incapable of identifying with the divine Intellect. He cannot do so because he is not pure spirit and therefore cannot reach an "intuition of the self by the self."[35] He is condemned to a kind of obscurity with respect to himself:

> The substance of a man is obscure to himself; it is in receiving and suffering things, in awaking to the world, that it awakes to itself. The poet, we have said elsewhere, cannot express his own substance in a work except on the condition that things resound in him, and that within him, in a single awakening, those things and his own substance rise together out of sleep.[36]

It is therefore only when man is identified with objects and when that identification is objectified as a work of art that he can grasp his self. Man knows himself through what he feels and what he produces; and even so, this knowledge remains somewhat obscure, precisely because it is mediated and indirect. Paradoxically, the poet becomes capable, through the process of creation, of "showing the Grail to others (while not seeing) it himself."[37] He

---

[34] Plato, *Alcibiades*, 133c, cited in Benjamin Jowett (trans.), *The Dialogues of Plato*, 2, p. 770.

[35] Jacques Maritain, *Art and Poetry*, p. 89.

[36] Jacques and Raïssa Maritain, *The Situation of Poetry*, p. 51.

[37] "It is thus as if all that he discerns and divines in things he discerns and divines as inseparable from himself and his emotion, indeed as himself, and so he grasps obscurely his own being, with a knowledge which will only come to fruition in being creative. That is why he shows the Grail to others and does not see it himself" (*Ibid.*, p. 51).

is a "prophet" who cannot see. Such a paradoxical situation coincides with the fact that poetry can be seen as a sort of by-product of the "rebellious" resistance and opacity of "matter" in man. For Plato, the accidental "materiality" of man does not utterly prevent him from knowing himself through unmediated contemplation; it may certainly be a hindrance in so far as man identifies with his outer shells, but such an identification finds its remedy in contemplation and self-investigation.

In the Thomistic epistemology of Maritain, on the contrary, the "sensualist" model of knowledge (there is no intellective knowledge that does not first proceed through the senses) presupposes the mediation of sensory knowledge. The intellectual act is a kind of reading of the intelligible in the sensory form. This mediation is instrumental both in noetic and in poetic knowledge. However, in the first case, the intellective form is so to speak "extracted" from the sensory form and it remains "entitatively" different from the knower (although being "intentionally" identified with him); whereas in the case of "poetic knowledge," the "object" becomes part of the knowing self in an intuitive mode. The self "contemplates" itself in and through the objective "actuality" of the poem.

It would however be inaccurate to conceive of the reaction of the self to the world as that of a "matter" that would be the substratum of the work of poetry. Maritain is very keen to distinguish between poetic emotions as the "material" substance of a work, and poetic emotions as the "intentional," efficient, and creative "energy" of a work. If emotional responses resulting from the contact between the self and the world are merely understood as the "subject matter" of poetry, then poetic creation is reduced to a "commercial or idealistic corruption of art";[38] commercial in the sense of a marketable psychologizing of sentimental "expressions of oneself," and idealistic in that the very "reality" of the catalytic encounter with the world is treated as an objective "idea" deprived of its own creative dynamics. In fact, the creative emotion is "an intuitive and *intentional* emotion, which bears within it much more than itself."[39] It bears more than itself because it is so to speak the catalyst of an actualization of both the subject and the poetic object. The idea of intentionality is therefore crucial to a real understanding of poetic practice: Scholasticism establishes a sharp distinction between the entitative reality of

---

[38] Jacques Maritain, *Art and Poetry*, p. 88.
[39] *Ibid.*, p. 88.

a being (its actual being) and its intentional reality, i.e., its intelligible form that is no less real than it is.

This doctrine entails an understanding of the intellectual form as a means of knowledge and not as the object of knowledge itself. The Peripatetic and Scholastic model of the intentional identification of the knower and the known in the act of knowing is here pregnant. To know is to actualize through identification what is *a priori* potential both in the knower and in what is known. The image of "awakening" is a direct expression of the Scholastic epistemological model of the passage from *potentia* to *actualitas*. Man reaches some intuition of what he is by actualizing his nature through an intentional intuition of what he knows or contemplates. We understand that such a knowledge is of necessity profoundly colored by the very act of being a person. Knowledge happens "in the act of exercising": the poet perceiving himself as the source of creation, as a subject—therefore not "clearly" and "distinctly"—and not as an object of reflection. In Maritain's view, the personal subject "I" is the "substantial depth of the living and loving subjectivity."[40] As sanctity, true poetry proceeds from an unadulterated selfhood that is founded upon the "straightforward gaze" of interior life and the "secret colloquy in which God alone takes part" and that remains unaffected by prohibitions, rules, and conventions; "if such a sincerity is not frequent, this is because it requires courage."[41] Whence the privileged "liberty" of the poet who is not bound by external social or psychological constraints, given his identification with the pure act of creation.

This liberty is a key to the understanding of the Aristotelian and Scholastic idea of poetry as an imitation of a pattern. The latter is defined as *id ad quod respiciens artifex operatur* ("that which the creative spirit looks at within itself in order to bring the work into existence)."[42] Now, Maritain strongly cautions his readers against the danger of misinterpreting this idea in terms of a mere imitation of a model. The essence of art—and sanctity—is not mimetic but "original" in the sense that the artist is to discover within himself the very "origin" of his being as willed by God. Imitation must here be taken as the imitation of a process and not the copying of a product. That process is actually a perpetuation of the process of Creation. In "imitating" the Creator, the poet "creates as it were in the second stage";[43] he does not usurp God's function in an illusory feeling of self-sufficiency, but rather

[40] *Ibid.*, p. 88.
[41] *Ibid.*, p. 50.
[42] *Ibid.*, p. 78.
[43] *Ibid.*, p. 45.

prolongs God's work by furthering His ways. If "to imitate the Saints is to become, precisely, an *original*, not a copy" and "like them, to become inimitable,"[44] it is also true, analogously speaking, that a true "copy" of a pattern is always an "original." It is "original" in so far as it involves the very subjectivity of the artist as Nature involves the very Subjectivity of God, so to speak. Accordingly, poetry cannot be an impersonal contemplation because it presupposes the reflexive actualization of the self. The latter is not a plenitude in itself; as with Plato or *Advaita Vedānta*, it is but a "void" deprived of any positive determinations. In Maritain's spiritual epistemology there is no pure consciousness of oneself; consciousness—as for the phenomenologists—is always consciousness of something else. Actually, the necessary presence of this "otherness" in the process of true poetic creation is the hallmark of its contemplativity. For Maritain, poetic contemplation requires another to contemplate lest it collapse into "the natural void of the human intellect when uninvaded by the *other*."[45]

We should understand at this juncture that we are confronted with two very different visions of the relationship between contemplation and poetry. On the one hand, we have a vision of poetry as a sort of supererogatory (in no way necessary) and symbolic (fundamentally allusive) "out-come" of an experience of pure consciousness—this is the general model of mystical poetry. On the other hand, we have an understanding of poetic contemplation that is predicated upon the necessity of creation as a *conditio sine qua non* for an intuitive consciousness of oneself. Raïssa Maritain has judiciously alluded to this point when referring—against those who would equate poetry and mystic contemplation—to the consistently recurring feeling of a failure that haunts those who would be "pure poets":

> It is strange, if poetry and mysticism are indistinguishable ... that all the poets should have the feeling of that great defeat which perpetuates itself and of which Aragon once spoke.[46]

The true poet is aware that his art—even if "inspired" and touched upon by grace—cannot give access to a stable enjoyment of poetic presence and

---

[44] *Ibid.*, p. 79.

[45] Maritain perceives in much of contemporary art, particularly that of the Cubists and Naturalists, an inability to "contemplate" the "object" or the "other," which is the symptom of a self-engrossed and Luciferian angelism.

[46] Jacques and Raïssa Maritain, *The Situation of Poetry*, p. 73.

consciousness, much less to a spiritual station. Raïssa Maritain accounts for the fundamental distinction between the poet and the mystic on the basis of the plausible assumption that the poet is chiefly interested in the Word whereas the mystic aims at Silence. The poetic word of the mystic is not an end but rather the superabundant flow that is added "by grace" to the full unfolding of his or her contemplative experience.[47] As for poets, one may still wonder whether some of them do not in a sense tend toward the same Silence that the mystic chooses as his goal. It is difficult to exclude *a priori* the possibility that a poet may conceive of his words as a kind of symbol of Silence, and a door opened onto It. Jacques Maritain has asked the question: "why should the song stop?"[48] The answer he proposes points to the reality of a silence that is not the absence of sound but the essence of words and music:

> As the time of the world shall one day emerge into the instant of eternity, so music should cease only by emerging into a silence of *another order*, filled with a substantial voice, where the soul for a moment tastes that time no longer is.[49]

However relevant the above distinction might be, and even if the genuinely poetic mode of consciousness cannot be understood as a purely spiritual perception, it is nonetheless not exclusive of transcendence since it presupposes the sudden appearance of something that is neither the subject nor the object, nor yet both of them. It is clear that for Maritain, poetry entails a mode of transcendence that is the very essence of its coming into being. With respect to this, the tripartite composition of man is used as a paradigm the better to understand the dynamics of creation. Maritain refers to the body (*soma*), soul (*psyche*), and spirit (*noūs*) of the poem in order to illustrate the respective functions of its constituents. In this respect, it may be useful to remember that, in Aristotelian psychology, the soul is the form of the body, and the spirit—or rather, the intellective aspect of the soul—is the form of the soul, i.e., in its vegetative and sensitive aspects. In Maritain's analysis, the body of the poem amounts to the prosodic and linguistic elements of which

---

[47] "Although it very often happens that the mystic feels the need to describe his experience, the fact remains that for him the expression is not a means of completing the experience, is in no way necessary to its conclusion and perfection; it is only a result of superabundance, a generous attempt at communication" (*Ibid.*, p. 34).

[48] Jacques Maritain, *Art and Poetry*, p. 82.

[49] *Ibid.*, p. 82.

it is constituted, whereas its soul corresponds to the "animic language" of the poet, the content of his soul, or else the intent he has in view. As for the spirit, which is also the intelligible form of poetry, Maritain cannot find a better way to define it than by referring to it as "poetry."[50]

It is interesting to note that the denotative identity between the art, its process, and its "spirit" clearly indicates that the latter element is the fundamental component of poetic creation. This "indefinable" element is almost independent from the other two, at least in the sense that its radiance utterly subsumes the body/soul of the poem. The vocabulary used by Maritain to express the relationship between body/soul and the spirit suggests a break from the purely Scholastic apparatus of his reflection upon poetry:

> I think … that there is "magic" in a work when the spirit transcends the soul, is a way separate from it—like the *Nous* of Aristotle that entered by the door—and when the soul and the body find themselves in regard to the spirit as it were annihilated, I mean to say they become together, the soul like the body of the work, the pure *instrument* of an alien spirit, a sign through which passes a superior causality, the sacrament of a separate poetry that makes a game of art.[51]

The reference to an "alien" reality is in itself the indication of a discontinuity that is the very hallmark of true poetry. The spirit of poetry descends upon the linguistic and psychic substance of the poem as if in a sudden fixation that is utterly independent of it and without which it is nothing but a conglomeration of words. We are not here in the domain of natural or mechanical "causality": there are so to speak no secondary causes to the inception of poetry. To speak of a sacrament is, for a Christian writer, the highest and most authentic expression of an experience that is after all outside the confines of the supernatural life to which the Church may give access. If art is understood as *technē*, then it is quite clear that poetry transcends this realm.

It is, however, quite interesting to note the fact that Maritain does not stop short at his tripartite division of the poem on the model of the human compound: by adding a fourth element, which he refers to as "grace," he

---

[50] *Ibid.*, p. 99.
[51] *Ibid.*, p. 100.

implicitly rejects the Platonic vision of the Divine as being one with the spirit (and therefore in a sense with the springing forth of poetry); the allusion to grace may be thus understood as a way of situating the Divine beyond the level of aesthetics. Quoting Plotinus, for whom "grace is superior to beauty,"[52] Maritain interprets this distinction in terms that make it impossible to equate poetry and religion or mysticism. In other words, there can be a truly "poetic" and "beautiful" poetry that is not suffused by "grace." The fact that Maritain refers to this fourth level under two very different terms, "grace" and "magic" seems to indicate a measure of uneasiness or at least uncertainty as to the status of the highest poetry. In the vocabulary of a Christian philosopher such as Maritain, the term "magic" is not without certain ambiguous or negative connotations. Magic may be black or white whereas grace is purely and exclusively a divine dispensation; this remark points to a fundamental dimension of the practice of poetry: "the danger of magic arises from the fact that it is the gift of an order exterior or superior to art."[53] It is not quite clear whether we should understand this sentence as referring to "art" as different from "poetry" (i.e., as "technique") or more generally to all that pertains to beauty and poetic creation. If we choose to understand it in the latter sense, we must then infer that "magic" comes very close to falling into the category of "inspiration" or "possession" as it is described in Plato's *Ion*.

For Maritain, as in Plato, poetry is not so much understood as a contemplative discipline *stricto sensu* but rather as a somewhat unintelligible "dispensation" that bears no direct causal relation to the technical and animic modalities that it entails. If Plato did not envisage a "danger" in poetic *mania* (apart from the possibility of being mistaken in confusing it with actual art or knowledge) the reason is no doubt that the spiritual climate of the Hellenic tradition did not foster a clear-cut spiritual and moral delineation between the Divine and the demonic. In keeping with the overall spirit of mythological and "shamanistic" traditions such as his, Plato was not intent on such a distinction; Bacchic *mania*, as erotic madness, is by definition ambiguous and cannot be envisaged from a moral standpoint. For Maritain on the other hand, the mediumistic function of the poet places him in a particularly perilous situation in that it leaves him without protection against, or control over, the most tenebrous sources of inspiration. Even celestial gifts may be too heavy to bear, inducing imbalance and fall.

---

[52] *Ibid.*, p. 100.
[53] *Ibid.*, p. 101.

As for "contemplative" and "artistic" techniques for the acquisition of grace, they are obviously doomed to fail since the latter has no common measure with its "material" substratum. The transcendence and "gratuitousness" of grace place the poet in a situation in which he can never rely on a stable center that he would contemplate; he must, on the contrary, exercise the *"eccentric* virtues" that are conducive to his constant striving toward the Source, which is constantly higher and further than himself. The contemplative practice of poetry is not a pure repose in being; it is rather an unending voyage in search of a transcendence that can only be the horizon of a longing gaze. There is little doubt that sensualist epistemology and the emphasis on the material nature of man—his separation from the Divine Spirit—are the foundations of such an understanding of the ways of poetry.

We also note that Maritain does not seem to explicitly raise the question of the finality of poetry outside of the context of knowledge. It is difficult to perceive what would be left of poetry if it were not for the intellective contemplation that it affords. We do not even find here the all too common idea, expressed by Etienne Gilson among others, according to which a poem is "desirable for its own sake,"[54] a definition that dangerously borders on the principle of art for art's sake. Another important point to stress is that the "body" of the work is not simply subordinate to its "spirit," it is also subsequent to it, as if the creative intellect were to be clothed in the linguistic and prosodic material that is its accompaniment. In fact, the "material" substance of the poem is rather conceived by Maritain as an unfolding of the creative idea itself. The latter is instantaneous, simple, "transcendent," and "unlimited" in regard to the produced work itself. In other words, it is quite clear that poetry is altogether dependent, at all of its levels, upon the creative knowledge from which it entirely proceeds. Poetry is not a kind of addendum to form, it is the essence of form. Poetic contemplation is "simple" in the sense that it contains *in potentia* its entire object, and it is transcendent and unlimited as God's infinite creative power.

Maritain is not as much interested in the horizontal relationship between the body and the soul of the poem as he is intent on unveiling the dynamics of the process of creation. The body of the poem is not essential to the definition of poetry, and there is in fact little mention of formal matters in Maritain's reflections upon poetry. By contrast, Etienne Gilson, another contemporary neo-Scholastic theorist of poetry, tends to apprehend poetry in the context of

---

[54] Etienne Gilson, *Forms and Substances in the Arts*, p. 211.

the particular relationship between language and meaning. Contrasting the prosaic use of language, based upon the primacy of conveying a meaningful message, and that of poetic language which is more or less independent of that primacy, Gilson suggests that the poet does not primarily seek to be understood but rather to "create a verbal structure whose real meaning is the beauty proper to it."[55] In poetic contemplation, beauty is clearly defined as an end in itself; beauty is the meaning of poetry. The element of gratuitousness that is part and parcel of poetic creation is not necessarily dependent upon the metrical form of a poem, since that element may be present even in prose while some poems that are too didactic may lack it. Now, the term "meaning" should not mislead us into thinking that poetry has no meaning of its own. This meaning is of a different nature, pertaining to the realm of aesthetics and not to that of thinking reason. In this sense, Gilson follows in the steps of the Platonic and Augustinian understanding of beauty as the "splendor of the truth." Poetic beauty, or in fact beauty in general, is indeed intelligible, but it is so in a way that is dependent upon formal manifestations:

> The true always partakes of the intelligible, but artistic beauty partakes in the intelligible perceived in sensible experience.[56]

Truth is not some element that would be added to beauty, as in didactic art, but the very essence of beauty. The more authentically truth is conveyed by beauty, the truer to its essence poetry will be. In the highest poetry, the "logical" expression (the *logos*) is simultaneously a "poetical" (the *poiesis*) utterance. In their essential core, "poetry" and "logic" are one; and it is through a profound attention to this mystery—which is all the more paradoxical for modern minds—that Emerson associated the Son of the Christian Trinity with the Sayer and with Beauty, the Father with the Knower and the True, and the Spirit with the Good and the Doer.[57] The *Logos* or the Word is both "revelation" and "beauty." It is like the outward manifestation of Divine

---

[55] *Ibid.*, p. 215.

[56] *Ibid.*, p. 225.

[57] "For the universe has three children, born at one time, which reappear, under different names, in every system of thought, whether they be called cause, operation and effect; or, more poetically, Jove, Pluto and Neptune; or theologically, the Father, the Spirit and the Son; but which we call here, the Knower, the Doer, and the Sayer. These stand respectively for the love of truth, for the love of good, and for the love of beauty" (Ralph Waldo Emerson, "The Poet," in *Self-reliance and Other Essays*, p. 67).

Knowledge. Likewise, poetry may appear to us as an aesthetic crystallization of intuitive knowledge. This is obviously not to say that all poetry is a pure manifestation of reality: in fact, its very "materiality," in terms of both conceptual and animic components, most often entails a kind of "impurity" that may distract the reader from its essential meaning. As A.E. Housman perceptively remarked, one may love a poem for all kinds of reasons that have nothing to do with poetry.[58] Poetry has achieved its highest potentiality when it presents us with a beauty that cannot be severed or dissociated from the insight into reality that it conveys. This ability presupposes that poetry may reach the very depth of human and terrestrial existence.

"A Poem is the very image of life expressed in its eternal truth," wrote Shelley in his *Defence of Poetry* (9.59); and the contrast that he draws between the factual "insignificance" of the narrative—"a catalogue of detached facts"—and the "unchangeable forms of human nature, as existing in the mind of the creator, which is itself the image of all other minds"[59] suggests that the function of poetry can be the quintessential meaning of existence. As spiritual contemplation, poetry is a sort of shortcut that takes us directly into the fundamental substance of things. Whence the contrast between the relative ontological "poverty" that is the reverse side of the outward plenitude of the narrative—the 19th century novel would be a case in point—and the inexhaustible richness of the synthetic mode of poetic expression.

It is interesting to note in this regard that the polysemic character of poetry, which clearly differentiates poetic language from narrative discourse, is akin to the inexhaustible dimension of sacred utterance in the traditional world. Poetic language, through its synthetic and essential mode of apprehension of reality, entails a tendency toward the plenitude of its potentiality. The contemplative apprehension of language is primarily an attention to the latent wealth of meaning that it contains and to its polyphonic verbal articulations.[60] This wealth of meaning and associations of meaning reaches beyond the

---

[58] "I am convinced that most readers, when they think that they are admiring poetry, are deceived by inability to analyze their sensations, and that they are admiring, not the poetry of the passage before them, but something else in it, which they like better than poetry" (A.E. Housman, *Selected Prose*, p. 185).

[59] Percy Bysshe Shelley, *Defence of Poetry*, 9.60.

[60] A poetical gift is akin to an acute sensibility to the unlimited meaning that is immanent in language: "Poetic genius certainly is attributable to this innate gift, a kind of co-naturality between a sensibility and the forms of a certain language which enables the writer to demonstrate the incantatory power of words by choosing them and by arranging them in such a way that their action is brought to bear in all its force and which no sin against their musicality prevents from coming into being, or destroys" (Etienne Gilson, *Forms and Substances*, p. 233).

intention of the poet; its synthetic and immediate character makes it akin to the eternal—it takes poetry out of the diachronic sequence as such—and allows for an unfolding that is never totally actualized. Following Shelley's intuition of the relationship between poetry and time, one can acknowledge that time "forever develops new and wonderful applications of the eternal truth which it (poetry) contains."[61] What Shelley does not make explicit—and this is the key to the infinite unfolding of poetry—is the intimate relationship between the original poetic intuition and the plenitude of the instant. In poetry, the instant is the key to eternity, as particularity is the key to the universal. As Baudelaire has pointed out in the preface to his *Flowers of Evil*, poetry is like an alchemical process through which the poet extracts a quintessential sap from phenomena, be they seemingly ugly or ordinary. Shelley's simile points to the same operation: "A story of particular facts is as a mirror which obscures and distorts that which should be beautiful: Poetry is a mirror which makes beautiful that which is distorted."[62] The distortion and obfuscation brought about by most of narrative fiction stems from the absence of a contemplative centering and synthesis that is part and parcel of an overly-literal attention to particulars. Reality becomes "obscured" by the mirror inasmuch as the narrative writer must inscribe his story in the accidental sequence of time and in the contingent diversity of occurrences and episodes.

It could of course be argued that the principles of selection and focus entail a kind of synthetic and meaningful rendering of reality that might reveal some of its essential dimensions. However, this "poetic" aspect of the narrative is always dependent upon the limitations inherent in the genre such as the prevalence of particulars and time sequences. In poetry, on the contrary, the distortion that results from the fragmented accidentality of the real is as if corrected by the contemplative lens of the poet, who is able to perceive and to convey a sense of depth, timelessness, and symbolic resonance. When Shelley alludes to the "secret alchemy (of poetry that) turns to potable gold the poisonous waters which flow from death through life,"[63] he no doubt has in mind the ability of poetry to keep reality from the "rotting" effect of time and death, an ability that is fundamentally the hallmark of symbolic imagination. The latter is a defense against death in the sense that it perceives the imperishable symbol within its envelope of flesh. Or again, as Shelley

---

[61] Percy Bysshe Shelley, *Defence of Poetry*, 9.62.

[62] *Ibid.*, 9.59.

[63] *Ibid.*, 43.303.

puts it in a most suggestive way: "it strips the veil of familiarity from the world, and lays bare the naked and sleeping beauty which is the spirit of its forms."[64] There could not be a clearer expression of the fact that poetry is *a priori* defined by the quality of its contemplative gaze. The practice of poetry does not consist in seeing another reality that would pertain to a distant realm of imagination, nor in projecting phantasmal associations, but in cultivating a sense of wonderment before the world.

Baudelaire has articulated this essential characteristic of poetry in referring to three states of consciousness that present us with a qualitative mode of contemplation which is analogous to that of genuine poetry. In his essay, "The Painter of Modern Life," Baudelaire mentions convalescence as a psychophysical state in which reality may be apprehended in all its immediacy, as it springs forth from the naught so to speak. Relating convalescence to childhood, Baudelaire emphasizes the importance of "curiosity" in the make-up of a true poet:

> Now, convalescence is like a return to childhood. A convalescent person enjoys to the highest degree, as a child, a faculty of being keenly interested in things, including those that may seem apparently the most trivial.[65]

This curiosity is not to be confused with the superficial feeling that may arise from mere passivity and boredom. On the contrary, it is founded upon a most lively and active attentiveness to the spectacle of the world. This receptivity is heightened by a sense of "novelty"; and here again novelty has no relationship with the need for variety that would result from a blasé perception of reality. On the contrary, the poetic and contemplative sense of novelty results from an ability to consider phenomena independently of the customary associations that tend to dull the originally sharp perception of reality with which mankind is endowed. "The child sees everything as for the first time (*en nouveauté*); he is always inebriated."[66] For inebriation, like convalescence and childhood, whether it be induced by stimulants or simply by a particular animic state, is characterized by a modification and an intensification of perceptions. However, the obvious difference between

---

[64] *Ibid.*, 43.303.

[65] Charles Baudelaire, "Le peintre de la vie moderne," in *L'art romantique*, p. 59 (my translation).

[66] *Ibid.*, p. 58.

childhood, drunkenness, and convalescence on the one hand, and poetic receptivity on the other hand, is that the latter may combine a heightened and refined sense of perception with a no less strong and lucid ability to translate that perception into concepts, images, and words. Poetry is therefore situated at the intersection of receptivity and creativity.

Baudelaire provides us with a major key to an understanding of poetic perception when he writes that in some occurrences a given phenomenon is the opportunity for an unveiling of the "profundity of life," thereby becoming a symbol of that profundity. The notion of symbol refers in this case to the power of phenomena to unveil a level of reality that could neither be perceived nor expressed without them. The symbol is by definition double: it has both a dimension of literalness and depth of meaning. Poetic vision is not characterized by dualism; it is rather an immediate and simple perception of both levels in one. This is precisely why the poet is particularly sensitive to the "novelty" of that which he contemplates: for what is blasé perception if not an inability to perceive the ground from which every phenomenon draws its freshness and its originality?

As far as the properly creative side of poetry is concerned, we are confronted with the same oneness in duality that we have just mentioned. As Octavio Paz has remarkably encapsulated the matter, poetic language is a way of restoring or suggesting a sense of ontological unity through language:

> Language (in poetry) goes beyond the circle of relative meanings, the *this* and *that*, and says the unsayable: stones are feathers, this is that.[67]

Far from the separative function of purely rational language, poetic language—which is akin to magic and to mystical modes of apprehending reality—suggests more than "imaginary" correspondences: rather, it suggests ontological identities.

The "this is that" is of utmost importance when considering the contemplative dimension of poetry: contemplation is a way of restoring a sense of ontological unity by transcending the segmented and oppositional perceptions of ordinary consciousness. In "saying the unsayable" poetry reveals its most profound affinity with contemplation, if the latter is to be understood (as it is in the Christian tradition), as a silent, synthetic, and

---

[67] Octavio Paz, *The Bow and the Lyre*, p. 97.

motionless consciousness of presence, a consciousness that is moreover not mediated by the discursive faculty. If one is to distinguish, as does Frithjof Schuon, between two fundamental modes of apprehension of the divine in human experience, one being centered on consciousness of truth and the intellective faculties, and the other on presence and existential totality,[68] then it seems that both poetry and contemplation lie at the junction of these two domains. On the one hand, contemplation presupposes a dimension of consciousness without which there could not even be any subjective foundation for the act of contemplating: contemplation in this sense results from an intellectual awareness that triggers the contemplative process. In Christian mysticism, discursive meditation is therefore often conceived as a preparatory stage for contemplation. On the other hand, unlike meditation that proceeds through the mind, contemplation cannot be limited to an activity of the latter since it is characterized by a sense of unity and wholeness that must pervade the entire subject and determine his total being. In a sense, contemplation can be defined as an effusion of spiritual consciousness within the entire existential space of man. In a kind of reverse analogy, it could be said that poetry stems from an experience that is crystallized into the intellectual beauty of the poem. The experience that we have in mind is one in which the instant appears in all clarity as the catalyst of a participation in the unity of being.

This unity is primarily experienced in and through the image. Far from being merely an indirect device of ornamentation, the image springs forth as an occurrence of the unity of the whole. As Octavio Paz has noted, "it does not dwell in the realm of succession, which is precisely the realm of relative opposites, but it is in each moment."[69] Succession is a mode of differentiation and otherness: in it identity is corroded by difference. The impermanence of being is a case in point. Only the present which is available to us in the form of the instant can deliver being in its indissociable unity. It is this instant which is the "timeless moment" in which the existential intuition must rest to produce the crystal of a poem. It would however be inaccurate to consider the intuition and the act of poetic creation as two distinct moments: in fact consciousness of presence and its formalization in the poem remain practically indivisible.

---

[68] "The saving manifestation of the Absolute is either Truth or Presence, but it is not one or the other in an exclusive fashion, for as Truth It comprises Presence, and as Presence It comprises Truth" (Frithjof Schuon, *Form and Substance in the Religions*, p. 1).

[69] Octavio Paz, *The Bow and the Lyre*, p. 88.

Proceeding from presence to consciousness, but in a way that is instantaneous in proportion to its profundity, poetry may be deemed as the exact complement of contemplation. We could also recapitulate the cycle of poetic creation as follows: meditation connects concepts and sharpens consciousness through repeated exercise until the mind is as if instantaneously fixed in the integral sense of presence that involves one's whole being. This presence may then become the foundation for a conscious crystallization that finds its perfect expression and outcome in the poem.

So we see that the process just described is akin to Maritain's understanding of poetry, if it is to be understood as a coming to consciousness, through poetry, of a non-articulated and supra-conscious mode of presence that is our essence, or our heart. To express the matter in Paz's words: "the poem makes us remember that which we have forgotten: this that we really are."[70] And again, this manifestation of the most remote aspect of ourselves— our forgotten self—emerges through the identification between subject and object. The object actualizes a hidden or potential dimension of the subject while the subject actualizes an implicit and unarticulated dimension of the object. Central to this process is the image, which brings together language and reality in the poetic unity of the instant, and consecrates agreement between the subject and the object. Or else, it could be said that the poem highlights the coincidence between language and being, a coincidence in and through which we know who we fundamentally are. It must be strongly emphasized that this double actualization through coincidence is in fact the very model of a contemplative and mystical reading of sacred scriptures. The phenomenological approach of Henry Corbin has masterfully unveiled this fundamental aspect of contemplative reading. In his analysis of Biblical and Qur'ānic hermeneutics in the context of contemplative mysticism, Corbin highlights the fact that the contemplative reader of the Scripture actualizes, through reading, potential aspects of his own self that had remained until then latent, and he does so by actualizing aspects of the limitless semantic treasury of the sacred text. There is a spiritual reciprocity in the encounter between the soul and the text; spiritual exegesis is a modality of inner contemplative rebirth.[71]

---

[70] *Ibid.*, p. 94.

[71] Cf. Henry Corbin, *Histoire de la philosophie islamique*, "L'exégèse spirituelle du Qorān," pp. 13-30.

Extrinsic explanation or justification can only point to or suggest the integral sense of unity that pervades such a poetic experience. To explain what the poem is and what its meaning is may be possible, and even necessary, within the realm of discursive understanding; but one must acknowledge the limits of this approach if one is to understand the poem as consciousness of presence. This is why the image can be considered as an end in itself, not that it would be an art for art's sake, but in the sense that being a symbol—in the plenary sense of this term—it incarnates the reality which it symbolizes; it thus reaches what it means in the very act of its crystallization. When speaking of presence, we implicitly speak of a mode of presentation, i.e., of making present, which is the hallmark of true poetry. In this connection, Octavio Paz seems particularly well inspired when he characterizes poetic language as a way of "presenting," in contrast to the "representative" dimension of common language:

> Language (in the poetic sense) goes beyond the circle of relative meanings, the *this* and the *that*, and says the unsayable: stones are feathers, this is that. Language indicates, represents; the poem does not explain or represent: it presents. It does not allude to reality; it tries to re-create it—and sometimes succeeds.[72]

This presentation must somehow be made possible by the very mode of contemplative presence of the poet in the world. It is by virtue of this attentive presence that the poet is able to "reveal" or "produce" the world, in and through the poem, in all its freshness and depth.

[72] Octavio Paz, *The Bow and the Lyre*, p. 97.

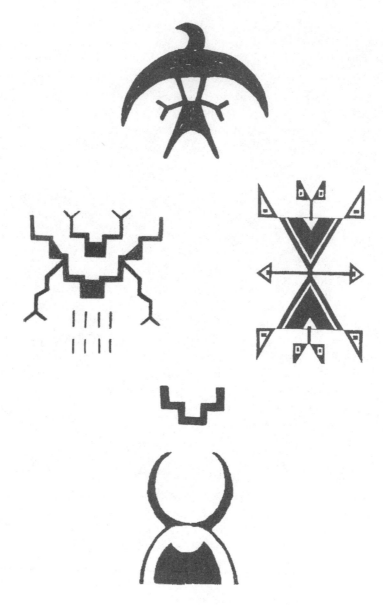

VI. American Indian pictographs

6. Singing the Sacred Way
Poetry and Shamanism

Trying to spell out the characteristics of the relationship between poetic language and the sacred within the context of the diverse body of beliefs and practices that have come to be referred to as shamanism is a complex task. This religious concept covers a very wide range of manifestations throughout time and space, making generalizations difficult, even hazardous. Still, it could be argued that the main characteristic that distinguishes it from other religious identities lies in the fact that it is less a "confession of faith" than a generic type of relationship with the invisible and the divine within and through nature. The term "shamanism" itself stems from a universalization of the local and specific sorts of religious belief and practice indigenous to the Ural-Altaic peoples of Central and Northern Asia. The word "shaman" was borrowed from the Tungus language.[1] A clear indication of the tension between the formal diversity of shamanism and its more universal traits or tendencies is evidenced in the fact that the term "shaman" is not widely recognized by shamanistic peoples themselves, and that they make use of their own vernacular term to refer to the central human figure of their religious universe.[2] The Yakut *ojun*, the Lakota *wicasa wakan*, the Mapuche *machi*, the Zulu *sangoma*, the Australian *karadji*, the Dayak *manang*, and the Korean *mudang*, are but a few examples of this fact.[3] Although there has been a great deal of debate among specialists concerning the proper definition of shamanism, or even the very possibility of such a generic definition, a relatively small number of components may be deemed to enter most, if not all, forms of religious practices referred to as shamanistic.

A first feature that distinguishes shamanism from most other religious phenomena, as indicated above, is a strong measure of *cultural particularity* that links each of its manifestations to a given people and a given land. Shamanism is not universalist in the sense in which Buddhism or Christianity are, although the specific people practicing it often consider themselves as

---

[1] An earlier etymological interpretation of the term had its derivation from the Pali *samana* by way of the Chinese *sha-men*. This interpretation is rejected by most scholars.

[2] See Jean-Patrick Costa, *Les Chamans, hier et aujourd'hui*, p. 16.

[3] Jean-Patrick Costa has included a fairly extensive list of these denominations in *Les Chamans, hier et aujourd'hui*, pp. 17-8.

the representatives of mankind and humanity *par excellence*. They are "the people," or "the real people." In shamanistic cultures the indigenous people tend to become the symbol of mankind in its totality, as this reinforces the divine "rooting" of the collective identity and experience. This characteristic has led some analysts to interpret shamanism as a preliminary step in the evolution of the religious consciousness of mankind, since the evolutionist outlook that determines the work of most scholars of religion always presupposes a "concrete" and phenomenal "simplicity" as antecedent to "abstract" universality. Accordingly, such an understanding of shamanistic religions tends to emphasize the "rudimentary" nature of its metaphysical concepts and its spiritual "dependence" upon the visible realm of nature. Needless to say, this "elementary" simplicity is in fact far from being exclusive of a high level of complexity and a profound spiritual and metaphysical insight.[4] In respect of shamanistic societies' use of language, as also their practice of archaic forms of poetry, the evolutionist line of interpretation is wont to stress the gross "naiveness" and lack of literary and conceptual sophistication. The "immediacy" of the poetic language of archaic cultures tends therefore to be interpreted along the lines of a lesser degree of "universality." In fact, within this perspective, the very appropriateness of the term "poetry" to refer to such forms of language can be called into question. When referring to an Inuit hunting song and a sonnet by Shakespeare are we entitled to use the term "poetry" to refer to both? This question cannot but be addressed, directly or indirectly, in the following pages.

A second feature, profoundly connected to the previous one, lies in a strong awareness of *nature and the cosmos* as repositories of divine and invis-

---

[4] Jean Servier has rightfully derided the "scientific naiveness" of a number of 20th century linguists who have correlated "primitive cultures" with "concrete language": "On s'est attaché à souligner le caractère concret des langues dites primitives. Pawell, dans *The evolution of language*, s'étonne du caractère concret des langues parlées par les Indiens d'Amérique du Nord: 'Un Indien Ponka, pour dire: un homme a tué un lapin, doit dire: l'homme, lui, un-debout, a tué-exprès-en-lançant-une flèche, le lapin,lui, un-assis....' Pawell n'a pas pensé un seul instant qu'un Indien Ponka aurait été péniblement surpris par l'imprécision de la phrase occidentale: l'homme a tué un lapin, qui laisse la porte ouverte à toutes les hypothèses et nécessite, pour être plus exacte, de nombreuses incidentes [Some have attempted to underline the concrete character of so-called primitive languages. Pawell, in *The Evolution of Language*, expresses surprise at the concrete character of the languages spoken by North American Indians: 'In order to say "a man killed a rabbit," a Ponka Indian must say, the man, him, one-standing, killed-on-purpose-by-throwing-an-arrow, the rabbit, him, one-sitted....' Pawell has not even considered that a Ponka Indian might have been surprised by the imprecise character of the Western sentence: the man killed a rabbit, which leaves the door open to all kinds of hypotheses, and requires, in order to be made more specific, numerous incident clauses]" (*L'homme et l'invisible*, pp. 194-95 [my translation]).

ible presences. In shamanism the Divine is envisaged in its psychic prolongations in man and in the animal, vegetal, and mineral realms. For shamanistic
peoples, nature is inhabited by invisible beings, and every being is endowed
with a spirit of its own, a spirit that can be addressed, used, or appeased
depending upon circumstances and needs. This, for example, is clearly illustrated by the Japanese Shintō worship of the *kami*. The Japanese word for
Shinto is *kami-no-michi*, or the "way of the *kami*," the latter referring to all
manifestations of invisible power and spiritual charisma within the natural
world, ranging from founding gods such as Ame-no-mi-naka-nushi-no-kami
to animals like foxes, as well as plants and minerals. In fact, it would be more
accurate to state that everything in creation is *kami*: "Everything, whatever its
nature, good or bad, is Kami-like," and "Whatever is, is divine spirit."[5] The
entire visible world is nothing but the outer layer of reality, many invisible
layers remaining hidden below it, or above it. There is nothing in nature that
is disconnected from the divine world. It could even be said, on the contrary,
that for men of shamanistic cultures, Nature constitutes the primary and fundamental "revelation."

The aspect of "primordiality" that has often been attributed to shamanism
is primarily connected with this "elemental reading" of the invisible within
the visible. Indeed, the shamanistic mentality is characterized by a perception
of the entire field of nature as "symbolic," thereby pointing to the reality of
the invisible world. This point of view does not merely consist in positing a
supernatural world beyond the realm of nature; nor does it amount to denying
that there is more to reality than the phenomenal envelope of nature. Both
these viewpoints would be ways of misunderstanding shamanism, either out
of a desire to project alien theological concepts onto it, or—often as a mis-
guided reaction to the previous attitude—out of a concern to keep any sense
of transcendence out of the shamanistic "picture." Spirits are both within and
beyond natural existence. As Gilbert Durand has suggestively put it, for the
symbolic psyche of men of the pre-modern era, the symbol is "the epiphany
of the mystery."[6] The symbol is not an abstract and arbitrary representation
of something else; it is the very presentation of the self-same invisible reality through the translucid veil of visible creatures. The implications of this
central idea for the study of shamanistic language and poetry can hardly be
overemphasized. As we will see, if there is a shamanistic "poetry" it stems

[5] J.W.T. Mason, *The Meaning of Shinto*, pp. 58 and 61.
[6] "Le symbole ... est l'épiphanie d'un mystère," Gilbert Durand, *L'imagination symbolique*,
p.13 (my translation).

from an ability to perceive and express the symbolic and sacred character of nature.

As a third characteristic, shamanism tends to place a particular figure, the *shaman*, or *medicine-man*, at the center of the religious life of the group. The shaman enjoys a particular knowledge of the invisible world that makes him able to communicate with other planes of reality; he thereby serves as an intermediary between the world of the spirits and that of men, between the underworld, the earth, and the celestial regions. Thus, for instance, the ability of the Siberian shaman to "fly" along the axis that binds these different worlds is essential to his function and to his prestige among members of the group. The shaman is endowed with psycho-spiritual gifts and has also mastered theurgic techniques, most often under the supervision of fellow elders; these allow him to "negotiate" and "intercede" with the spiritual world in order to solve difficulties such as disease, climactic crises, and individual or collective problems that might arise within the tribal community.

With regard to our particular focus, the shaman is the manipulator of language *par excellence*, and although he is by no means the only member of the community connected to the sacred power of language, he neverthe-less enjoys the highest expertise in dealing with the virtues and dangers of the spoken word. The mode of election of the shaman varies greatly from one cultural context to the next but it more often than not entails a period of profound inner crisis that is characterized by a state of psychic chaos during which language itself is so to speak freed from its usual, ordinary, concep-tual forms and meanings. This crisis may even give rise to various modes of verbal delirium, which manifest the irruption of the invisible world within the psychic substance of the future shaman.[7] More generally speaking, the heightened inner receptivity of the shaman, particularly on the threshold of rituals, is characterized by a kind of psychic dissolution that is not uncom-monly linked to like phenomena of linguistic "explosions" and logorrhea.[8]

---

[7] "Même le symbolisme (du chaos) se laisse déchiffrer dans la 'folie' des futures chamans, dans leur 'chaos psychique': c'est le signe que l'homme profane est en train de se 'dissoudre' et qu'une nouvelle personnalité se prepare à naître [Even the symbolism of chaos can be deciphered in the 'madness' of future shamans, in their 'psychic chaos': this is a sign that the profane man is in the process of 'dissolving' and that a new personality is in the making]" (Mircea Eliade, "Expérience sensorielle et experience mystique chez les primitives," *Du corps à l'esprit*, p. 75 [my translation]).

[8] This is not to be interpreted as a loss of consciousness or a kind of ventriloquism, for it involves an acute consciousness, albeit of a different order and mode. Cf. Nora Chadwick, *Poetry and Prophecy*, pp. 17-18.

This undoubtedly amounts to reaching a *materia prima* of language through what Nora Chadwick has called "manticism," suggesting thereby a state of pure potentiality that is the prelude to the act of "poetic" creation.

A fourth recurrent character of shamanistic cultures is the presence of a *mythology*, or more often segments of mythology,[9] which account for the existence of the world as it is, and define the identity of the group within the economy of this world, particularly in terms of a specific eminence or difference. The Greek notion of *mythos*, from the meaning of word or story, is particularly apt to convey a sense of this association between word and creation. The idea that the world was "spoken out" or "sung" is to be found in many shamanistic and archaic cultures of the world. There is perhaps no better illustration of this idea than the beautiful Australian myth of the "singing" and "making" of the various places that constitute the Australian continent;[10] a myth teaches that all places on the continent were "qualified" and "named" by the songs of the divine-animal Ancestors, who wandered across the land, singing along tracks and ending their mythic journeys in places and beings into which they "transformed" and in whom they have remained "present" till this day. Poetry and song appear as a form of spiritual memory, as confirmed by the fact that shamanistic peoples are most often characterized by extraordinary powers of memorization.[11]

These four characteristics of shamanism—as has been suggested above—have an important bearing upon the way in which shamanistic people conceive of language, particularly language as a source of sacred power. This mysterious power is evident, for example, in the African *griot*'s use of language; so much so that it could be considered the distinctive feature of the traditional practice of the word, in contradistinction with poetry in its modern usage.[12] This is one of the reasons why the term poetry might not

---

[9] "There is a myth for each set of songs, and this myth is the key. The song myths of the tribe are very numerous, and few songs, except extemporaneous compositions, exist independently of a myth" (Washington Matthews, "Songs of Sequence of the Navajos," *The Journal of American Folklore* 7, no. 26 (July-September 1894):186).

[10] Cf. Ronald M. and Catherine H. Berndt, *The Speaking Land: Myth and Story in Aboriginal Australia*.

[11] "[The accomplished Navajo shaman] ... must commit to memory many hundreds of songs, and some of these are so sacred that not the slightest mistake can be made in repeating them without rendering void an elaborate and costly ceremonial" (Washington Matthews, "Songs of Sequence of the Navajos," p. 185).

[12] Thomas A. Hale has stressed this point in his study on the Mande *griot*: "What distinguishes the verbal art of griots and griottes from those who fulfill some of the same functions in other societies—such as poets in the Western tradition—is that the speech of these African

be quite appropriate to refer to the traditional use of language, which transcends the realm of its daily communicative function. Another reason why one might be reticent to make use of this term in our current context lies in the contemporary associations of ideas between poetic language and a higher register of discourse, one that may in fact be inaccessible to many. Now such a distinctive factor is not representative of archaic and shamanistic "poetry." This is not to say that "poems" of these kinds—or the songs, spells, prayers, and invocations that may be referred to as such—do not exhibit in their own right specific qualities that entitle aboriginal people to distinguish them, up to a point, from ordinary language. However, the simplicity, directness, and lack of "literary" effects in these pieces can be considered one of their hallmarks. There is no question here of a social delimitation of poetry in terms of class distinctions. In fact, if the social dimension is to be considered apart, the chances are that the practice of "poetry" will be associated either with "outcast" individuals—such as many shamans—who do not fit into the ordinary categories of society, or with a social omnipresence of "poetic creation" along virtually all tribal categories, or again with some social stigma attached to the "poet" as representative of the lower classes. The latter case is exemplified in the Korean world of shamanism, that of *kut* and *p'ansori*. The Korean shaman (most often a woman, a *mudang*, rarely a man, a *p'ansu*), who creates and performs shamanistic incantations and hymns, is consistently considered as belonging to the lower strata of society.[13] This social situation is reflected in the relative lack of literary qualities (as defined by the "literate" culture) of her creation.[14] This granted, it must be added that the aesthetic value intrinsically attached to our current understanding of poetry is certainly not absent from the shamanistic use of language—which we might refer to as "primordial poetry"—while yet not occupying a place as central as it does in poetry as commonly understood today.

Having laid out these preliminary orientations, we can now turn to the question of determining which forms of shamanistic language possess the

---

wordsmiths combines both poetic art and, in many cases, a much less clearly defined power. In the Mande world it is known as *nyama*" (*Griots and Griottes*, p. 114).

[13] This may be due in part to the contrast between the "aristocratic" Confucian culture and the shamanistic, archaic practices that predate the latter and tend to be associated with the popular classes. The Chinese contrast between "literate" Confucianism and popular Taoism presents us with an analogous case.

[14] "Since the *mudang* belongs to the lowest social class and has almost no formal education, her songs, oracles and prayers are neither eloquent nor refined" (Jung Young Lee, *Korean Shamanistic Rituals*, p. 40).

quality of "poetry," the latter being defined, for our current purpose, as a type of language that cannot be reduced to the communicative function of daily social interaction and involving, moreover, an aesthetic sense for the sacredness of both language and nature. In considering the shamanistic way of being in the world, we can discern an initial category which has to do with prayer, understood here in the general sense of spoken words addressed to invisible beings, or to the Supreme Mystery. There is virtually no shamanistic poetry that is not informed by a sense of prayer. Prayer, in this context, is neither strictly personal nor truly collective in the sense in which "canonical" prayers are universally accessible to and in fact "prescribed" for all members of a given religious community. In a sense, most of the prayers that we find in anthologies of Amerindian poetry pertain to modes of sacred expression that fall somewhere between the two aforementioned categories. If personal prayer is to be understood as a free and "informal" expression of gratitude and petition before the Divine, one can consider many of these as shamanistic "poems."

It must be added, however, that what makes them "poems" is not so much their character of "personal prayer" as it is the "archetypical" value that is inherent in them; it is this which gives them a meaning and effectiveness beyond the purely individual instance in which they arose. This "archetypical" value stems primarily from a sense of adoration, respect, and deep attentiveness to creatures and natural forces. To be more specific, the intention of "shamanistic poetry" is not primarily to produce a beautiful song or poem, since the functional aspect of the art comes first. This function may be spiritual properly speaking, as with prayers and ritual songs, or psycho-spiritual as with protective spells, or else simply psychological in the case of extemporaneous songs. This does not mean that beauty is not an important aspect of such productions; it simply means that beauty is not self-consciously sought as such; rather, it proceeds from a kind of adjustment between man, nature, and their common "language," which is "beauty" in a deeper sense.

The language of shamanism being oral, it is fundamentally connected to the voice and to the breath, thereby sharing in the air as a principle of unity[15] between all beings.[16] The human language of poetry and the language of

---

[15] This is the connecting function of breath and air. It is exemplified by the Cheyenne *taxtavoom*, the domain of wind and air, which connects *votostoom* (the middle world) and *setovoom* (the near sky). See Karl H. Schlesier, *The Wolves of Heaven*, p. 6.

[16] "As the experiential source of both psyche and spirit, it would seem that the air was once felt to be the very matter of awareness, the subtle body of the mind. *And hence that awareness,*

creation meet in this enveloping omnipresence of the "air."[17] The beauty of human language lies in an harmonious connection between human feelings, nature, and the particular function, situation, or context that associates them. In this sense shamanistic poetry is nearly always akin to "spells," the Latin term for the latter, *carmina*, referring in fact to poetry, and stemming from the same traditional understanding of the function of sacred language. Whether it be defined as "prayer" or as "spell," shamanistic poetry is consistently characterized by a sense of power. As John Bierhorst puts it within the context of Native American shamanism:

> The belief that words in themselves have the power to make things happen—especially words in extraordinary combinations—is one of the distinguishing features of native American thought; and it may be said that for the people who share this belief a connection exists between the sacred and the verbal, or, to put it in more familiar terms, a connection between religion and poetry.[18]

In shamanistic songs and "poetry" the conceptual content of the words is far less important than their animic "charge." This is why the poem may very well preserve most of its effectiveness in a translation into another language.[19] In fact, the "song" may be comprised, at least in part, of sounds that have no intelligible meaning.[20] These sounds are not entirely meaningless, however, since they are a means of "projecting" a spiritual mood or feeling via

---

far from being experienced as a quality that distinguishes humans from the rest of nature, was originally felt as that which invisibly joined human beings to other animals and to the plants, to the forests and to the mountains. For it was the unseen but common medium of their existence" (David Abram, *The Spell of the Sensuous*, p. 238).

[17] "You see the sky now
 but the earth
 is lost in it
 and there are no horizons.
 It is all
 A single breath" (Leslie Marmon Silko, *Storyteller*, p. 177).

[18] *The Sacred Path, Spells, Prayers and Power Songs of the American Indians*, ed. John Bierhorst, p. 3

[19] "For the outsider, their [Indian poems'] values lies in their vivid, highly condensed portrayal of Indian costumes, on the one hand, and, on the other, their authoritative language, which even in translation has the ability to exert an influence on the mind, if not on the physical world" (*Ibid.*, p. 3).

[20] "[The *Atsa'lei* song] … consists almost exclusively of meaningless or archaic vocables which convey no idea to the mind of the singer" (Washington Matthews, "Songs of Sequence of the Navajos," p. 185).

elemental vibrations of sound. Sounds without any apparent meaning have, in fact, a significance that transcends concepts and words, as testified by the fact that "they [the American Indians] will readily classify songs of other tribes in unknown tongues into songs of love or war or magic."[21] Two of the three categories of Lakota songs involve so-called "vocables" that have no specific meaning in Lakota language.[22] In an African context, the Mande *nyama*, or power of words, is all the stronger in that it is both unintelligible and non-referential. In praise poetry, this power stems in part from an extremely quick elocution and frequent shouting.[23] The animic "charge" is thus the truly meaningful element. It is like the projection of a mode of being, a state of soul. The singer, the orant, or the speaker exteriorizes a mode of being that is most often a result of an encounter with the power or beauty of a natural being. There is a sense of elation, or inebriation, in singing the praises of nature while participating in its aura and energy, as in these excerpts from a Navajo song honoring the earth:

All is beautiful,
All is beautiful,
All is beautiful, indeed.

Now the Mother Earth
And the Father Sky,
Meeting, joining one another,
Helpmates ever, they.
All is beautiful,
All is beautiful,
All is beautiful, indeed....

And the night of darkness
And the dawn of light,
Meeting, joining one another,

[21] Mary Austin, introduction to *American Indian Poetry: An Anthology of Songs and Chants*, ed. George W. Cronyn, p. xxxiii.

[22] Ben Black Bear Sr. and R.D. Theisz, *Songs and Dances of the Lakota*, p. 13.

[23] "The obscurity of its referential content in the performance context is an important aspect of the *nyama* of *jelikan* [speech of the griot] ... They are uttered very rapidly, at times like verbal gunfire, bombarding the noble with more sound than can be assimilated, causing confusion.... The emotion thus stirred is literally dripping with *nyama*" (Barbara Hoffman, "Power, Structure, and Mande *Jeliw*," in David Conrad and Barbara Frank [eds.], *Status and Identity in West Africa: Nyamakalaw of Mande*, pp. 41-2).

Helpmates ever, they.
All is beautiful,
All is beautiful,
All is beautiful. Indeed....[24]

Mircea Eliade has suggested a profound connection between shamanistic techniques of ecstasy and poetic creation in his classic work on the subject.[25] The central phenomenon consists in reaching a "second state" of consciousness which informs an inner language that will be the principle of poetic creation. The ecstatic state of consciousness is most often brought about by the rhythm of a drum, or by an imitation of the sounds of nature; sometimes the two means are associated. Imitative magic plays an important role in shamanistic rituals and use of language. At its height it constitutes an ability to understand the language of nature, thereby recovering, on an individual basis, the situation of harmony and connectedness between all living creatures that marked the mythological origin of mankind.[26] These uses of imitation are predicated on the belief that qualitative powers are attached to sounds and motions from the natural world, and that human beings may enter a state of participation with them. This is a manifestation of the traditional law that "like attracts like," in the sense that certain external kinds of behavior representative of animal creatures or cosmic forces may open the way to a manifestation of spirits attending these creatures and forces. In other words, and to put it very plainly, "behaving" as a bear may be a key to a precipitation of the bear spirit.[27] A Cheyenne scouting song may help suggest this phenomenon:

Wolf I am.
In darkness
In light
Wherever I search

---

[24] Cited in *American Indian Poetry*, ed. George W. Cronyn, p. 118.

[25] Cf. Mircea Eliade, *Shamanism: Archaic Techniques of Ecstasy*, pp. 510-11.

[26] "During his trance the Tungus shaman is believed to understand the language of nature" (*Ibid.*, p. 96).

[27] "Castagné describes the Kirgiz-Tatar *baqça* running around the tent, springing, roaring, leaping; he 'barks like a dog, sniffs at the audience, lows like an ox, bellows, cries, bleats like a lamb, grunts like a pig, whinnies, coos, imitating with remarkable accuracy the cries of animals, the songs of birds, the sound of their flight, and so on, all of which greatly impresses his audience.' The 'descent of the spirits' often takes place in this fashion" (*Ibid.*, p. 97).

Wherever I run
Wherever I stand...[28]

Such a possibility is based on an understanding of the psychic *materia* as a kind of plastic form that can become impregnated with cosmic qualities such as those manifested in the natural order. This also applies, *mutatis mutandis*, to the ability of many shamans to speak languages unknown to them outside of ecstatic mode.[29] In this connection, Eliade refers to the shamanistic access to a "secret language" that characterizes shamans in pre-ecstatic or ecstatic mode. This is nothing other than the language of their inner experience; it is a language that Eliade sees as a kind of "recreation" of language, a recreation that may be considered the archetypal foundation of poetic creation. Mallarmé's definition of the poet's function as "to render a purer meaning to the words of the tribe" (*rendre un sens plus pur aux mots de la tribu*), would echo this shamanistic conception of language as "poetic." This aspect of poetic creation is not unrelated to the etymological genius of a given language, in the sense of the poet's ability to reach the original semantic charge of words—even beyond concepts—at the level of the most archaic strata of language. The creative awareness and use of the etymological implications and associations of words is also, no doubt, a way of enlightening the riches of language by unveiling its principial source.

However, etymology is only one aspect, and in fact a relatively external one, in this process of the poetical renewal of language. Each authentic poet "recreates" language, not so much in the sense of "creatively" stamping the language of the community with his own individual "mark" so to speak, but rather in that he experiences afresh the nature of language as symbolic access to archetypical realities.[30] Or to put it differently, in genuine poetry a "recovery" of reality occurs which is intrinsically connected to a "rediscovery" of language. Poetic language is nothing other than the exteriorization of an ontological rediscovery. There lies the mystery of the individual nature of poetry. This mystery is distinct from—and in fact ultimately opposed to—the

---

[28] Cited in Karl H. Schlesier, *Wolves of Heaven*, p. 3.

[29] "The famous shaman Ilighin, of the vanished Kangienci tribe, who are said to have lived till the advent of the Russians on one of the eastern tributaries of the River Kolyma in north-eastern Siberia, is traditionally described as uttering incomprehensible words, 'speaking *khorro* (i.e. shaman) language,' at the climax of his incantations. This sometimes consists of a mixture of Koryak, Yakut, and Yukaghir" (Nora Chadwick, *Poetry and Prophecy*, pp. 18-19).

[30] This is also illustrated by the existence of "hidden languages" which are the exclusive province of shamans. Cf. Karl H. Schlesier, *Wolves of Heaven*, p. xiv.

individualistic claims that characterize most of contemporary poetry, even if the latter might be thought to proceed from it as a kind of shadow reflection. In shamanistic and shamanistically oriented poetry, the individual experience results from a profound encounter with the universal core of reality in a way that actualizes the particularity of a given outlook as an integrated part of that universal whole.[31] This point of view cannot be defined as individualistic, since it does not have as its starting point the insular difference of a self-reflexive consciousness mirroring the indefinite play of its own limitations and tendencies. It is why shamanistic poetry is both highly personal and fundamentally universal: it stems from a personal "opening" onto reality, and yet the poetic fruits of this opening are readily accessible to others, at least on the basis of sufficient conditions of receptivity on their part, since the "poetic" experience involves a connection with psycho-spiritual realms that are "subjectively objective" in the sense of being ontologically grounded while apprehensible "from within."

The individual, or personal, nature of this type of creative language raises the question of the "prophetic" nature of shamanistic ways. As Frithjof Schuon has pointed out, each and every American Indian of the Northern Plains is in a sense a "prophet."[32] The discovery of the invisible realm is an individual odyssey: it is achieved through "revelations" that are specific to each individual, as in the famous "vision quest" of the Indians of the Great Plains. Accordingly, a sacred "song" is sometimes revealed to the individual in a dream or a vision. Among Australian Aborigines, each and every human being receives at birth a part of the spiritual "landscape" of the spirits for which he is responsible. This landscape is also associated with a given song. There is, therefore, a profound connection between the mythic and collective entity of the Dreamtime and the most profound nature of the individual. The individual is faithful to himself by keeping his "song" integrated within the collective myth.[33] Accordingly, the world of spirits is one and the same

---

[31] The relationship between the individual and the larger group is often "mediated" by the existence of secret societies that share a common language unknown to the rest of the community. "Among the Kwakiutl tribe, girls, young women, and old women have separate secret societies from those of the men, and these, no doubt, have their own peculiar songs" (Alexander F. Chamberlain, "Primitive Woman as Poet," *Journal of American Folklore* 16, no. 63 [October-December 1903]:208).

[32] "An original feature of the Indian tradition is that the 'prophetic' element, which elsewhere crystallizes in rare *avatāras*, is spread out so to speak over all the members of the tribes, without for that abolishing the differences in degrees and the crucial manifestations" (Frithjof Schuon, *The Feathered Sun: Plains Indians in Art and Philosophy*, p. 19).

[33] "Every Aboriginal person, at birth, inherits a particular stretch of song as his private property,

for all members of a given spiritual collectivity or tribe, but the modalities, aspects, and goals of human contact with it greatly vary from one individual to the next, as they define the function of a given person within the spiritual economy of the whole. However important the social dimension might be, it is still always the individual function that involves the most essential duties.[34] The "revealed" song shares the same dual character: it partakes in a spiritual "style" that characterizes the genius of a given tribe or a given people while being the "gift" specifically bestowed upon a particular individual. In a manner analogous to the way in which "our people" *is* mankind, each individual *is* "our people." It is as if "universality" were reached by and through a spiritual deepening of particularity.

Among American Indians the individual dimension of spiritual vocation is linked to a strong emphasis on solitary worship, and more generally a sense for each and every soul's station before the Great Mystery. The constant confrontation of man, in his metaphysical "bareness," with the immensity and majesty of Nature also confers upon the individual a kind of mystical station that relativizes collective mediations and belongings. It should be understood that this is in a sense independent from the issue of the "specialization" or "gifts" of the shaman or medicine-man, since the latter by no means has a monopoly on mankind's connection with the invisible world. Even Mircea Eliade, who tends to place a great emphasis on the role of the shaman as primary intermediary between the world of man and the supernal realm, acknowledges that the shaman is not necessarily the only "technician" of the sacred, as testified by the recurrent presence of priestly figures devoted to sacrificial duties, the central role of each and every head of family in the domestic cult of the spirits, and the involvement of every human being with the invisible since no soul may remain "foreign," to the invisible that envelops everything.[35]

---

a stretch of song that is, as it were, his title to a stretch of land, to his conception site. This land is that part of the Dreaming from whence his life comes—it is that place on the earth where he most belongs, and his essence, his deepest self, is indistinguishable from that terrain" (David Abram, *The Spell of the Sensuous*, p. 167).

[34] "But the essential in this social context is fidelity to oneself, to one's own vision, one's own pact with a particular theophany, or in other terms, with one's own 'medicine' or one's own 'totem'" (Frithjof Schuon, *The Feathered Sun*, pp. 19-20).

[35] "Throughout the immense area comprising Central and North Asia, the magico-religious life of society centers on the shaman. This, of course, does not mean that he is the one and only manipulator of the sacred, nor that religious activity is completely usurped by him. In many tribes the sacrificing priest coexists with the shaman, not to mention the fact that every head of a family is also the head of the domestic cult" (Mircea Eliade, *Shamanism*, p. 4).

In respect of the shaman, it must be noted that the same principle of spiritual "individualism" is to be found, as testified by the fact that he enjoys the inner privilege of certain prayers or spells specific to himself. Among the Ojibwa or Chippewa members of the Midéwiwin, or society of shamans,

> ... each Midé priest usually invents and prepares his own songs, whether for ceremonial purposes, medicine, hunting, exorcism, or any other use, he may frequently be unable to sing them twice in exactly the same manner.[36]

Generally speaking, it can be said that the relationship American Indians, and shamanistic peoples in general, keep up with tradition is based upon the principles of faithful transmission and individual creativity. In this respect one can speak of an harmonious complementarity between a scrupulous attentiveness to traditional heritage and a cultivation of enriching differences and adjunctions. In terms of our specific focus, it can be asserted that the "poetical" tradition that is comprised of songs, prayers, and spells is like an ever changing stream flowing along an ever identical river. A. L. Soens has told some interesting stories to illustrate this point. One of them stages "an Inuit singer (who remarked that) his best songs came to him when he left the village, sat alone on a hill, and tried phrases from the songs he liked until he had arranged them into a new song." Another is about an Apache "maker of songs" who liked to compile and modify a stock of old songs following his own inclinations and inspirations. He "used about three and worked one new song out of them."[37] There is, in this attitude, no quest for an artificial sense of artistic originality; yet neither is there any scruple about reconfiguring traditional data along one's own sense of creative freedom.

Most of what is referred to as shamanistic poetry is sung. In such a context, the act of singing can best be defined as an exteriorization of the individual soul. In a certain sense each song refers to a given soul, and every man has his song, or his songs; such is the man, such is his song.[38] Words are expressions of the individual because they exteriorize the self through their power. Poetry is a kind of growth in being. Mary Austin mentions an

---

[36] W.J. Hoffman, cited in Alexander F. Chamberlain, "Primitive Woman as Poet," p. 208.

[37] A.L. Soens, *I, the Song: Classical Poetry of Native North America*, p. xvi.

[38] "Poetry is valued primarily by the aboriginal for the reaction it produces within himself rather than for any effect he is able to produce on others by means of it" (*American Indian Poetry*, ed. George W. Cronyn, p. xxxiii).

instructive story about the nature of aboriginal "poetry" in narrating the following episode:

> On one occasion in the high Sierras I observed my Indian packer going apart at a certain hour each day to shuffle rhythmically with his feet and croon to himself. To my inquiry he said it was a song which he had made, to be sung by himself and his wife when they were apart from one another.[39]

Even when songs are shared by the group, as is often the case, the power of a given soul is manifested in the "animation" of the song by the voice of the individual. The animic projection that is actualized by the song is indicative of the identity and the function of the individual; it is an affirmation of self, not in an individualistic and prideful manner, but through a kind of "instinctive" knowledge of oneself. As for the collective dimension of "poetry," it appears in the fact that many songs are fragments, variations, and additions to a tribal story that is a kind of foundational myth. The epic character of much of what is considered as "shamanistic poetry" is in this sense not intrinsically different from the great mythological epics of Indo-European peoples, such as the Homeric poems or the Finnish *Kalevala*. The "poetic myth" encapsulates the vision of the universe of a particular group and is often integrated into major ceremonies and rituals, thereby reminding shamanistic peoples of the archetypical interconnections between the world of man and the world of the gods and nature.[40]

Shamanistic epic poetry can be characterized as a return to the origin of time, and the origin of both land and tribe. Singing the founding myth amounts to returning to the origin. It is a symbolic restoration of the "present," the ever present beginning that defines the group and its identity. This is illustrated by the opening segment of the Seneca Thank-You Prayer, narrated by the culture hero Good Mind:

> I will make the Earth where some people can walk around.
> I have created them, now this has happened.
> We are walking on it.

[39] Mary Austin, introduction to *American Indian Poetry*, ed. George W. Cronyn, p. xxxi.

[40] Cf. Paul Zolbrod, "Cosmos and Poesis in the Seneca Thank-You Prayer," in *Earth and Sky, Visions of the Cosmos in Native American Folklore*, eds. Ray. A Williamson and Claire R. Farrer, p. 26.

Now this time of day.
This is the way it should be in our minds.[41]

Most often, this myth is not narrated in its entirety; rather, it is sung in fragments that may not even be connected into a coherent whole. The repetition of certain words or expressions is often used—besides its mnemonic function—as a reminder of things as they were *in illo tempore*. Sometimes no more than a few syllables are enough to bring some of the basic events of the founding story to the mind of the auditors. Rhythmic repetition is akin to memory both as a device that makes the narration easier to "remember" and as a symbolic reinstatement of the original manner of being.[42] Singing is a way of connecting with the primal creative energy by telling of what happened at the beginning and sharing in the "magic" of this liminal creation. This principle is beautifully expressed in the following piece from the Pima creation myth:

The world is sung,
The world is finished.
The world is sung,
The world is finished.
Now it moves,
Now it stirs.[43]

In addition, the "poetry of the beginning" is a way of keeping this world going according to the principles and rules that governed its coming into existence. Poetic language is the matrix of culture, it preserves and transmits the integrity of the world in which "the people" lives. David Abram mentions, for example, how the Koyukon people from Alaska would spend many evenings telling stories of the "Distant Time," thereby making "explicit the proper etiquette that must be maintained by the (Koyukon) people when dealing with the diverse presences that surround them, the kinships that must be celebrated and the taboos that must be respected if the human community

[41] Cited in Paul Zolbrod, "Cosmos and Poesis in the Seneca Thank-You Prayer," p. 29.

[42] A.L. Soens mentions how the frequent repetition of three syllables in two verses of an Apache mourning song (*Emu kayovbak kange Tiyam onge kanga*) reminds the audience of the steps (*vak*) that the first people had to take by going (*tiym*) on their legs (*mu*) to return to the mountain Avikome after burning the body of the founding hero Matevilye. In these two verses, all other syllables have no conceptual meaning and serve simply as phonetic "fillers" (Cf. *I, the Song*, p. xvi).

[43] Cited in A.L. Soens, *I, the Song*, p. 30.

and the land are to support and sustain one another."[44] This concept is also epitomized by the Dreamtime of the Australian Aborigines, a time that precedes "our time" and that was, or is, characterized by the pre-emergence of the subtle world from which the current world issued forth. Chronologically "anterior," since it refers to the beginning of time as humans now know it, this "aboriginal" time is also ontologically "simultaneous" to the world since access to it remains a possibility—a possibility that is precisely connected to the power of the word. The near-universal association between the word—whether spoken or sung—and the appearance of the world through emanation or creation bears witness to the deepest dimension of poetry as a symbolic rehearsal and a prolongation of the cosmogonic process.

In keeping with this "poetic" focus on the origin, shamanism can be considered, at least in its highest forms, as a repository of a primordial religion antecedent to recorded history. In some cases, particularly the North American Indians of the Plains, this primordial aspect is quite clearly expressed in a metaphysics of nature and in various modes of collective and solitary orison before the Great Mystery. Some historians of religion such as Mircea Eliade have denied the "primordial" nature of shamanism on the grounds of a "diffusionism" that assigns to this religious phenomenon a specifically Siberian and Mongolian origin. In fact, Eliade is still obliged to recognize the omnipresence of shamanistic elements in virtually all archaic religions, thereby reluctantly bearing witness to the reality of a primordial shamanistic strata in the human religious experience. What seems most strikingly to characterize this primordial layer of religion is a tendency among its practitioners to envisage all invisible forms pertaining to the psychic realm as prolongations and manifestations of the highest Reality. In many cases, such an emphasis may relegate the Supreme to the status of a *deus otiosus*, who forms only the distant background of reality, and from whom mankind is, for all practical purposes, more or less disconnected.[45] The extent of this "practical disconnection" may account for the extreme diversity of "spiritual levels" in the world of shamanism.[46]

The recurrence of rhythmic numbers is a not unimportant dimension of the shamanistic "poetic spell." Some fundamental numbers, primarily three

---

[44] David Abram, *The Spell of the Sensuous*, p. 151.

[45] This "disconnection," however, is not akin to a negation, although it may result in a kind of "forgetfulness." Shamanism is never pantheistic as such since it does not reduce the Divine to Nature.

[46] With respect to shamanism at large, Frithjof Schuon mentions that "the general impression is one of the very widest differences of level" (Cf. *The Feathered Sun*, p. 23).

and four, tend to enter into the sonoral alchemy that takes place at the occasion of poem and spell singing. One can, among many other possible examples, mention the primordial value of the number four among the Navajo.[47] As for the number three it is particularly emphasized in shamanistic rituals and prayers, as in Korea where it expresses the perfection of the sacred process.[48] The centrality of the mystical numbers 7 (4+3) and 9 (3x3) in shamanistic myths and practices pertaining to the Cosmic Tree and the Celestial Ascent has also been highlighted by Mircea Eliade in his classic study.[49] Independently of the question of the specific number of phrases that are in fact repeated, it is the very principle of rhythmic repetition that is the hallmark of a magical understanding of words. The role of repetition is a complex and manifold issue in sacred poetry: its main significance appears to lie in its connective function as a nexus between unity and multiplicity. As we have suggested above, this connection flows from the traditional understanding of time as a succession of "instants" that takes us back to the first moment of creation. In this view of things, repetition is a cyclical reinstatement of the origin, a return to what has in fact never ceased to be in the upper realm of the archetypes. On a lower level, repetition is also the means of a kind of animic appropriation of the power inherent in the words. The inebriation that is often associated with repetition, particularly in prayers and spells, flows from a sharing in the vital and energetic substance of the spoken phrases. This phenomenon can be compared to an accumulation of psychic forces that is analogous to the "recharging" of a dynamic battery. This is particularly clear in shamanistic poems that sing the uplifting beauty and majesty of nature, and involve a kind of ecstatic celebration. A.L. Soens has encapsulated the deeper meaning of this celebration in beautifully suggestive terms:

> Their songs helped the singers pay attention, not to a transcendent Holiness that spurned our visible universe, but to the immanent Holiness

[47] "Among the Navajo the magic effect is made certain by the fourfold repetition of the affirming phrase, four being a sacred number" (*American Indian Poetry*, ed. George W. Cronyn, p. xxxiv).

[48] "We have noticed that one dance and *Gongsu* (divine oracle) are constantly repeated three times. The number 'three' seems to occupy an important place in Korean shamanism. It signifies completion, the fulfillment of the beginning. Thus to repeat three times means to complete or fulfill the initial intention of the ritualistic function" (Jung Young Lee, *Korean Shamanistic Rituals*, p. 38)

[49] Mircea Eliade, *Shamanism*, pp. 274-79.

that saturated it. This poetry led the singers to delight in their world as in a beatific vision.[50]

Sometimes, such celebratory rhythm and anaphora refers to this same sense of awe while focusing, subjectively, on the powers of nature as expressed through man's high deeds and the animals' energy. Such is the case in hunting songs, like this Omaha Song of the Buffalo Dance:

One I have wounded, yonder he moves,
Yonder he moves, bleeding at the mouth.

One I have wounded, yonder he moves,
Yonder he moves, with staggering steps.

One I have wounded, yonder he moves,
Yonder he falls, yonder he falls.[51]

The African genre of praise poetry demonstrates some analogous characteristics.[52] The religious attitude of awe also informs repetition in the form of the reiterative address to the spirit of an animal, just as when the hunter tries to approach his prey, or when he speaks to the soul of the animal he has killed in order to ask its forgiveness.

More generally speaking, shamanistic poetry can be characterized as effecting a "conciliation" of the highest metaphysics and the most minute practicality. The latter is generally the starting point of the contemplative attitude, the shamanistic perspective placing an emphasis on the most immediate immanence.[53] The two dimensions of attention to the most earthly phenomena and awareness of transcendence meet in a poetic observation of Nature. The attentiveness to natural cycles in motion, like the transition between winter and spring, or the succession between night and day, is one

---

[50] A.L. Soens, *I, the Song*, p. xix.

[51] Cited in *The Sacred Path*, ed. John Bierhorst, p. 128.

[52] Cf. Thomas A. Hale, *Griots and Griottes*, pp. 123-25.

[53] Commenting on the Seneca Thank-You Prayer, Paul Zolbrod notes that "the poem's focus radiates steadily outward from the centrally immediate, the stationary, the earthbound, and the concrete to the distant, the mobile, the celestial, and finally the abstract. This orderly way of observing from the nearest at hand to the most distant, or from the most immediately concrete to the most remotely abstract, is apparently fixed in the Iroquois world view" ("Cosmos and Poesis in the Seneca Thank-You Prayer," p. 46).

of the fundamental characteristics of a mentality that is still vitally associated with the phases of natural life. These kind of pieces bear witness to the attentiveness of archaic peoples to the messages of nature, but also to a "poetic sense" that has the ability to connect discrete expressions of the same qualities, like colors for example. Let us mention two beautiful occurrences of such a "reading" of nature. The first is a Navajo song:

> The Magpie! The Magpie! Here underneath
> In the white of his wings are the footsteps of morning.
> It dawns! It dawns![54]

The whiteness of dawn (*alba* in Latin) seems to emerge with the white feathers of the magpie from under the black and greenish blue cloak of his plumage. The demiurgic character of the tri-colored bird is thus seized and expressed in action—as that of a messenger—a function that is very often attributed to birds in general. There is also a kind of "demiurgic" function of the song, in the sense that it expresses and in some measure "re-creates" the dynamics of creation. It may either be suffused with majesty and attentiveness, when it expresses a sacred purpose; or it may be illustrated by a somewhat unintelligible cosmogonic unfolding, as in numerous tricksters' stories and songs. Either way, the re-occurring interconnection between singing (and breathing) and walking is at the center of this "demiurgic" power. There is no better illustration of this phenomenon than the episode of the gift of the Sacred Pipe in Black Elk's words. The Buffalo Cow Woman came walking to the tepee while singing:

> With visible breath I am walking.
> A voice I am sending as I walk.
> In a sacred manner I am walking.
> With visible tracks I am walking.
> In a sacred manner I walk.[55]

Sacred walking and sacred singing are enveloped in a spiritual aura that "ritualizes" both gesture and song. The symbolism of smoke, air, and breathing is fundamentally connected to ascending blessings. The recurrent allusion to the "sending of the voice," emanating from the "breath" or the

---

[54] Cited in *American Indian Poetry*, ed. George W. Cronyn, p. 66.
[55] Cited in John Neihardt, *Black Elk Speaks*, p. 4.

spirit indicates the connection between the word and a "new beginning" marked by a divine gift. This kind of spiritual utterance is also illustrated by a song from the *Heyoka* ceremony quoted by Black Elk:

> In a sacred manner they have sent voices.
> Half the universe has sent voices.
> In a sacred manner they have sent voices to you.[56]

There is moreover a kind of spiritual complementarity between walking on Mother Earth in a sacred manner and "sending one's voice" toward Heaven. "Tracks" and "breath" are the respective visible manifestations of two "archetypical" and therefore "invisible" ways of linking heaven and earth.

In cosmogonic accounts, singing and walking are usually associated with a "roaming" and adventuresome context that suggests the amorality of creation, while paradoxically involving moral lessons. This is true of such narratives as those involving the wandering Coyote and Iktomi, and their cosmogonic function. In this Maidu song, for example, Coyote sings of the possibilities that are about to be brought to existence by his wandering:

> My world, where one travels by the valley edge,
> My world of many mountains,
> My world where one zigzags here and there,
> Range after range.[57]

In an altogether different register, but not without analogy to the theme of exploring freedom and hardships, a word should be said about travelers' songs. They often evoke a thirst for action, deeds of courage, and high adventure, which characterizes the nomadic hunter, the warrior, or the pilgrim, as in the initial words of this Papago song that evokes the yearly odyssey of young men across the desert to the ocean in search of salt, and in quest for a vision:

> This is the story of my desire
> There was my wife's cooking that I didn't carefully eat
> My child that I didn't carefully hold
> "What does he know that he acts this way?"
> Through this my days were completed and so I could go.[58]

[56] *Ibid.*, p. 192.
[57] Cited in A.L. Soens, *I, the Song*, p. 24.
[58] Cited in *The Sacred Path*, ed. John Bierhorst, p. 72.

Drum and dance are other phenomena that both parallel and highlight this "demiurgic" power of songs. The words of the song are "energized" by the drum, which awakens the spirits and animates the soul through the voice that is its channel of expression. The drum seems to be traditionally connected to the tree, out of which it is made, as also to the animals—through its hide— and as such is a fitting symbol of the connection between heaven and earth. In many mythical poems, the drum is associated with creation and inspiration, as also is thunder, of which it is in fact a manifestation. An Alaskan Tsimshian song encapsulates the relationship between demiurgic creation, the rolling sound of the drum, and the "voices" of nature, particularly that of "demiurgic" animals—here the Raven:

> We hear only its large voice,
> A voice like a great brightness!
> The Raven Drum has returned,
> The Great Cawing,
> The great Voice of the Raven,
> Covered with pearls!
> Ahead of me, the large voice,
> Nothing but the large voice![59]

This song, which is sung in the context of a funeral, refers to an image of the Raven on the drum that accompanies the song. It therefore aptly conveys the identification between the sound of the drum and the spirit. The expressions "a voice like a great brightness" and "nothing but the large voice" probably allude to the psycho-spiritual transition between this life and the next, the Raven performing the role of psychopomp.

A word should be said about the relationship between song and dance since shamanistic poetry is often "acted out," either through dance or mime. First of all, the imperatives of dance often have a bearing on the form of songs, since one has to take into account the rhythmic dimension of dance, its repetitive patterns, and its changes of pace. More profoundly, it bears stressing that singing and dancing, poetry and dance, are both modes of exteriorization that are inspired by the "revelation" of the Spirit, or spirits, the one corresponding more closely to the soul, the other to the body. In rituals and ceremonies in which the drum "informs" and accompanies song and dance, it could be said that it manifests the Spirit, whereas the voice of

---

[59] Cited in A.L. Soens, *I, the Song*, p. 18.

the singers expresses the soul, and the motions of dancers the body. Although the song is in a way more "interior" than the dance, the latter could be seen, paradoxically, as closer to the Spirit given its character of totality.

As we indicated above, the symbolic understanding of the universe that is the hallmark of the shamanistic mentality is at the core of "primordial poetry." In this symbolic context, some parts of the natural landscape take on a striking spiritual value. One can mention, among other possible themes, the mountain and the rock on the one hand, and rain, thunder, and lightning on the other hand. The mountain is a particularly central symbol in shamanistic songs: it symbolizes the *axis mundi*, the vertical axis that links heaven and earth. Other symbols such as the ladder and the rainbow partake of this symbolic constellation. Korean shamanism shows, for example, a very strong affinity with mountains. The appearance of the Holy Mother, the spiritual ancestor of the *mudang*, takes place on Mount Chiri; and the presence of altars in the mountains of Korea is also evidence of the strong connection between the *mudang* and mountains.[60] Mountains are also symbols of power, stability, and purity, as indicated by the fact that some shamanistic hymns are placed under their auspices; as in this *Sansang Gongsu* (Oracle of the Mountain Goddess):

> There are eight peaks within the inner mountain,
> And thirteen famous places in the outer mountain,
> Within these famous mountains and the great heavens of all Buddhas,
> The great altar of the nation is protected by the great generals.[61]

Or this hymn,

> Shades are formed from mountains,
> But brooks are fashioned after the dragon.
> Like the deep brook,
> The divining power of *Sansang* is deep.
> Your nation is healthy, the government is stable,
> And the people of *Nimgom* (Korea) are peaceful and prosperous.[62]

---

[60] Jung Young Lee, *Korean Shamanistic Rituals*, pp. 5 and 11.

[61] Cited in Jung Young Lee, *Korean Shamanistic Rituals*, p. 50. It is interesting to note how a "national" shamanistic religion such as the Korean *Sinkyo* readily includes and adapts elements taken from "universal" religions such as Buddhism. This phenomenon is worldwide.

[62] *Ibid.*, p. 51.

Spiritual worship is itself informed by the mountain:

> To worship the *Pyolsang* ("deity of star from another world"),
> Let us climb up a mountain.
> We pass through the ninety-nine peaks of the mountain,
> As if searching through the falling plum flowers on the snow.[63]

Numerous Amerindian songs and poems involve mountains and rocks as embodiments of permanence, endurance, courage, and the refuge of eternity, like the Cheyenne war song "Friends, stone always remains firm, forward," or the primeval rock of the Omaha Creation myth.[64] The mineral nature of the rock is an emblem of its eternity within the realm of time; the rock is invincible and impugnable as all waters break on it. As such it represents the cosmogonic principle, while its spiritual qualities are strength and constancy. Finally, the spirit may spring forth from it as an inspiring source, or as incensing sparks. As a kind of symbolic summary of the spiritual archetype that is manifested in mountains and rocks, let us mention the following Navajo prayer to the Mountain Spirit:

> Hear a prayer for courage.
> Lord of the thin peaks,
> Reared amid the thunders;
> Keeper of the headlands
> Holding up the harvest,
> Keeper of the strong rocks
> Hear a prayer for staunchness.[65]

As already suggested by the preceding prayer, there is often a fundamental complementarity between mountains and thunder or lightning. To the motionless permanence of the mountain, in its receptive inviolability, responds the shaking and dazzling instantaneity of the celestial drum and light. Thunder, lightning, and rain are consistently associated with a complex symbolic constellation that revolves around the twofold spiritual mystery of fear and blessing. This twofold reality is also epitomized, in the world of Japanese shamanism, by the Shintō god of the tempest, Susano-o-Mikoto, whose name is akin to "impetuousness" and who embodies both the rough

---

[63] *Ibid.*, p. 55.
[64] Cf. A.L. Soens, *I, the Song*, p. xx.
[65] *American Indian Poetry*, ed. George W. Cronyn, p. 187.

and gentle aspects of the Divine Spirit (respectively Ara-Mitama and Nigi-Mitama).[66] Like the mountain and the rock, lightning and thunder have both a rigorous and a merciful aspect. The terrifying aspect is quite apparent in the *Heyoka* visions and songs; as Black Elk explains, "when a vision comes from the thunder beings of the west, it comes with terror like a thunder storm." This aspect is symbolized by the humility shown toward the thunder beings, as manifested in the shaving of the right side of the head before the *Heyoka* ceremony.[67] But, as Black Elk himself says, "when the storm of vision has passed, the world is greener and happier."[68] Many shamanistic ceremonies, as is well known, are intended to invite the rain—a blessed downpouring which revivifies nature.

A.L. Soens has perceptively spoken of "flashes of timeless vision and absolute perception"[69] with reference to traditional Native American poetry. The timelessness of this poetry lies in the fact that it radiates from a genuine relationship with the world of nature in its perennial cycles and permanent aspects. It also stems from a complete ignorance of the self-reflexive "creativity" that unavoidably "situates" most of contemporary poetry in the most fleeting psychological dimension of time, and often the most artificial virtuosity, as if man had become an ontological island and language an entity in itself and for itself. It is not without reason that self-referentiality has become a sort of obsession for writers, poets, and critics of our age, as also the mania for constant change and motion. Shamanistic or "primordial" poetry is the product of a kind of fusion between subject and object that transcends time. It is not because man feels himself different from what surrounds him that he creates; poetry results from a spiritual and psychic alignment between mankind, nature, and the universe,[70] which is suffused with invisible presence. Poetry is the air breathed in and out by shamanistic man.

---

[66] Cf. J.W.T. Mason, *The Meaning of Shinto*, p. 115.

[67] "This looked very funny, but it had a meaning; for when we looked toward where you are always facing (the south) the bare sides of our heads were toward the west, which showed that we were humble before the thunder beings who had given us power" (Black Elk, cited in John Neihardt, *Black Elk Speaks*, p. 191).

[68] *Ibid.*, p. 188.

[69] A.L. Soens, *I, the Song*, p. xiv.

[70] This is beautifully expressed in the spiritual art of navigation taught to James Barr by Bora-Boran and Maori master sailors, a way which teaches that "in order to have one's mind 'filled with the sea,' one must learn to 'see with the heart,' and to 'breathe with the feet'" (James Barr, "Of Metaphysics and Polynesian Navigation," in *Seeing God Everywhere: Essays on Nature and the Sacred*, ed. Barry McDonald, p. 166).

The impression of timelessness that emanates from most shamanistic poems also suggests a pristine integrity or "absoluteness" that is none other than the purest meaning of existence. One could compare this shamanistic intuition of pure existence in poetry with the Zen experience expressed through the *haiku* form. They share a laconic and straightforward style of expression and a same alert attentiveness to nature and being. The diversity of shamanistic poetry, even in the Amerindian world alone, cannot easily fit the high degree of formalization of Japanese poetry;[71] still, its affinity with a clarity of soul and speech that mirrors the untainted truth of existence sometimes strikes a resounding Zen note; as in this Sioux Buffalo Dance song:

> In the north
> The wind
> Blows
> They are walking
> The hail
> Beats
> They are walking.[72]

Shamanistic poetry, whether it be directly ritual or not, can be characterized as being centered on vision and action in their concrete phenomenality. Most Amerindian poems, for example, are directly connected to a human activity like hunting, planting, traveling, or warfare. The poetic word "accompanies" action as a kind of blessed "attendant" and helping spirit. At the same time, action itself is not essentially different from poetry since it proceeds from the same spirit of attentiveness to nature, and a deep awareness of the sacred as present in all things. The contemplativeness of shamanistic poetry is not only—nor even primarily—the result of a motionless gazing, although it entails a receptivity resulting from an inner silence; this poetry expresses, and in fact *is* a way of being, a way of singing the sacredness of existence from an inner place of quiet awe.

---

[71] One could draw a parallel concerning the relationship between American Indian poetry and *haiku* on the one hand, and the Indian warrior and the samurai on the other hand. As Frithjof Schuon has noted, the latter manifest a primordial combination of priestly and combative virtues, with the difference that the Japanese figure is characterized by a culture of refined perfection that amounts to a quintessential "formalization" of primordiality and nature, whereas the Indian manifestation may be deemed to express the same values in the context of a greater diversity and freedom (Cf. Frithjof Schuon, *The Feathered Sun*, pp. 20-21).

[72] Cited in *The Sacred Path*, ed. John Bierhorst, p. 127.

CONCLUSION

As a conclusion, we would like to highlight a few general observations concerning the ways wherein poetry acts as a means of spiritual and contemplative transformation.

A first point of view considers poetry in its rhythmic and auditory dimension. In this connection, poetry is conceived as a passage from multiplicity to unity. The repetition of rhythmic patterns and sounds is akin to the contemplative conversion of multiplicity into unity. This approach also touches upon the significant connection between poetry and silence. We have examined the ways in which various traditions, particularly in India, have conceived of the bridge between sacred sounds and contemplative silence. In this respect the methodical use of recitation, psalmody, and incantation in traditional spiritual contexts demonstrates the contemplative potentialities of sound patterns in poetry as an instrument of meditation and concentration.

A second perspective has allowed us to understand poetry as the language *par excellence* of intuition and discontinuity. In contrast with the discursive *continuum* of narrative and conceptual expression, the brevity and density of the poem expresses an immediate insight into the nature of things. Particular attention has been paid to the theory and practice of the Japanese *haiku* and *waka* as literary media of the Zen contemplative experience, two outstanding illustrations of this profound dimension of poetry. The relationship between poetic expression and visual contemplation is crucial to this aspect of the discussion since, as we have suggested, it is particularly important to understand poetry as a "vision" of reality and not simply as a representation of reality.

Parallel to its intuitive dimension, poetry needs to be envisaged as an existential participation in reality. Poetry is an "experience," as is plainly illustrated by its all too common exclusive association with feelings and emotions. As such, it involves not only the mental faculty, but also the animic domain of sentiments and aesthetic vibrations. Studying poetry therefore amounts to studying a very mode of being. Baudelaire spoke of the poetic experience as one in which "childhood (is) recovered at will."[1] He also equated it to a perception of symbols as ontological realities. In the mystical

---

[1] "L'enfance retrouvée à volonté," Charles Baudelaire, "L'artiste homme du monde, homme des foules et enfant," in *L'art romantique, Oeuvres complètes*, III, p. 58 (my translation).

realm of contemplation, the works of Sufi poets like Rūmī have served as an exemplar for the subjective and objective aspects of this understanding.

The function of poetry as the sacred or mythical language of cultural foundation is also intimately connected to the language of symbols. In particular, we have considered how poetry has been theorized and practiced as an art pertaining to the essential and primordial reality of language. In the wake of this exploration of poetry as "essential" and primordial language, the polysemic nature of poetic expression has also been emphasized. The contemplative and symbolic inclusiveness of poetry should be set in contrast to the exclusivity of conceptual discourse. Most profoundly, the hermeneutics of poetry implies that the reader "contemplates" his own reality as actualized by the layers of meaning in the text.

*   *   *

The spectrum of poetry spans a vast expanse of expressive phenomena. At one end of this expanse—which is in fact its beginning—there is the voice; at the other end, there is the idea, the conceptual and linguistic articulation. The voice is the soul, it is intimately connected to breathing,[2] and it is most directly involved in the "magical" process that presides over the poetic work.[3] Poetry is first of all recited or sung; it flows from the breath, the manifested presence of the soul. Voice, breathing, and creation are in a sense one, as expressed by the great Sufi Ibn al 'Arabī in his *Futūhāt al-Makkiyya* ("The Illuminations of Mecca").[4] On this level of manifestation, the voice and the breath are analogous to the songs and cries of animals; they are primal exte-

---

[2] "Atmen, du unsichtbares Gedicht!" ("Breathing, thou invisible poem!"), Rilke writes in his *Sonnets to Orpheus.*

[3] As Toshihiko Izutsu has put it: "It is the voice, i.e. the breath, that actualizes the magical force contained in potency in the world and launches it in whatever direction the magician desires. It is in the breath that the main virtue of all verbal magic is believed to reside" (*Language and Magic: Studies in the Magical Function of Speech*, p. 26).

[4] In his commentary on the *Futūhāt* (II, 395), Pierre Lory writes: "Il y a homologie constante entre création divine et parole humaine. Dieu crée par le moyen d'une 'expiration divine' dite 'souffle de miséricorde'—*nafas al-rahmān*—qui sous-tend perpétuellement l'existence de l'univers. C'est cette expiration qui rend possible l' 'articulation' des paroles divines [There is a constant homology between divine creation and human speech. God creates through a 'divine expiration' called 'breath of the compassionate'—*nafas al-rahmān*—that perpetually underlies the existence of the universe. This expiration is what makes the 'articulation' of divine words possible]" ("Le symbolisme des lettres et du langage chez Ibn 'Arabi," *Connaissance des Religions* (winter 1999):93).

riorizations of the soul. Their immediacy pertains to the mode of apprehension of the Intellect, which is characterized by directness and totality. This is the most "incarnated" and substantial pole of poetry, which is also the most intimately connected with the essences and energies of the cosmos. It fundamentally coincides with the shamanistic and elemental source of poetry.

As for the notional and verbal articulation, it is a reflection of the Intellect in the mirror of the rational faculty. It is a crystallization of the vertical and intellective perception on the horizontal plane of rational concatenation. In poetry, however, this crystallization is different from the purely discursive exposition that occurs in non-poetical texts. In prose—in so far as the distinction between prose and poetry can be meaningful—the conceptual structure is more detached and distant from the experience of the soul than it is in pure poetry. Poetry thrives on a conjunction of the conceptual and the animic, both being reflections of the Intellect in their two respective modes. The spiritual power of poetry lies in this conjunction, which highlights the convergence of truth and presence.

It is important to recall in this connection that many traditional cultures—this is eminently true for the Vikings, Celts, and Arabs—associate war, magic, and poetry.[5] This connection is obviously not accidental, since it brings out the coincidence of word and power. In so far as the warrior caste, or class, functions within the realm of dynamic and combative energy, it bears a particular affinity with animic power as a *shakti* of the Spirit. The "manipulation" and exteriorization of this energy is closely related to the magic of the word. Poetry plays a central role in battle by connecting warriors to the psycho-spiritual source or spirit of power. It also constitutes an animic weapon against the enemy in the form of spells and magic entities. As a whole, poetry becomes a dynamic way of participating in the cosmic energies that are essentially none other than the Divine quality of Power itself.

From another perspective, inasmuch as poetry emphasizes truth, it pertains to the realm of the pure contemplative, that of the priestly function. In this case, the interiorizing and contemplative power of poetry stems from its ability to synthesize doctrine and method, intellective certainty and "rhythmic" methodical assimilation. Accordingly, poetry functions as a powerful means of integration, bringing together the positive tendencies of the soul under the aegis of the Spirit. Poetry is transformative because it brings the

---

[5] "The *kshatriya* readily turns poet or aesthete, he lays very little stress on matter as such" (Frithjof Schuon, *Language of the Self*, p. 117).

soul and all its faculties under the catalytic "spell" of the Spirit through the mediation of imaginal and verbal beauty. It "lures" the soul, so to speak, and fixes her by the gem that is cleft by truth into presence.

BIBLIOGRAPHY

Abe, Masao. "Buddhism." In *Our Religions*. Edited by Arvind Sharma, 69-137. San Fransisco, 1993.

Abram, David. *The Spell of the Sensuous*. New York, 1996.

'Alawī, Ahmed Ben Mustapha al-. *Extraits du Dīwān*. Paris, 1984.

Anandavardhana. *Dhvanyāloka*. Edited by K. Krishnamoorthy. Delhi, 1982.

Anawati, G.C. and Louis Gardet. *Mystique Musulmane*. Paris, 1961.

Aristotle. *Theory of Poetry and Fine Art*. Translated by S.H. Butcher. London, 1927.

Bakhtiar, Laleh. *Sufi: Expressions of the Mystic Quest*. London, 1976.

Barnstone, Tony and Chou Ping. *The Art of Writing: Teachings of the Chinese Masters*. Boston/London, 1996.

Barr, James. "Of Metaphysics and Polynesian Navigation." In *Seeing God Everywhere: Essays on Nature and the Sacred*. Edited by Barry McDonald, 161-68. Bloomington, 2002.

Barthes, Roland. *L'empire des signes*. Paris, 1970.

Bary, Theodore de. "The Vocabulary of Japanese Aesthetics." In *Japanese Aesthetics and Culture*. Edited by Nancy G. Hume, 43-76. Albany, 1995.

Baudelaire, Charles. *L'art romantique*. Paris, 1949.

Berndt, Ronald M. and Catherine H. *The Speaking Land: Myth and Story in Aboriginal Australia*. London, 1989.

Bhagavad Gītā. Translated by Winthrop Sargeant. Albany, 1994.

Bhagavad Gītā with the Commentary of Sri Sankaracharya. Translated by Alladi Mahadeva Sastry. Madras, 1981.

Bierhorst, John (ed.). *The Sacred Path, Spells, Prayers and Power Songs of the American Indians*. New York, 1983.

Black Bear, Ben Sr. and R.D. Theisz. *Songs and Dances of the Lakota*. Rosebud, 1976.

Black Elk. *Black Elk Speaks*. As told through John G. Neihardt. Lincoln/ London, 1979.

Blyth, R.H. *A History of Haiku*. 2 Vols. Tokyo, 1964.

Boileau Despréaux, Nicolas. *Art Poétique*. Edited by Henri Bénac. Paris, 1946.

Burckhardt, Titus. *Sacred Art in East and West*. Bloomington/Kentucky, 1999.

Cave, George. *Sufi Poetry*. Rawalpindi, 1975.

Chadwick, Nora Kershaw. *Poetry and Prophecy*. Cambridge, 1942.

Chaitanya, Krishna. *Sanskrit Poetics*. Bombay, 1965.

Chamberlain, Alexander F., "Primitive Woman as Poet." *Journal of American Folklore* 16, no. 63 (October-December 1903).

Cheng, François. *L'Ecriture poétique chinoise*. Paris, 1982.

Chittick, William. *The Sufi Path of Love, The Spiritual Teachings of Rūmī*. Albany, 1983.

Chuang-tzu. *Inner Chapters*. Translated by Gia-fu Feng and Jane English. New York, 1974.

Coleridge, Samuel Taylor. *The Portable Coleridge*. New York, 1950.

Conrad, David and Barbara Frank. *Status and Identity in West Africa: Nyamakalaw of Mande*. Bloomington, 1995.

Coomaraswamy, Ananda K. *The Transformation of Nature in Art*. New York, 1956.

——. *Spiritual Authority and Temporal Power in the Indian Theory of Government*. Delhi, 1993.

Corbin, Henry. *Histoire de la philosophie islamique*. Paris, 1964.

——. *Creative Imagination in the Sufism of Ibn 'Arabī*. Princeton, 1969.

——. *En Islam iranien*. Paris, 1972.

Costa, Jean-Patrick. *Les Chamans, hier et aujourd'hui*. Paris, 2001.

Cronyn, George W (ed.). *American Indian Poetry: An Anthology of Songs and Chants*. New York, 1991.

Daumal, René. *Rasa or Knowledge of the Self: Essays on Indian Aesthetics and Selected Sanskrit Studies*. Translated by Louise Landes Levi. New York, 1982.

Deutsch, Eliot. *Advaita Vedānta*. Honolulu, 1969.

Driessen, Georges and Yonten Gyatso. *Traité du Milieu*. Paris, 1995.

Durand, Gilbert. *L'imagination symbolique*. Paris, 1964.

Eliade, Mircea. *Shamanism: Archaic Techniques of Ecstasy*. Princeton, 1964.

——. *Du corps à l'esprit*. Paris, 1989.

Emerson, Ralph Waldo. *Self-reliance and Other Essays*. New York, 1993.

Geertz, Clifford. *The Religion of Java*. New York, 1960.

Gilson, Etienne. *Forms and Substances in the Arts*. New York, 1966.

Granet, Marcel. *La pensée chinoise*. Paris, 1934.

Guénon, René. *The Reign of Quantity & the Signs of the Times*. Translated by Lord Northbourne. Ghent, 1995.

——. *Man and his Becoming according to the Vedānta*. Translated by R.C. Nicholson. Delhi, 1999.

Gupta, Rakesh. *A Dictionary of Sanskrit Poetics*. Delhi, 1987.

Hafiz. *The Subject Tonight is Love, 60 Wild and Sweet Poems from Hafiz*. Translated by Daniel Ladinsky. London, 2003.

Hale, Thomas A. *Griots and Griottes*. Bloomington, 1998.

Al-Hallāj, Husein Ibn Mansur and Zuhair ibn Abi Sulma. *Selections from the Poems of Zuhair ibn Abi Sulma and Husain ibn Mansur al Hallaj*. Translated by Arthur Wormhoudt. Oskaloosa, 1975.

Hatem, Jad, *Travaux et Jours*. Beyrouth, 1998.

Heine, Steven. *The Zen Poetry of Dōgen*. Boston, 1997.

Housman, A.E. *Selected Prose*. Edited by John Carter. Cambridge, 1961.

Hume, Nancy G (ed.). *Japanese Aesthetics and Culture*. Albany, 1995.

Ikkyū. *Crow With No Mouth, Ikkyū, 15th Century Zen Master*. Translated by Stephen Berg. Washington, 1989.

Ikkyū, *Zen Poems of China and Japan*. Edited by Lucien Stryk, translated by Takashi Ikemoto. New York, 1988.

Izutsu, Toshihiko. *Language and Magic: Studies in the Magical Function of Speech*. Tokyo, 1955.

——. *Ethico-Religious Concepts in the Qur'ān*. Montreal, 1966.

——. "The Absolute and the Perfect Man in Taoism." In *The Unanimous Tradition*. Edited by Ranjit Fernando, 39-54. Colombo, 1991.

Izutsu, Toshihiko and Toyo. *The Theory of Beauty in the Classical Aesthetics of Japan*. The Hague, 1981.

Jain, Nirmala. *A Dictionary of Sanskrit Poetics*.

Keene, Donald. "Japanese Aesthetics." In *Japanese Aesthetics and Culture*. Edited by Nancy G. Hume, 27-41. Albany, 1995.

Lao-tzu. *Tao Te Ching*. Translated by Liou Kia-Hway and Etiemble. Paris, 1980.

——. *Tao Te Ching*. Translated by Man-Ho Kwok, Martin Palmer, and Jay Ramsay. New York, 1993.

Lee, Jung Young. *Korean Shamanistic Rituals*. The Hague, 1981.

Lings, Martin. *Symbol and Archetype: A Study of the Meaning of Existence*. Cambridge, 1991.

——. "Mystical Poetry." In *The Cambridge History of Arabic Literature: 'Abbasid Belles-Lettres*. Edited by Julia Ashtiany et al., 235-64. Cambridge, 1990.

Livingston, Ray. *The Traditional Theory of Literature*. Minneapolis, 1962.

Lorca, Federico Garcia. *In Search of Duende*. Edited and translated by Christopher Maurer. New York, 1998.

Lory, Pierre. "Le symbolisme des lettres et du langage chez Ibn 'Arabi." *Connaissance des Religions* (Winter 1999).

Lu Chi, *Wen Fu, The Art of Writing*. Translated by Sam Hamill. Portland, 1987.

Maistre, Joseph de. *Les soirées de Saint-Petersbourg*. Paris, 1821.

Marchiano, Grazia. "What to Learn From Eastern Aesthetics." *Canadian Aesthetics Journal/Revue canadienne d'esthétique* 2 (Winter 1998). http://www.uqtr.uquebec.ca/AE/vol_2/marchiano.html.

Maritain, Jacques. *Art and Poetry*. New York, 1943.

Maritain, Jacques and Raïssa. *The Situation of Poetry*. New York, 1955.

Mason, J.W.T. *The Meaning of Shinto*. New York, 1935.

Matthews, Washington. "Songs of Sequence of the Navajos." *The Journal of American Folklore* 7, no. 26 (July-September 1894).

Muhammad Ali, Maulana. *The Holy Qur'ān*. Lahore, 1995.

Nasr, Seyyed Hossein. *Jalāl ad-Dīn Rūmī: Supreme Persian Poet and Sage*.

Tehran, 1974.

——. *Islamic Art and Spirituality*. Albany, 1987.

——. *Sufi Essays*. Albany, 1991.

——. "Oral Transmission and the Book in Islamic Education: the Spoken and the Written Word." *Journal of Islamic Studies* 3:1 (1992):1-14.

Al-Niffarī, Muhammad Ibn 'Abdi'l-Jabbār. *The Mawāqif and Mukhātabāt of Muhammad Ibn 'Abdi'l-Jabbār al-Niffarī*. Edited and translated by A.J. Arberry. London, 1978.

Noss, David and John. *A History of the World's Religions*. New York, 1984.

Okakura, Kakuzo. *The Book of Tea*. New York, 1964.

Owen, Stephen. *Readings in Chinese Literary Thought*. Harvard, 1992.

Parimoo, B.N. *The Ascent of the Self: A Reinterpretation of the Mystical Poetry of Lalla Deb*. Delhi, 1978.

Paz, Octavio. *The Bow and the Lyre*. Austin, 1973.

Plato, *The Dialogues of Plato*. 2 Vols. Translated by Benjamin Jowett. New York, 1937.

Renondeau, G (ed.). *Le Bouddhisme japonais, textes fondamentaux*. Paris, 1965.

Rilke, Rainer Maria. *A Rilke Trilogy: Duino Elegies/Letters to a Young Poet/ The Sonnets to Orpheus*. Translated and edited by Stephen Mitchell. Boston, 1993.

——. *Letters to a Young Poet*. New York, 1987.

Robinet, Isabelle. "*Xin Fa*, l'art du coeur et de la connaissance dans le Taoïsme." *Connaissance des Religions* nos. 57/58/59 (January-September 1999):246-65.

Rolland, Romain. *Prophets of the New India*. Translated by E.F. Malcolm Smith. New York, 1930.

Rūmī, Jalāl ad-Dīn. *Mathnawī*. Edited and translated by R.A. Nicholson. London, 1925.

——. *Mystical Poems of Rūmī*. 2 Vols. Edited and translated by A.J. Arberry. Chicago, 1968.

——. *Birdsong*. Translated by Coleman Barks. Athens, 1993.

——. *The Essential Rumi*. Translated by Coleman Barks. San Francisco, 1997.

——. *Teachings of Rumi*. Translated by Andrew Harvey. Boston, 1999.

——. *Rumi Daylight*. Translated by Camille and Kabir Helminski. Boston, 1999.

——. "One-Handed Basket Weaving." http://www.armory.com/~thrace/sufi/poems.html.

Schimmel, Anne-Marie. *As Through a Veil, Mystical Poetry in Islam*. New York, 1982.

——. *I am Wind You are Fire, The Life and Work of Rumi*. Boston/London, 1996.

Schlesier, Karl H. *The Wolves of Heaven*. Norman, 1987.

Schuon, Frithjof. *Christianity/Islam: Essays on Esoteric Ecumenicism*. Bloomington, 1985.

——. *The Feathered Sun: Plains Indians in Art and Philosophy*. Bloomington, 1990.

——. *Treasures of Buddhism*. Bloomington, 1993.

——. *Understanding Islam*. Bloomington, 1994.

——. *Language of the Self*. Bloomington, 1999.

——. *Roots of the Human Condition*. Bloomington, 2002.

——. *Form and Substance in the Religions*. Bloomington, 2002.

Sells, Michael A. *Mystical Languages of Unsaying*. Chicago/London, 1994.

Servier, Jean. *L'homme et l'invisible*. Paris, 1980.

Shelley, Percy Bysshe. *Defence of Poetry*. Boston, 1891.

Silesius, Angelus, *Cherubinischer Wandersmann*. Edited by H. Plard. Paris, 1946.

Silko, Leslie Marmon. *Storyteller*. New York, 1981.

Soens, A.L. *I, the Song: Classical Poetry of Native North America*. Salt Lake City, 1999.

Stoddart, William. *Outline of Hinduism*. Washington DC, 1993.

Suzuki, D.T. *Essays in Zen Buddhism*. London, 1933.

——. *Zen and Japanese Culture*. Princeton, 1970.

Takahashi, Shinkishi. *Triumph of the Sparrow*. Translated by Lucien Stryk. Urbana/Chicago, 1986.

Ueda, Makoto. "Bashō on the Art of the Haiku: Impersonality in Poetry." In *Japanese Aesthetics and Culture*. Edited by Nancy G. Hume, 151-175. Albany, 1995

Varenne, Jean. *Upanishads du Yoga*. Paris, 1971.

Von Denffer, Ahmad. *'Ulūm al-Qur'ān*. Leicester, 1983.

Wei-ming, Tu. "Confucianism." In *Our Religions*. Edited by Arvind Sharma, 139-227. San Francisco, 1993.

Wilde, Dana. "Poetry and Sufism: A Few Generalities." http://www.unc.edu/depts/sufilit/Wilde.htm.

Williamson, Ray. A and Claire R. Farrer (eds.). *Earth and Sky, Visions of the Cosmos in Native American Folklore*. Albuquerque, 1992.

Yourcenar, Marguerite. "Comment Wang-Fō fut sauvé." In *Nouvelles orientales*. Paris, 1963.

Zaehner R.C. *Hinduism*. Oxford, 1975.

BIOGRAPHICAL NOTE

PATRICK LAUDE is Professor of French at Georgetown University. Born of Gascon and Basque stock in 1958 in Lannemezan, Hautes Pyrénées, France, he later studied history and philosophy at Paris-Sorbonne and was a Fellow at the Ecole Normale Supérieure in Paris (1979-1982). His academic career took him to the United States where he obtained a Ph.D. in French literature, specializing in poetry and mystical literature. He is the author of numerous articles and books dealing with the relationship between mysticism, symbolism, and literature, including *Music of the Sky: An Anthology of Spiritual Poetry* (co-edited with Barry McDonald, World Wisdom, 2004). Dr. Laude is also the author of several studies on important contemporary spiritual figures such as Jeanne Guyon, Simone Weil, and Louis Massignon. He recently co-edited a work (with Jean-Baptiste Aymard) on Frithjof Schuon, the renowned Swiss metaphysician and expositor of the Perennial Philosophy, entitled *Frithjof Schuon: Life and Teachings* (SUNY Press, 2004). He is presently preparing *Cracks of Light: Demiurgic Gods and Tricksters, Sacred Clowns and Holy Fools* for publication. Dr. Laude's articles appear regularly in the traditional journals *Sophia* and *Sacred Web*.

INDEX

Abe, Masao, 116-117
Aboriginal Australia, 187
Abraham, 125
Abram, David , 190, 195, 198-199
Absolute, 12, 16, 26-28, 34, 44, 47, 60, 65, 89, 91, 116, 136, 178, 207
Adam, 67
Advaita Vedānta, 17-18, 29, 42-43, 168
Aesthetic, 17, 19-20, 22, 36, 63, 73, 93, 98, 110, 115, 118-119, 136, 138, 174, 188-189, 209
Aesthetics, iv, 8, 20, 22, 115, 117, 120, 135, 137-139, 141-143, 145-146, 171, 173
African, 187, 191, 201
Agni Purana, 8
Alawī, Ahmad Ben Mustafa, Al-, 60
Alcibiades, 152, 164-165
Ame-no-mi-naka-nushi-no-kami, 185
Amida, 128-129
Amidism, 129
Amrtābindu Upanishad, 35
Analects, 110
Ananda Moyi, 44
Anawati, Paul, 61
Angelus Silesius, 117
Apache, 196, 198
Arabic, 7, 47, 61, 67, 159
Arberry, A. J., 62, 64, 66-67
Archaic Techniques of Ecstasy, 192
Archetype, 10, 37, 52, 154, 206
Aristotelian, 40, 86, 167, 169
Aristotle, 86, 170
Art of Writing, 83-84, 95, 99, 103,

109-110
Art Poétique, 110
Art, 4, 9-10, 15-17, 19, 21, 23, 26, 33, 36-37, 40-41, 50-53, 56, 63, 67, 69, 74, 83-84, 86-87, 91-92, 95, 99, 103, 107-110, 112, 115, 117-119, 126, 131, 137, 141, 143-146, 150, 153-156, 159, 163-173, 176, 180, 187-189, 194, 207, 209-210
Arunachala, 42
Augustinian, 173
AUM, 27, 32

Bacchic, 102, 151, 171
Bakhtiar, Laleh, 74
Barks, Coleman, 53, 69, 74
Barnstone, Tony, 84, 95, 99, 109
Barr, Michael, 207
Barthes, Roland, 115
Baudelaire, Charles, 10, 175-177, 209
Beauty, 4, 8, 19, 24, 52, 54, 69, 72-73, 115, 120, 135, 137-139, 143, 146, 154, 171, 173-174, 176, 178, 189-191, 200, 212
Bedouin, 48
Berg, Stephen, 124, 126, 130-132
Bhagavad Gītā, vii, 14, 28-29
Bible, 5
Black Elk, 202-203, 207
Blyth, Reginald Horace, 119, 121-122
Boileau, 110
Book of Tea, 118
Brahma, 26, 28

For a glossary of all key foreign words used in books published by World Wisdom, including metaphysical terms in English, consult:

www.DictionaryofSpiritualTerms.com.

This on-line Dictionary of Spiritual Terms provides extensive definitions, examples and related terms in other languages.

Titles in The Perennial Philosophy Series by World Wisdom

The Betrayal of Tradition: Essays on the Spiritual Crisis of Modernity,
edited by Harry Oldmeadow, 2005

Borderlands of the Spirit: Reflections on a Sacred Science of Mind
by John Herlihy, 2005

A Buddhist Spectrum by Marco Pallis, 2003

The Essential Ananda K. Coomaraswamy,
edited by Rama P. Coomaraswamy, 2004

The Essential Titus Burckhardt: Reflections on Sacred Art, Faiths, and Civilizations,
edited by William Stoddart, 2003

Every Branch in Me: Essays on the Meaning of Man,
edited by Barry McDonald, 2002

Islam, Fundamentalism, and the Betrayal of Tradition: Essays by Western Muslim Scholars, edited by Joseph E. B. Lumbard, 2004

Journeys East: 20th Century Western Encounters with Eastern Religious Traditions
by Harry Oldmeadow, 2004

Living in Amida's Universal Vow: Essays in Shin Buddhism,
edited by Alfred Bloom, 2004

Paths to the Heart: Sufism and the Christian East,
edited by James S. Cutsinger, 2002

Returning to the Essential: Selected Writings of Jean Biès,
translated by Deborah Weiss-Dutilh, 2004

Science and the Myth of Progress, edited by Mehrdad M. Zarandi, 2003

Seeing God Everywhere: Essays on Nature and the Sacred,
edited by Barry McDonald, 2003

Singing the Way: Insights in Poetry and Spiritual Transformation
by Patrick Laude, 2005

Ye Shall Know the Truth: Christianity and the Perennial Philosophy,
edited by Mateus Soares de Azevedo, 2005